ZAMBIA IN MAPS: Graphic Perspectives of a Developing Country

ZAMBIA IN MAPS: Graphic Perspectives of a Developing Country

edited by
D. Hywel Davies MA PHD
formerly Professor of Geography
University of Zambia

AFRICANA PUBLISHING CORPORATION · NEW YORK

Published
in the United States of America 1972
by Africana Publishing Corporation
101 Fifth Avenue
New York, N.Y. 10003

Library of Congress Catalog Card No. 73-653626
ISBN 0-8419-0081-7

Printed in Great Britain

CONTENTS

LIST OF CONTRIBUTORS

G H ADIKA AIST *Cartographer and Chief Draughtsman; formerly Chief Technician in Geography, University of Zambia*

D R ARCHER BA (HONS) MSC *formerly Lecturer in Geography, University of Zambia*

J G CHILESHE *Draughtsman; Assistant Technician in Geography, University of Zambia*

I DAPPRICH (Miss) *Draughtswoman; formerly attached to Geography, University of Zambia*

D HYWEL DAVIES MA PHD *formerly Professor and Head of Geography, University of Zambia*

J E GARDINER MA *formerly British (ODM) 'Study and Serve' staff, attached to Geography, University of Zambia*

M E JACKMAN (Mrs) BSC (HONS) DIP ED *Technical Officer (I) Zambian National Council for Scientific Research (Cartographic and Location Analysis Unit)*

J JENKINSON (Mrs) BA *formerly Research Assistant in Geography, University of Zambia*

M M KAUNDA BA *Director of Correspondence Studies, University of Zambia*

G KAY MA PHD *formerly Research Affiliate, Rhodes-Livingstone Institute, Lusaka*

H W LANGWORTHY MA PHD *formerly Lecturer in History, University of Zambia*

N D McGLASHAN MA PHD CERT ED *formerly Lecturer in Geography, University of Zambia*

R MÄCKEL DIP GEOG PHD *Lecturer in Geography, University of Zambia*

S NDHLOVU *Draughtsman; formerly Assistant Technician in Geography, University of Zambia*

D W PHILLIPSON MA *Secretary/Inspector, National Monuments Commission of Zambia*

H L ROBART-MORGAN (Miss) *Draughtswomen; formerly of Geography, University of Zambia*

D. J. SIDDLE BA (HONS) M LITT PHD DIP ED *formerly Lecturer in Geography, University of Zambia*

J W SNADEN MA PHD *formerly Senior Lecturer in Geography, University of Zambia*

LILLI STEIN (Mrs) MA PHD FRSS *Senior Statistician, Department of Health*

E WILSON (Miss) MA LTD *formerly Headmistress, Kabulonga Girls' School, Lusaka*

R A YOUNG MA *formerly Lecturer in Political Science, University of Zambia*

ACKNOWLEDGMENT

Two of the maps in Section 19—Age-structure, sex ratio and migrations—have been reproduced by kind permission of Professor George Kay. These maps are reproduced from *A Social Geography of Zambia*

INTRODUCTION

This volume is one of a series on developing African countries arising from the success of the pioneer study, *Sierra Leone in Maps*, published in 1966. It follows the general format of that work in presenting over fifty pages of maps and supplementary illustrations, each map supported by a short text. There are, however, significant differences in presentation, particularly relating to choice of topics, reflecting real differences between the two countries. The present study provides a variety of information on natural and human resources in Zambia at a time when the First National Development Plan, 1966—70 (following independence in 1964) is ending, while the second plan still awaits formulation. It is basically a portrayal of contemporary Zambia, but certain studies are included to provide historical context.

It was anticipated that this would be essentially an exercise in the compilation of existing data but, as gaps in knowledge emerged, it has also given rise to much original investigation on many topics. It is hoped that the book may interest the general reader abroad concerned with the development of Africa, and also administrators, businessmen, teachers, students and others in Zambia itself: it may also provide some background information for those engaged in Zambia's national and regional development planning.

The unusual format—half atlas, half book, and divided into fifty-five short 'chapters'—permits many topics to be quickly located and examined. An attempt is made to increase the book's reference value by permitting limited overlap of subject-matter between chapters and considerable cross-referencing. In this broad descriptive study involving sixteen authors, there has been little attempt at correlations between the distributions plotted; however, use of only three basic scales for maps of all Zambia should help the reader to make his own comparisons and draw his own conclusions.

As the editor of *Sierra Leone in Maps* rightly emphasized, such a format also imposes limitations. Limitations of space naturally affect the handling of topics. Since topics cannot be introduced unless they can be mapped, the study cannot claim to be comprehensive, but only usefully far-ranging. Furthermore, some topics suitable for cartographic treatment are omitted because of inadequate present knowledge. Inevitably the maps vary in accuracy of detail, a point easily lost on the over-casual reader. Some maps, based upon detailed official mapping or careful field research, are accurate within limitations imposed by scale and format; others are little more than sketch-maps, depicting distributions too important to be omitted but concerning which insufficient detailed information is yet available. (The status of such tentative maps is indicated in their accompanying texts.) The book seeks to portray Zambia as a whole: at the published scale it has rarely been possible to provide detail significant at a regional level, and almost never at a local level.

The format stresses the geographical or spatial viewpoint in the handling as well as in the selection of topics: unmapped factors may therefore be passed over in the process. For example, the brief discussion of provincial variations in secondary school places per 1000 (p. 104) could well have ignored the fact that mobility of the pupils (mostly boarders) and a national (as opposed to provincial) educational policy significantly reduce the effects of spatial inequalities in physical facilities, as mapped. This particular point has, in fact, been noted in the text.

The contributors have compiled both maps and facing texts. The long list of contributors reflects the interdisciplinary range of the work; the need to produce it relatively quickly in face of rapid change in a fast-developing country; and a high rate of turnover of potential authors (more than a half of the contributors are no longer in Zambia as publication approaches). The bulk of the work, however, is by geographers at the University of Zambia. It is pleasing to note contributions, academic and technical, by Zambian citizens. It is hoped that the output of graduates from the new university will help to ensure that there will be many more in any subsequent editions. Several draughtsmen have been engaged on the project at various times; none, unfortunately, from beginning to end. Except for Godwin Adika, the project has lacked senior skilled draughtsmen, and some juniors have received much of their basic training while engaged on it. The few maps not drawn in the university geography drawing office are acknowledged. Mr E C Francis, MBE (who replaced Mr Adika as Chief Technician in Geography) provided skilled assistance with the population maps, the last to be drawn.

For a developing country Zambia is quite well served with maps (p. 12) and grateful acknowledgment is made of generous co-operation from the Department of Surveys, Ministry of Lands and Natural Resources, who allowed full use of their publications for basemap material and certain distributional plots. With plotting scales of 1:2 500 000; 1:3 000 000; and 1:5 000 000, it was possible to use the old *Federal Atlas* and the *National Atlas of Zambia* for basemaps—a great convenience. The authors, however, are responsible for any mapping errors.

In a work of this breadth it seems inevitable that some errors will have crept in, for which the authors accept responsibility. To limit these it has been editorial policy to subject submitted draft texts and plates to detailed scrutiny by many experts not directly involved with the project. The editor particularly wishes to thank these persons for their invaluable assistance: G D Anderson, Reader in Agricultural Sciences, University of Zambia; M H Bailey, Meteorological Department; J Baillie and J Thomson-Jacob, Department of Mines; M F Beattie, formerly Chief Fisheries Officer, Department of Wildlife, Fisheries and National Parks; A Beesly, Senior Electrical Engineer, Ministry of Power, Transport and Works; M Blackall, Director, Zambian National Tourist Bureau; H F Buckle, Chief Livestock Officer, Ministry of Rural Development; T A Coombe, Senior Lecturer in Education, University of Zambia; P R Dallosso, Chief Operations Officer, Department of Civil Aviation; J M Denham and D E R Jones, Roads Branch, Ministry of Power, Transport and Works; A. R. Drysdall, Director, Geological Survey; D B Fanshawe, Forestry Department; A F Greenwood, formerly United Nations Advisor in Public Administration to the Zambian Government; C Gertzel and I Scott, respectively Reader and former Assistant Lecturer in Political Science, University of Zambia; C Harvey and A Young, respectively Lecturer and

Research Fellow in Economics, University of Zambia; M H King, Professor of Social Medicine, University of Zambia; D A Lehmann, Senior Research Fellow in Linguistics, Centre for African Studies, University of Zambia; Rev. F McPherson, Dean of Student Affairs, University of Zambia; L Mumeka, Commission for Land Resettlement, Ministry of Rural Development; P O Ohadike, formerly Research Fellow in Demography, Institute for Social Research, University of Zambia; J F A Russell, Chief Farm Management Officer, Ministry of Rural Development; G D Shaw, Director of Veterinary and Tsetse Control Services; D R Spargareen, Mount Makulu Agricultural Research Station; G A N Starmans, Senior Hydrological Engineer, department of Water Affairs; The Surveyor-General and colleagues, Survey Department, Ministry of Lands and Natural Resources; M Tague, Senior Hydrogeologist, Department of Water Affairs; W Verboom, Senior Conservationist-Biologist, Ministry of Rural Development; A A Wood, Forestry Research Station, Kitwe; and in particular I Henderson, Senior Lecturer in History, University of Zambia, who gave invaluable assistance with the historical chapters.

Most of these experts work in government, and it is appropriate to acknowledge sincere appreciation for the interest shown, and the very willing co-operation received, in all ministries and departments approached.

Thanks are also due to the many people who assisted individual authors with information; to the Zambian National Council for Scientific Research, for permission to use map plots of population distribution and density prepared by Mrs M E Jackman; to the geography teachers and students of the Dominican Convent School, Lusaka, who kindly made and checked over 1200 area calculations for the population density map; and to the Geography Clubs and Teachers of Chassa, Nchelenge and St Francis (Mansa) Secondary Schools, and the Agricultural Experiment Station, University of Maryland, for permission to reproduce amended versions of village plans.

D HYWEL DAVIES
Lusaka
March 1970

EDITORIAL NOTES

1. Currency

In January 1968 Zambia changed from British style currency (pounds, shillings and pence) to a decimal system comprising the *Kwacha* (K), worth ten old shillings, and the *ngwee* (n), worth one hundredth part of a Kwacha. However, since Britain devalued the pound sterling in November 1967, the exchange value of one Kwacha is now 58 pence sterling (1·39 US dollars). In this book all monetary figures are expressed in Kwachas irrespective of date, but their actual exchange values accord with the dates given in each case.

2. Metrication

This book appears during an awkward period of transition regarding systems of weights and measures in Zambia. Until now Zambia has followed the imperial system but (like Britain) plans to convert to metric units. Because this process will not be complete until 1973, both types of units are quoted in this book although, to avoid undue disruptions to the short texts, some minor metric equivalents are omitted here and there. Because current data sources all use imperial units, actual measurements are usually made in them, the metric figures being calculated equivalents (e.g. contours have been *measured* in feet until recently). However, where measurements are conventionally expressed in metric units (e.g. soil depths), these alone have been used in the texts. Map keys normally contain both types of unit, but actual measurements are normally given in imperial units.

3. Nomenclature

Since this book was prepared the names of two districts and of their administrative centres have been changed: Balovale has been renamed Zambezi and Mankoya has been renamed Kaoma.

4. Corrigenda

In 1970 fee-paying wards in hospitals (p. 100) and fee-paying schools p. 104) were abolished, and the Shell/BP Company (p. 106) came under state control.

ERRATUM

On the Population Density map on p. 43, the square kilometres/ square miles equivalents should read as follows:

Population per sq. km. (nearest equivalent)	Population per sq. mile
193	500
43	110
21	55
10	25
4	11
2	5

1 POLITICAL GEOGRAPHY

The Republic of Zambia, born on 24 October 1964, is a youthful state striving for nationhood. At independence the country's not inconsiderable natural resources were, except for copper, grossly under-utilized and the limited development was over-concentrated along the solitary railway line. With over 75 per cent of the population living close to subsistence level in the rural areas and with a weak mass educational structure, Zambia's human resources had also been neglected during colonial rule. Inevitably and rightly, therefore, the keyword in the national vocabulary since independence has been 'development'.

To many, national development is virtually synonymous with economic development, a theme recurring throughout this book and specifically, although briefly, considered in the final chapter. It is quite widely recognized in Zambia, however, that there are social and political, as well as economic, components of development. Major social problems include the processes and consequences of transforming the rural population from a semi-subsistence to a commercial way of life and combating (or accommodating) the powerful drift of rural folk into shanty settlements around the major towns.

At least in the short run, however, both economic and social considerations tend to take second place to political imperatives and are in large measure regarded as a means to the end of nation-building (as expressed in the national motto 'One Zambia, One Nation'), which is basically a political exercise. The test of this assertion lies in situations where political and economic ends are in the short run incomptaible: events since Rhodesia's Unilateral Declaration of Independence (UDI) prove the paramountcy of political considerations in decision-making.

Underlying the policies of the Zambian Government are, among others, two geopolitical factors. Firstly, Zambians are culturally diverse and historically disunited, with perhaps seventy tribal groups and numerous tongues—none fully a *lingua franca*—scattered thinly and unevenly across a large land with poor communications, encircled by a grotesque boundary of colonial origin that cuts with fine indifference through tribal group and 'natural region' alike. This situation provides a fragile basis indeed for nation-building; as in so much of Africa, tribalism persists in retarding national unity. Secondly, Zambia is located in the heartland of south-central Africa, remote from the sea and in the cockpit of the racial cold war that today dominates the scene south of the Congo. Militarily weak and vulnerable, she is partly dependent still, though decreasingly, upon routes through states she regards as hostile.

Both these basic sets of political problems—parochialism and locational vulnerability—are largely rooted in geography. Their geopolitical significance thus warrants examination at the outset as a context for what follows. Space permits brief consideration of only the classic criteria of size, shape and location and mere mention of the policies of trade re-orientation and autarchy that stem in part from them. Trade is further discussed on p. 114, while the national power base, which cannot be specifically considered here, emerges from a general perusal of the book.

Size and shape

In geographical size Zambia stands in the middle ranks of African states. Its area of some 291,000 sq. miles (753,000 sq. km.) is occupied by 4 057 000 people (1969 Census) at the very low overall density of 14 to the square mile (5 per sq. k.m.). This comparatively large size in relation to a small population is both advantageous and disadvantageous. The general availability of land offsets limitations imposed by large tracts of inherently infertile soils, unproductive bush vegetation and tsetse-fly infestation, in that an ample usable 'land bank' remains for development. In consequence, a comparatively gradual change-over from space-wasting traditional rural economies to more intensive systems can be accepted in rural planning, with at least potential gains in efficiency. On the other hand, Zambia's long interior distances, highly irregular shape and impediments to communication in the form of lake, swamp and escarpment zone aggravate tribal diversity, foster separatism and add to the problems of maintaining order, security and the pace of development from Lusaka. Geographically, Zambia is not an easy country to organize, to educate or to unify, while its long, largely remote boundary is far beyond its present military capacity to patrol adequately, let alone defend.

Location

Location is one of the two most crucial geographical factors in Zambian life today, the second being regional inequality (p. 116). There are at least four distinct aspects of location, all significant.

The first is that Zambia is a *tropical* country, lying within latitudes 8 to 18 degrees south and subjected to a modified tropical climatic régime. Both opportunities for, and hazards to, the basic farming economy are broadly characteristic of much of tropical Africa. Secondly, Zambia lies mainly on the interior African *high plateau* which, mostly developed on old rocks, is rich in minerals but generally rather infertile of soils. This limits the base for productive farming (although ample development possibilities exist) while providing valuable resources for extractive industries. Furthermore, the altitude causes climatic amelioration, permitting a range of temperate crops to supplement tropical varieties and attracting, along the line of rail, European settlers who, in seventy years of colonial rule, laid the foundations of the modern economy.

Perhaps the most crucial location factor is that Zambia is *land-locked*. Its economic heartland lies some 1250 miles (2000 km.) from Lobito Bay, Beira and Lourenço Marques. Dar es Salaam is 1000 miles (1600 km.) away along a road only very recently tarred for much of its length (p. 110). Thus Zambia's economy, depending heavily upon copper exports and the importation of capital and consumer goods, hangs upon slender transport lifelines. The best developed but politically disfavoured of these pass through the white-ruled territories to the south.

Fourthly, Zambia is *surrounded* by no less than eight neighbours, including territories both independent and colonial, friendly and potentially hostile, politically unstable and stable. She thus finds herself geopolitically vulnerable. This situation became critical at UDI, when Zambia could effectively have been economically strangled by blocking the railway and road to the south and cutting off Kariba power to the copper mines at the Rhodesian-controlled power station. Although this did not happen, the push of this vulnerability, added to the strong pull of her Pan-Africanist policies and her friendship with Tanzania, led Zambia more vigorously to realign her trade routes from south to north and at the same time to seek to widen her options of available routes (p. 114). This process, carried out quickly since 1965 but still incomplete, was expensive in terms of diverted resources and increased costs, but can ultimately benefit Zambia economically as well as politically by opening up her northern and north-eastern hinterlands. The real costs of this vast exercise have also given impetus to the drive for autarchy, with its emphasis on a wide spread of resource development. A further consequence of Zambia's surrounded position is vulnerability to incursions by foreign elements—subversive agents, freedom fighters and refugees—all of whom bring potential political embarrassment in their train.

Zambia has been placed by a cruel geography in the front line in the cold war to oust the distinctly stubborn 'last vestiges' of minority rule from southern Africa. Her undeniable ideological commitment to this struggle is tempered by continued, if fast diminishing, dependence on southern routes and by present feeble military capacity and strategic vulnerability. In her continuing drive towards nationhood Zambia nevertheless disposes of considerable natural wealth in minerals, farmland, climate and water (superior to many young African states), suffers only very localized population pressures, and benefits from energetic leadership that has won friends in Africa and overseas.

D HYWEL DAVIES

ZAMBIA AND HER NEIGHBOURS

2 PROGRESS IN MAPPING

The principal mapping agency in Zambia is the Survey Department in the Ministry of Lands and Natural Resources. Directed by the Surveyor-General, the department is charged with producing a wide variety of maps. To this end it is divided into six sections: geodetic survey, regional survey, mapping, cadastral, photogrammetric and photo-reproduction.

Basic field data are obtained from field survey and air photographs. The geodetic survey section provides general ground control for the photogrammetric section, while the regional survey section provides cadastral information. Ground control is based on the Universal Transverse Mercator Projection. The photogrammetric section is headed by a qualified photogrammetrist and its equipment includes Wild B8, A7 and A8 plotters and a Kelsh plotter. Photo-reproduction work required for photogrammetric purposes is carried out by the photo-reproduction section at actual scale and, at present, without a process camera, using contact prints.

The aforementioned sections provide the data from which the mapping and cadastral sections compile and produce the maps. Basically similar work is carried out in both. From pencil compilation derived from field notes, air photographs and map sources, a blue line plate is made on a photo-sensitive base and a contact print of the compilation is made for final ink draughting. A guide image is then produced by photographic process for each colour in left-reading image on coated sheets: from this the cartographer scribes the detail required for each colour. Lettering is printed on adhesive-backed film. This produces a series of engraved negatives which are then turned over to the Government Printer, where photo-reproduced offset plates are made for printing.

There is some shortage of available trained personnel, most critically in the surveying field. In an attempt to combat this situation, the department runs a training programme in the mapping, cadastral and photogrammetric sections, under the direction of qualified supervisors.

The bulk of the mapping at the important 1:50 000 scale is provided by the British Directorate of Overseas Surveys, Ministry of Overseas Development, under the Zambia–United Kingdom Technical Aid Programme. Directorate surveyors supply ground control, while their photogrammetric and cartographic sections compile the maps in England from air photographs. Proofs are returned to Zambia where field detail and place-names are carefully checked. Printing of the first edition is then undertaken by the British Ordnance Survey, while reprinted and revised editions are prepared by the Zambian Survey Department.

Various maps ranging in scale from 1:2500 to 1:1 500 000 are produced and maintained by the department. Coverage is relatively complete at smaller scales, but at larger scales considerable gaps remain. The maps include a particularly useful 1:1 500 000 sheet of the entire country as well as the 1:1 000 000 International Map of the World (Zambia) and the 1:1 000 000 ICAO Civil Aviation Map. A new 1:750 000 Provincial Series is in the compilation stage. One of the most important series is the uncontoured 1:250 000 (fig. b), which covers the entire country except for the extreme south and west and shows useful topographic detail. The basic 1:50 000 topographic series unfortunately achieves much less coverage, although this is steadily being increased. However, contoured sheets are available in a broad band along the comparatively developed line of rail and the Copperbelt and in some outlying areas, other existing sheets at this scale being uncontoured (fig. a). Major cities and towns have been mapped at 1:5000. Specialty maps appear in the National Atlas of Zambia, for which over 20 sheets had been produced by late 1969 on conventional atlas topics, such as rainfall, soils, population density, medical facilities and many others.

Air photography is available for virtually the entire country at various scales and ages. Nearly all photography falls within the 1:20 000 to 1:40 000 scale range (fig. c). Photography from Western Province and the Kafue Basin mostly dates from 1960 or earlier, but for the remainder of the country much of the coverage has been flown since 1965 and represents a valuable source of information on Zambia.

Maps and air photographs are on sale to the public at Map Sales, Survey Department, PO Box RW 397, Lusaka, Zambia, where complete catalogues may be obtained.

The only other Zambian agency producing maps for sale in any quantity is the Geological Survey Department of the Ministry of State Participation. Here some twenty-two field geologists provide data to the department's draughting section. The Geological Survey undertakes no control work and all their maps are produced on controlled bases provided by the Survey Department. The basic 1:50 000 geological map has been published for the area around Lusaka, generally southward along the line of rail, and towards the Copperbelt: a few other sheets are available for outlying areas (fig. d). A number of special maps have been produced, including the 1:1 000 000 Geological map of Northern Rhodesia, the 1:500 000 Copperbelt map, the 1:125 000 Karroo System and Coal Resources of the Gwembe District map (two sheets), twenty-six geological maps of special areas at 1:100 000, and a number of sheets at 1:75 000. In addition, the Geological Survey has produced numerous scholarly geological reports, bibliographies and economic and technical reports, many containing maps and other illustrations. A list of publications is available from the Director, Geological Survey Department, Ministry of State Participation, PO Box RW 135, Lusaka, Zambia.

Various other maps are produced for special purposes in Zambia, particularly by the mining companies, government departments (such as Agriculture), and by planning bodies and consultant groups. Such maps usually meet the special requirements of the bodies concerned and are not generally available. The Ministry of Power, Transport and Works, the Automobile Association of Zambia, and the Zambia National Tourist Bureau all produce a few uncontrolled maps of roads, and the latter body publishes some popular maps of tourist attractions. The new University of Zambia (1966) is beginning to contribute to progress in mapping through research publications.

J W SNADEN

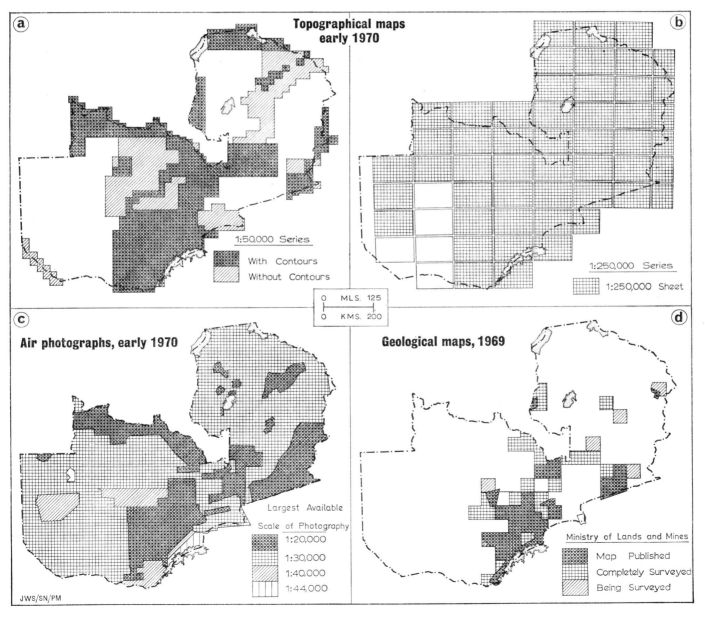

a Topographical maps early 1970

1:50,000 Series
▦ With Contours
▨ Without Contours

b

1:250,000 Series
▦ 1:250,000 Sheet

O ____ MLS. 125
O ____ KMS. 200

c Air photographs, early 1970

Largest Available
Scale of Photography
1:20,000
1:30,000
1:40,000
1:44,000

d Geological maps, 1969

Ministry of Lands and Mines
▦ Map Published
Completely Surveyed
▨ Being Surveyed

JWS/SN/PM

13

3 RELIEF

The relief of Zambia consists mainly of a series of gently undulating to flat plateaux, occasionally broken by isolated hills or low ranges of resistant rocks. Plateaux at different levels may merge gradually or may be separated by intensely dissected escarpment zones. The highest of these plateau surfaces lies in the east and north-east and reaches a maximum height of 7100 feet (2164 m.) on the Malawi border. The plateaux decrease in height towards the south and south-west, the lowest point in the country, at 1030 feet (325 m.), occurring where the Zambezi River enters Mozambique. Most of Zambia lies between 3000 and 5000 feet (1524 m.) and the average altitude of the country is 3700 feet (1127 m.) above mean sea level.

The plateaux of Zambia result from the processes of gradation acting over a long period of time on a relatively stable land mass. Cycles of erosion have been able to progress to a late stage and nearly level peneplains have been produced across rocks of varying resistance (cf. pp. 15 and 19). Uplift of these peneplains on a subcontinental scale initiated new cycles, this sequence of planation and uplift occurring several times so that remnants of plateaux of different ages can be found at different levels. Plateaux formed in this way are termed 'erosion surfaces'. Since uplift was frequently accompanied by warping and rift faulting, erosion surfaces of similar age are not necessarily at the same height, but the oldest are usually the highest and most restricted in area. These surfaces are covered by a mantle of weathering debris, usually between 50 and 100 feet (15–30 m.) deep, and deeper on the older undisturbed surfaces than on those produced more recently.

The exact ages and relationships of the erosion surfaces of Zambia are open to different interpretations, but the following is the most widely accepted.

The oldest surface, represented only by hill remnants over 7000 feet (2134 m.) in the Mafinga Hills and adjacent highland areas on the Malawi border, is believed to be part of the Gondwana surface—a remnant of the original surface of the ancient super-continent of Gondwanaland before the present continents drifted apart. This surface formed mainly during the Jurassic period and its formation ended with uplift in the early Cretaceous.

The erosion surface that developed during the ensuing Post-Gondwana cycle occurs in the Mbala area at a height of 5400 feet (1646 m.) and also along the Malawi border and in the higher parts of the Muchinga Mountains. This Post-Gondwana surface was formed during the Cretaceous period.

The next in sequence of formation, the early Tertiary African surface, forms very flat landscapes over wide areas of Zambia. It forms the greater part of the Muchinga Mountains and the higher plateau watersheds of Northern and Luapula Provinces. The African surface is also exhibited in the north-west, and large remnants also occur in the Lusaka, Southern Province and Malawi border areas. It is most commonly around 4000 feet high (1219 m.) in the south, but rises to 4800 feet (1463 m.) in the north due to warping since its formation.

Later Tertiary surfaces occupy most of the lower areas of all the main basins of the country. They usually stand 500 to 1000 feet (152 to 305 m.) below adjacent early Tertiary surfaces, but again there is variation in elevation due to uplift and warping. They are often undulating rather than flat, due to the shorter time available for their formation than for the earlier surfaces. In the north the later Tertiary surface has been downwarped to form the Bangweulu Lake and Swamps.

Uplift closed the Tertiary phase and carried the land surfaces to their present positions. Subsequently, during the Pleistocene period, the main land-forming activities were the incision of the major river systems and the formation of river terraces. In western Zambia, aggradation, mainly by wind, has gone on intermittently and the plateau is covered by semi-consolidated or unconsolidated sands up to 200 feet (61 m.) in thickness.

Parts of the Zambian plateau have been affected by trough faulting and several rift valley systems can be identified (p. 15). The Luangwa rift valley is the largest of these, extending 350 miles (560 km) from north-east to south-west in the eastern part of the country. It is bounded on the north-west by the impressive Muchinga Escarpment, but the south-eastern flank of the valley has a more subdued topography and the position of the fault is not always evident. Branching off to the west at the southern end of the Luangwa trough are the subsidiary rift valleys of the Lukusashi, Lunsemfwa and Rufunsa Rivers, while the middle Zambezi valley appears to be a south-westerly continuation of the Luangwa trough.

The main faulting that initiated these troughs occurred during the Karroo period, but faulting has occurred to a reduced extent since that time. After the period of most active faulting, the whole surface underwent peneplanation and the original fault scarps were erased. With subsequent uplift new valleys were formed in the same positions on the weaker Karroo rocks. The present valleys are thus secondary features and their present outlines are the result of differential erosion adjusted to variations in structure rather than the direct effect of faulting. The valleys are more correctly referred to as 'rift block valleys' and the scarps as 'fault line scarps'.

The southern end of the Lake Tanganyika rift valley is, in contrast, of more recent age and it is bounded by true fault scarps which are still quite youthful in character. The scarps may be as much as 2000 feet (610 m.) in height and streams are sharply incised into them. The faulting activity responsible in this case reached a maximum in the late Tertiary.

Small scale faulting in the Pleistocene and Recent periods has been responsible for the formation of fault scarps on the plateau between Lake Tanganyika and Lake Mweru.

D R ARCHER

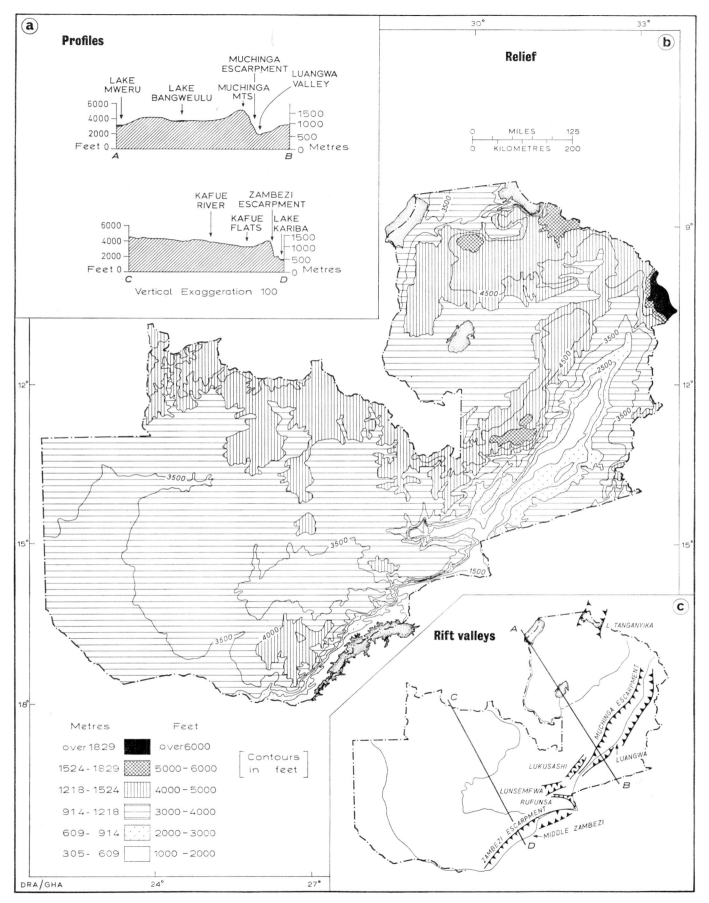

a

Profiles

LAKE
MWERU

LAKE
BANGWEULU

MUCHINGA
ESCARPMENT

MUCHINGA
MTS

LUANGWA
VALLEY

6000
4000
2000
Feet 0

1500
1000
500
0 Metres

A   B

KAFUE
RIVER

ZAMBEZI
ESCARPMENT

KAFUE
FLATS

LAKE
KARIBA

6000
4000
2000
Feet 0

1500
1000
500
0 Metres

C   D

Vertical Exaggeration 100

b

Relief

30°   33°

0   MILES   125
0   KILOMETRES   200

3500

4500

4500

2500

3500

3500

1500

9°

12°

12°

15°

15°

3500

3500

3500

4000

18°

Metres   Feet

over 1829   over 6000

1524 - 1829   5000 - 6000

1218 - 1524   4000 - 5000

914 - 1218   3000 - 4000

609 - 914   2000 - 3000

305 - 609   1000 - 2000

Contours
in feet

c

Rift valleys

A   L. TANGANYIKA

C

MUCHINGA ESCARPMENT

LUKUSASHI

LUANGWA

LUNSEMFWA

B

RUFUNSA

ZAMBEZI ESCARPMENT

MIDDLE ZAMBEZI

D

DRA/GHA   24°   27°

15

4 DRAINAGE

Zambia is drained by parts of two of Africa's major river systems, the Zambezi and the Congo. The Zambezi system covers about three-quarters of the total area and the Congo system about one-quarter. Besides these there is only the small area in the north-east that forms a part of the internal drainage system of Lake Rukwa in Tanzania. The major systems may be divided into eight basins as mapped and listed below:

System	Basin	Approximate area in Zambia	
		sq. miles	km²
	Zambezi (excluding main tributaries)	106 000	170 554
Zambezi	Kafue	59 900	96 379
	Luangwa	38 500	61 946
	Lunsemfwa	16 800	27 031
Congo	Chambeshi	19 900	32 019
	Bangweulu/Luapula	40 000	64 360
	Lake Tanganyika	6 300	10 136
	Rukwa	300	482

The main Zambezi system occupies most of the west of the country and some discontinuous areas in the south, separated from one another by the main tributary basins. The Zambezi rises in north-west Zambia, crosses into Angola and swings back into Zambia. Here its gradient is low and extensive flood-plains and swamps occur in Western Province. South of these the river turns sharply eastward, forming Zambia's southern border, and flows towards the Victoria Falls and the Batoka Gorge below. The valley opens out downstream to the rifted middle Zambezi valley now occupied by the vast man-made Lake Kariba, approximately 170 miles (274 km.) long and up to 30 miles (48 km.) wide. Another gorge below Kariba dam gives way to a wide flood plain that continues to the Mozambique border.

The Kafue River, tributary to the Zambezi, rises north of the Copperbelt, where the Kafue–Congo watershed forms the national boundary, and flows in a generally southward direction. Gradients are low and extensive swamps, notably the Lukanga and Busanga Swamps, occur along the main river and its tributaries. The river turns sharply eastward to the Kafue Flats, a vast floodplain zone with adjacent areas of poorly drained soils. Below the Flats, the Kafue enters a gorge and drops some 2000 feet (610 m.) in 20 miles (32 km.) over a series of rapids and waterfalls before joining the Zambezi.

The Luangwa River and its main tributary, the Lunsemfwa, drain much of eastern Zambia. The Luangwa follows a fairly direct course from north-east to south-west along a rifted zone and the main tributaries also follow the lines of rift block valleys. The Luangwa has on average a steeper gradient than the other Zambian rivers and has few swamps along its course. Tributaries fall steeply from the Muchinga Escarpment (p. 15) and from the high plateau on the Malawi border.

The Congo drainage in Zambia comprises the basins of the Chambeshi, the Luapula and Lake Tanganyika. The Luapula River is a continuation of the Chambeshi, but they are separated by Bangweulu Lake and Swamps, which for convenience are mapped as part of the Luapula drainage system.

The Chambeshi River follows a north-east to south-west course. It has a gentle gradient and extensive swamps, but it tumbles over a series of shallow rapids as it approaches the Bangweulu Swamps. These swamps consist of two basic units: an outer belt of 25 miles (40 km.), which is flooded annually during the rains, and the main swamp, permanently flooded and covered by floating vegetation. The Chambeshi waters are distributed in an intricate system of channels across the swamps, some finding their way to Lake Bangweulu but most being discharged directly into the Luapula River.

The Luapula River has a gently sloping profile in its upper course, but as it swings northward it becomes incised and flows over a series of falls. The valley widens again into a broad swampy zone before flowing into Lake Mweru.

The drainage into Lake Tanganyika consists of one main river, the Lufubu, and some short streams steeply incised into the surrounding scarps, with many rapids and waterfalls, including the spectacular Kalambo Falls, 710 feet (216 m.) high.

The distinctive characteristics of the drainage and hydrology of Zambia depend principally on three factors: the seasonal distribution of rainfall, the areal distribution of 'surplus water' and the characteristics of the plateau surfaces.

Almost all rainfall throughout the country falls during the rainy season from November to April, the dry months contributing no water to streamflow. Most small streams dry up, while in many larger streams flow is reduced to a small fraction of wet season discharge (fig. a). Thus maximum discharge of the lower Luangwa River is frequently one hundred times minimum discharge. The peak flow usually occurs during February in the headwaters, but downstream it may be delayed as late as May, particularly in rivers with swampy courses.

Surplus water (fig. c), i.e. the amount of precipitation that goes to streamflow and deep percolation as calculated by the Thornthwaite method, shows marked regional variations depending on variations in rainfall and evapotranspiration. It decreases from a maximum of about 25 inches (633 mm.) in the north to zero surplus in parts of the Luangwa and Zambezi valleys. Most of the discharge of the main rivers is therefore derived from the wetter northern part of Zambia, little being added by tributary drainage in the south.

The third factor determining drainage character is the gently sloping nature of the plateaux, which has given rise to the very widely spaced drainage network. Drainage of the low plateau interfluves may be effected mainly by sheet flow, and infiltration may account for a considerable proportion of the rainfall, especially in areas of Kalahari sands. Characteristically, the headwaters of plateau streams take the form of broad, shallow linear concavities known as dambos, which retain water and maintain streamflow well into the dry season. Dambos cover perhaps five per cent of the area of the country and are important for rural settlement since they provide a perennial water supply (p. 96).

D R ARCHER

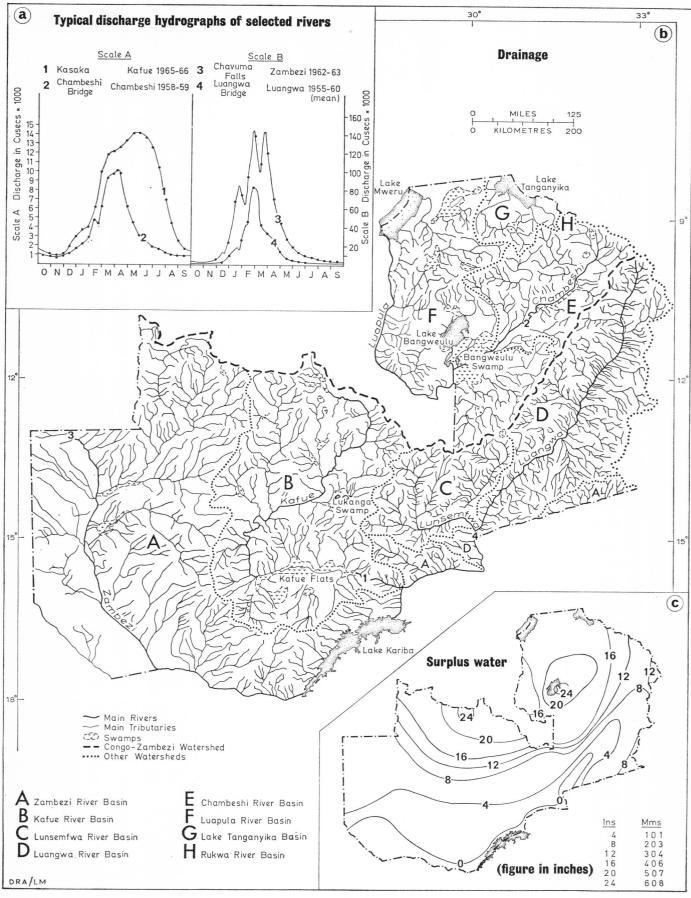

(a) Typical discharge hydrographs of selected rivers

Scale A
1 Kasaka   Kafue 1965-66
2 Chambeshi   Chambeshi 1958-59
  Bridge

Scale B
3 Chavuma   Zambezi 1962-63
  Falls
4 Luangwa   Luangwa 1955-60
  Bridge   (mean)

Scale A Discharge in Cusecs × 1000

Scale B Discharge in Cusecs × 1000

O N D J F M A M J J A S O N D J F M A M J J A S

(b) Drainage

MILES 125
KILOMETRES 200

Lake Mweru
Lake Tanganyika
G
H
F
Lake Bangweulu
Bangweulu Swamp
E
Chambeshi
D
Luangwa

Luapula

B
Kafue
Lukanga Swamp
C
Lunsemfwa
A
D
A
Zambezi
Kafue Flats
1
Lake Kariba

— Main Rivers
⌇ Main Tributaries
⌇⌇ Swamps
– – Congo-Zambezi Watershed
···· Other Watersheds

A Zambezi River Basin
B Kafue River Basin
C Lunsemfwa River Basin
D Luangwa River Basin

E Chambeshi River Basin
F Luapula River Basin
G Lake Tanganyika Basin
H Rukwa River Basin

(c) Surplus water

Ins	Mms
4	101
8	203
12	304
16	406
20	507
24	608

(figure in inches)

DRA/LM

5 GEOLOGY

The oldest rock system of Zambia, the Basement Complex, is most extensively exposed in the east and south-east of the country. Proceeding westward, successively younger rocks outcrop. These systems and their approximate European equivalents are outlined in the key to the map.

The *Basement Complex* in Zambia may be divided into upper and lower parts, separated by a major unconformity. The rocks of the lower Basement Complex, known on the Copperbelt as the Lufubu system, are structurally complex. They have been folded and faulted and have undergone repeated metamorphism, so that their original character has been completely obliterated. The main rock types are gneisses, mica, hornblende and kyanite schists and micaceous quartzites. The lower Basement Complex occupies a large part of Eastern and Northern Provinces. It is also exposed on the higher plateau areas of Southern Province, while isolated domelike outcrops occur elsewhere on the plateau, e.g. Solwezi and Luswishi.

The Muva group, representing the upper part of the Basement Complex, has a much lower grade of metamorphism. It is separated from the lower Basement by an unconformity which is believed to represent a period of as much as 1000 million years. The most characteristic rock types of this group are quartzites, schists and conglomerates. The quartzites are clean and are fairly easily distinguishable from quartzites of other systems. The Muva group is represented areally by fairly small scattered outcrops bordering the lower Basement. It is again most common in Eastern and Northern Provinces, in Southern Province near Zimba, and on the Copperbelt. A belt of porphyritic rock, largely rhyolitic in character and associated with volcanic breccias, is thought to be equivalent in age to the Muva group. It extends along the eastern side of the Luapula River and from Lake Mweru to Lake Tanganyika.

The Basement Complex has been extensively intruded by granites and parts of the lower Basement have been granitized. These older granites are recognizable where they are unconformably overlain by sediments of Katanga age, their main occurrence being in the south-east, east and north.

Mineralization of the Basement Complex is limited, but some gold, silver, mica and iron have been worked, and tin, asbestos and graphite are also present.

After the deposition and folding of the Muva group, there was considerable erosion of the entire Basement Complex. This left an irregular surface on which *Katanga* sediments were deposited late in the Pre-Cambrian era. Rocks of the Katanga System occur extensively in Northern, Luapula, Copperbelt, Northwestern and Central Provinces.

On the Copperbelt the Katanga System has been divided into Roan, Mwashia and Kundelungu groups. In the remainder of the country, it has been usual to divide the Katanga simply into upper and lower divisions, since it is not yet possible to make precise correlations with the Copperbelt area. Part of the Roan group is highly mineralized, and copper occurs in local synclinal basins in shales, sandstones, dolomites and quartzites on the margins of the broad Kafue anticline (p. 93 [g]). Copper minerals include chalocpyrite, bornite, chalcocite, malachite and azurite.

The Mwashia group consists largely of carbonaceous shales, argillites and interbedded quartzites. The Kundelungu group is believed to rest conformably on the Mwashia. The lithology of the Kundelungu varies greatly from place to place, but in some areas it is divisible into a lower part consisting of a conglomerate of glacial origin, dolomites, limestones and carbonaceous shales and an upper part predominantly of sandstones, quartzites and shales. The lead and zinc deposits in dolomites and argillites at Kabwe are now believed to belong to the Kundelungu group. Limestone from the Katanga System is widely used for metallurgical processing, for cement, agricultural lime and road stone.

No sediments in Zambia can be attributed to the Lower Palaeozoic. However, there is a younger granite, intrusive into the Katanga sediments, which has been dated to the early Ordovician period. These granites are best displayed in a batholithic outcrop west of Mumbwa.

The next youngest group of rocks, the *Karroo* system, extends in age from the Upper Carboniferous to the Jurassic period. This system is best represented in the rift block valleys of the east and south—the valleys of the Luangwa, Lukusashi, Lunsemfwa, Rufunsa and mid-Zambezi, although further outcrops occur on the plateau to the west. The lowest part of the sequence is represented by a possible tillite indicating a glacial phase of Carboniferous age. This is followed by sandstones and then by the Gwembe coal formation. These coal seams are best represented in the Maamba-Nkandabwe area of the Zambezi valley, but thin seams occur elsewhere in the mid-Zambezi valley and also in the Luangwa valley. Higher in the sequence, the Karroo consists mainly of mudstones, grit and sandstones with an upper layer of basaltic lava of Jurassic age. The basalt outcrops around Livingstone and is exposed in the walls of the Batoka Gorge below Victoria Falls. It is covered in the west by sands of the Kalahari system.

The *Kalahari* system, consisting of poorly consolidated sandstones and unconsolidated windblown sands, mantles the greater part of Western Province, together with smaller areas of Northwestern, Central and Southern Provinces. These sands originated during the later Tertiary and Pleistocene periods. They were deposited during an arid phase, when the limits of the Kalahari Desert were greatly extended.

Recent deposits of *alluvium* are most extensive in the upper Zambezi and its tributaries, on the Kafue Flats, the Lukanga and Bangweulu Swamps and along the upper Chambeshi River.

D R ARCHER

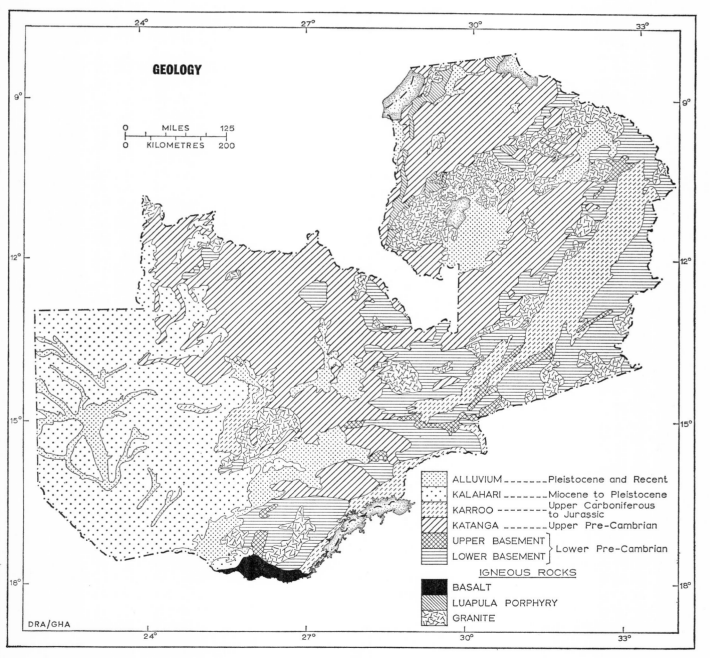

GEOLOGY

O ___ MILES ___ 125
O ___ KILOMETRES ___ 200

ALLUVIUM_____Pleistocene and Recent
KALAHARI_____Miocene to Pleistocene
KARROO_____Upper Carboniferous to Jurassic
KATANGA_____Upper Pre-Cambrian
UPPER BASEMENT ⎫
LOWER BASEMENT ⎭ Lower Pre-Cambrian
IGNEOUS ROCKS
BASALT
LUAPULA PORPHYRY
GRANITE

DRA/GHA

6 RAINFALL

The climatic régime, and particularly the seasonal distribution of rainfall, imposes a strong rhythm on most of Zambia's rural population. For the subsistence farmer, cultivation is concentrated in the rainy season lasting from November to March or April, while the long dry season is a period of dependence on stored crops.

The rainfall of Zambia is of several origins, the most important being related to the southward movement of the equatorial low pressure belt in the summer months in association with apparent migration of the overhead sun. Airstreams converge on this belt from the semi-permanent sub-tropical anticyclonic cells either in a distinct line or in a broad zone with an intervening area with light winds (fig c). The meeting-place of these airstreams is referred to as the Inter-Tropical Convergence Zone (ITCZ). The three principal airstreams affecting Zambia in the rainy season are:

1. Congo air

This is believed to originate at least partly in the south-east trades of the South Atlantic Ocean, which curve inland over the Congo as they approach the equator, reaching Zambia from the north-west. This airstream is very humid in its lower levels and can produce widespread rain when subjected to convergence. The forward edge of the airmass is known as the Congo Air Boundary and it typically lies across the country from south-west to north-east during the rainy season.

2. The south-east trades of the South Indian Ocean

These are the dominant winds during the dry season, but in summer, with a mainly sea track over the northern tip of Madagascar, they hold more moisture. By the time they reach Zambia they have often been deflected to easterly or even north-easterly paths.

3. The north-east monsoon

This originates in the Asiatic high pressure system, crosses the northern Indian Ocean and may reach north-eastern Zambia in midsummer.

Most rainfall occurs near the margins of the ITCZ along the Congo Air Boundary and at the northern limit of the south-east trades. Rainfall is particularly prevalent when there are surges in the airstreams and the boundaries are being actively moved forward. Precipitation occurs to a lesser extent in the central area of the equatorial trough or within the airstreams where there is sufficient depth of humid air.

A second but related group of circumstances leading to precipitation in Zambia occur when high pressure cells detach themselves from the semi-permanent Atlantic Ocean anti-cyclone and move eastward across the continent. Counter-clockwise circulation around such highs often brings an invasion of cool moist air from the south-east or south and causes surges in the south-east trades. The associated weather may be cloudy to overcast with persistent rain or drizzle where the air is lifted orographically. This condition is most common in the east and south and is referred to as the *guti*. These incoming highs may also be accompanied by upper westerly waves bringing cold air at high levels. This may produce instability and give rise to thundery showers. The infrequent occurrences of precipitation during the dry season are normally of this type.

Thirdly, tropical cyclones originating in the southern Indian Ocean may very occasionally penetrate inland as far as Zambia. Here they are usually slow moving and very high windspeeds are uncommon, but they may release heavy precipitation.

Mean annual rainfall

The most notable feature of the distribution of mean annual rainfall is the general decrease in amount from north to south, which may be attributed to the shorter time the south is influenced by the ITCZ. Superimposed on this pattern are areas of higher rainfall resulting from above-average altitude or from proximity to lakes and swamps. The northern half of the country has annual totals ranging from 40 to 60 inches (1015 to 1520 mm) with the maximum north-west of Lake Bangweulu. An average rainfall of 50 inches (1270 mm) in the neighbourhood of Lake Tanganyika is somewhat higher than adjacent areas farther from the lake. The southern half of Zambia has rainfall totals usually between 25 and 40 inches (635 to 1015 mm), the lower figures being recorded in the middle Zambezi valley. Altitude effects are best shown in the contrasting rainfall of the Muchinga Mountains (over 48 inches [1220 mm] in places) and the adjacent Luangwa valley (less than 32 inches [815 mm]).

Seasonal distribution of rainfall

Figure *d* (after Lineham) shows the 80 per cent probability date for the beginning of the wet season as defined by one inch of rain occurring in five days: i.e. this amount of rainfall may be expected to occur by the date noted on four years out of five. The rains commence in the north-west (followed shortly by the north-east), and progress south-eastward, generally arriving a month later in the south-east. The beginning of the rains at a given place can vary from year to year by as much a month.

Over most of the country there is a single rainfall peak, the rainiest month being January. At a few stations in the north-east and north-west, however, there is a tendency towards the double maxima typical of lower latitudes, with peaks of rainfall in December and March.

The average length of the rainy season varies from more than 190 days in parts of Luapula and Northern Provinces, to less than 120 days in the middle Zambezi valley. The end of the rains comes first in the south-west and moves almost directly nothward, the last rains coming in early May in the Mbala area.

Rainfall variability

There are substantial variations from year to year in the duration and amount of rainfall. This variability can be expressed in terms of the coefficient of variability, i.e. the standard deviation expressed as a percentage of the mean rainfall (fig. *a*). With a few local exceptions the variability is greatest in areas of lowest rainfall and least in areas of high rainfall.

D R ARCHER

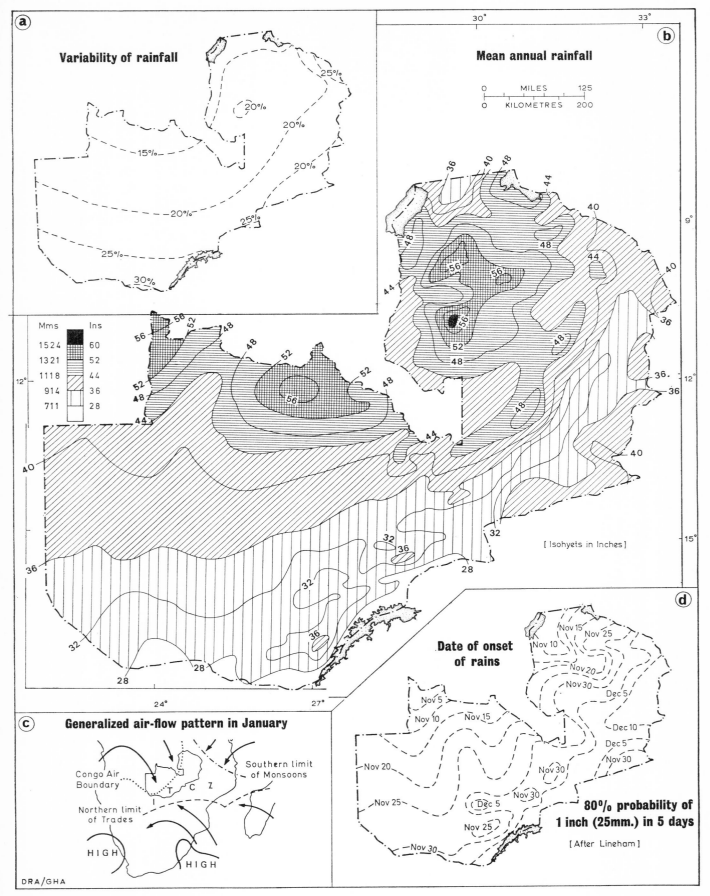

a Variability of rainfall

25%
20%
20%
15%
20%
20%
25%
25%
30%

b Mean annual rainfall

30°   33°

0   MILES   125
0   KILOMETRES   200

Mms	Ins
1524	60
1321	52
1118	44
914	36
711	28

[Isohyets in Inches]

c Generalized air-flow pattern in January

Congo Air
Boundary
Southern limit
of Monsoons
Northern limit
of Trades
T C Z
HIGH   HIGH

DRA/GHA

d

Date of onset
of rains

Nov 15   Nov 25
Nov 10
Nov 20
Nov 30   Dec 5
Nov 5
Nov 10   Nov 15   Dec 10
Dec 5
Nov 20   Nov 30
Nov 30   Nov 30
Nov 25
Dec 5   Nov 30
Nov 25

**80% probability of
1 inch (25mm.) in 5 days**

[After Lineham]

Nov 30

21

7 TEMPERATURE, HUMIDITY, SUNSHINE AND WINDS

Although rainfall is the most important element in seasonal differentiation in Zambia (p. 20), other climatic factors also have marked seasonal rhythm. These, together with rainfall, define Zambia's three seasons, namely:

1 The cool dry season (April to August)
2 The hot dry season (August to November)
3 the warm wet season (November to April)

The various climatic elements may conveniently be described in terms of their seasonal progress.

In the *cool dry season* the sun is overhead far in the northern hemisphere and Zambia experiences its lowest temperatures. In July (fig. *a*), which vies with June as the coldest month, night temperatures fall to between 45°F and 50°F (7°C and 10°C) in the west of the country, the coldest temperatures being experienced in the Sesheke District in the south-west of Western Province, where temperatures of less than 20°F (−7°C) have been recorded. Over the east and north-east, minimum temperatures tend to be higher, ranging from 50°F to 55°F (10°C to 13°C) except in the Muchinga Mountains and along the Malawi border. Clear skies at night throughout the country permit rapid loss of heat from the surface and temperature inversions frequently develop in the main valleys. Shallow but intense inversions may also occur occasionally in lower-lying areas on the plateau and associated frosts may occur locally over a substantial part of the country between June and August (fig *f*). The Sesheke area records the highest average number of frost days (10) while parts of Northwestern, Copperbelt, Southern and Central Provinces also experience on average a few days of frost a year. The occurrence of ground frost is even more widespread and probably only parts of Northern and Luapula Provinces escape entirely.

Mean maximum temperature distributions in July mainly demonstrate the effects of altitude. Highest temperatures of 80°F to 87°F (27°C to 31°C) are recorded in the low-lying Luangwa and middle Zambezi valleys and in the north between Lake Tanganyika and Lake Mweru, with lower temperatures (68°F to 72°F: 20°C to 22°C) in the Muchinga Mountains.

In the cool dry season, winds are usually light and predominantly from the east and south-east through the country (fig. *c*). Relative humidities in July range from 20 per cent to 40 per cent during the afternoon and between 60 and 80 per cent in the early morning, values being locally higher in the vicinity of lakes and permanent swamps. Mean relative humidity decreases steadily from the end of the rainy season, usually reaching a minimum in September. Bright sunshine is usually in excess of eight hours throughout the dry season, representing 70 per cent to 80 per cent of the total possible, and the cloud cover is correspondingly low. From June onwards visibilities may be reduced by smoke haze produced by grass fires.

At the end of August temperatures rise rapidly, marking the arrival of the *hot dry season*. October is usually the hottest month, although in some years, when the rains are delayed, November may be hotter. The highest maxima occur in the low-lying areas in the south (fig. *b*) and stations in the lower Luangwa valley may have mean daily maximum temperatures of over 100°F (38°C) in October and November. Mean minimum temperatures are highest in the same areas, but even there the night temperatures only occasionally remain above 70°F (21°C), so that at the hottest season conditions are still generally quite comfortable. From August onwards winds strengthen and back gradually to the north-east.

In October the humidity begins to rise with incursions of maritime Congo air and thunderstorms occur in the north-west, gradually spreading to the rest of the country during the following month. The *warm wet season* has usually arrived throughout the country by the end of November.

With the arrival of the rains, there is a sharp decrease in temperatures in spite of the continued high potential heating power of the sun with the approach of the solstice. In January, mean daily maximum temperatures are 10°F (6°C) lower than in October throughout the country. This is because incoming solar radiation is reduced by the greater cloud cover, while temperatures are also temporarily decreased by the effects of falling rain. However, the cloud cover also reduces the loss of heat from the surface at night, so that January mean minimum temperatures are slightly higher than those in October over most of the country.

At this season, there is a much greater variation in wind direction, indicating the increased importance of the Congo airstream and the presence of the convergence zone (p. 21[c]). Easterly winds are still dominant in the south and east but winds from the north-west quadrant become dominant over much of the north and west (fig *d*). Winds are usually light, but there may be heavy squalls associated with thunderstorms. Relative humidity increases sharply with the onset of the rains and in January it reaches 95 per cent in the early morning, declining to 60 to 70 per cent by mid-afternoon. Mist and fog patches may develop in the early morning but they are quickly dispersed after sunrise. During the wet season the sun still breaks through sufficiently often to provide an average daily sunshine ranging from five hours in the south to three hours in the north.

The rains gradually die out by the end of March in the south but linger on through April in the north. The cloud cover decreases and there is an increase in daytime heating. Mean daily maxima in March and April are similar to those in February in spite of the northward movement of the overhead sun. There is also a decrease in relative humidity. By May there is a general return to cool, dry conditions and the yearly cycle is complete.

D R ARCHER

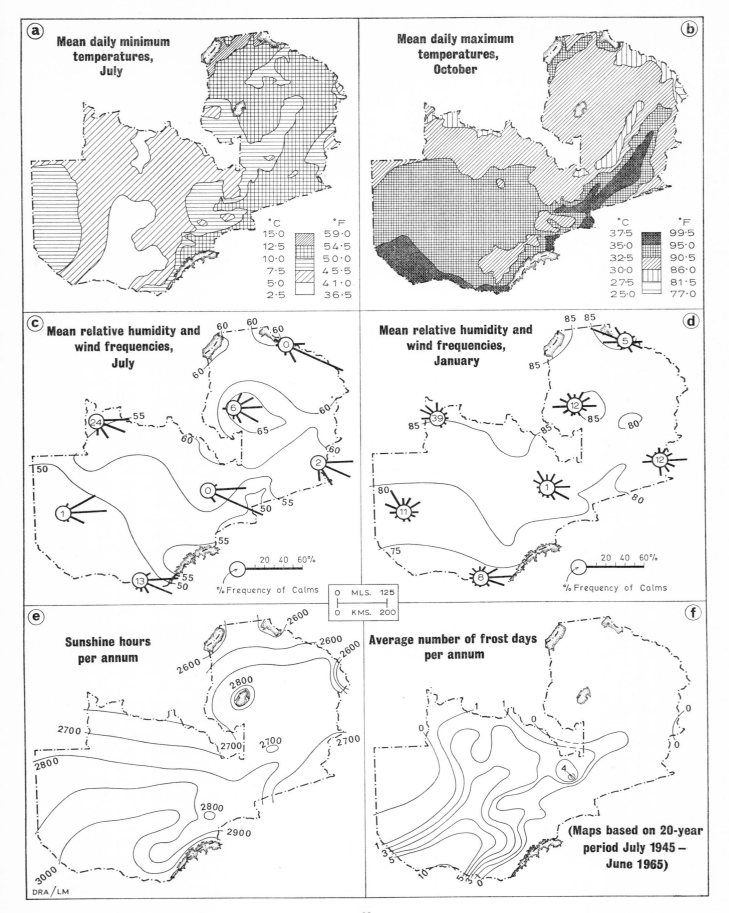

a Mean daily minimum temperatures, July

°C	°F
15·0	59·0
12·5	54·5
10·0	50·0
7·5	45·5
5·0	41·0
2·5	36·5

b Mean daily maximum temperatures, October

°C	°F
37·5	99·5
35·0	95·0
32·5	90·5
30·0	86·0
27·5	81·5
25·0	77·0

c Mean relative humidity and wind frequencies, July

20 40 60%
% Frequency of Calms

d Mean relative humidity and wind frequencies, January

20 40 60%
% Frequency of Calms

O ⊢⊢⊢⊢⊢ MLS. 125
O ⊢⊢⊢⊢⊢ KMS. 200

e Sunshine hours per annum

f Average number of frost days per annum

(Maps based on 20-year period July 1945 – June 1965)

DRA/LM

23

8 VEGETATION AND THE FOREST ESTATE

Zambia's vegetation can broadly be divided into 'forest', 'woodland' and 'grassland'. In the forests the upper tree layer is mostly closed and the middle layer often characterized by a dense thicket understorey. There is at best a discontinuous grass cover. Woodlands show a dense tree cover with more or less closed canopy. The middle layer, however, is open and there is only a sparse grass cover. True woodlands often merge into open grassy woodlands, in which the canopy is not closed, and there may be a complete grass cover ('woodland savanna'). Grasslands encompass areas with scattered trees and/or shrubs and treeless plains.

Together with climatic (precipitation, flooding) and edaphic (soils) factors, man has influenced the natural vegetation and helped to degrade forests and woodlands by burning and cultivation. Fire is undoubtedly the dominant single factor in maintaining a fairly open vegetation.

Livunda Forest covers parts of north-western Zambia. It is a dry evergreen low forest characterized by *Chryptosepalum pseudotaxus* ('Livunda'), with lianes forming a fairly dense understorey. Southward it merges into Mushibe Woodland, while other dry evergreen forests in northern Zambia have degraded to fire-hardy Chipya Woodland under the influences of drier climate, fire and cultivation. **Mutemwa Forest** is a dry deciduous forest confined to areas of Kalahari sand (p. 19), occurring widely in southern Western Province and as relics in Balovale, Kabompo and Sesheke Districts. It is dominated by *Baikiaea plurijuga* ('Zambian Teak') and *Pterocarpus antunesii*. A similar forest, with a poorly developed upper storey and a dense thicket layer, is found in the Mweru–Chishi–Tanganyika lowlands of Northern Province as **Itigi Forest**, closely related to the great Itigi Thicket of Tanzania. Characteristic species are *Bussea massaiensis*, *Baphia massaiensis* and *Combretum ssp*.

Woodland of various types covers four-fifths of Zambia. **Mushibe Woodland** occurs widely on Kalahari sand in Western Province, with evergreen species increasing northward. Typical species are *Guibourtia coleosperma* ('Mushibe'), *Burkea africana* and *Erythrophleum africanum*. **Miombo Woodland** covers over half Zambia, mainly on plateau and escarpment country, and is characterized by *Brachystegia*, *Jubelnardia* and *Isoberlinia* species. In the west, Miombo species, especially *Brachystegia spiciformis*, have invaded Mushibe Woodland. **Munga Woodland,** dominated by *Acacia*, *Combretum* and *Terminalia* species among tall grass, occurs in Central Province, Mazabuka–Monze Districts and in Petauke District. **Mopane Woodland** covers much of the hot, dry southern valleys of the Zambezi and Luangwa. Dominated by *Colophospermum mopane*, it is almost monotypic, but may be mixed with *Kirkia accuminata*, *Sterculia africana* and other species and have significant stands of baobab.

Chipya Woodland occurs particularly around Lake Bangweulu and also around Lake Mweru, in the Luapula valley and north-east of Mwinilunga. It reveals mixed tree growth of *Pterocarpus angolensis*, *Erthrophleum africanum*, *Parinari curatellifolia* and others, with small trees (*Terminalia*, *Combretum*, etc.) standing in very tall grass and herbs. Another open grassy woodland is **Lusese Woodland** in Western Province and Namwala District, dominated by *Burkea africana*, *Dialium engleanum* and species of *Baikiaea* and *Colophospermum*. In Western Province this shades into *Diplorhynchus* shrub savanna or into Loudetia grassland in flooded areas of the Zambezi and tributary valleys.

Grassland and swamp. Larger grasslands occupy seasonally flooded Kalahari sands (*Loudetia grassland*) and great swampy depressions such as Lukanga, Bangweulu and Kafue (*Hyparrhenia grassland*). Smaller grasslands line dambos, streams and rivers. Virtually permanently flooded areas of *Hyparrhenia* grassland are occupied by swamp and papyrus sudd.

The Forest Estate

Some 25 000 sq. miles (64 750 sq. km.) of Zambia fall under Forest Reserves, comprising reserved forest areas on state land and protected forest areas elsewhere (fig. *a*), as against over 120 000 sq. miles (310 800 sq. km.) of unreserved forests. (In this legal sense 'forest' includes woodland.) Reserves are classed as Protection Reserves (protecting hill ranges, headwaters, etc.) and Production Reserves (to assure future timber supplies), the latter comprising two-thirds of the total area. Because of potential export value certain trees are protected both in and out of reserves, including *Entandrophragma candatum* (Mupumena), *Khaya nyasica* (Mululu), *Petrocarpus angolensis* (Mukwa), *Afzelia quanzensis* (Mupapa), *Faurea saligna* (Saninga) and *Baikiaea plurijuga* (Makushi or 'Zambian Teak').

Utilization of indigenous forests is patchily distributed. In the south-west, 'Zambian Teak' and Mukwa are extensively logged along a private railway from Livingstone (p. 111) and used for construction, flooring, railway sleepers, furniture and props in mines, some being exported. A little quality timber is also produced in the north. Larger quantities of wood, mostly from Copperbelt Province, are used for mining construction and pit props. The rather limited and scattered useful trees and archaic production methods force Zambia to import much timber.

Inadequate local production, particularly for the mines during wartime (when outside supplies were disrupted) led to extensive development of exotic softwood plantations in reserves in the Copperbelt, especially around Ndola and near Kalulushi. After much experimentation, most planting has been of *Eucalyptus* and of tropical pines. Older plantations are niw beginning to produce timber. Eucalypts are used for fencing, telephone and other poles and for boxwood and processed boards. Pines are mainly for structural, general purpose and mine timbers. Recent manufacturing developments have led to further planting under the First National Development Plan, especially in Northwestern Province and along the line of rail.

Charcoal is of greater immediate value to many Zambians than timber. Many urban dwellers cook with charcoal and a few thousand people live by making and selling it, mostly under licence in forest reserves. Because of its bulk, virtually all charcoal making occurs near towns and major roads, being located by markets rather than vegetation types. Beeswax is quite an important forest product and production is expanding, about half coming from Western and Northwestern Provinces, where it is traded into Angola. The bushland widely permits collection of supplementary food, including edible berries, roots and cater-pillars. Medicinal herbs are also gathered for traditional remedies.

R MÄCKEL

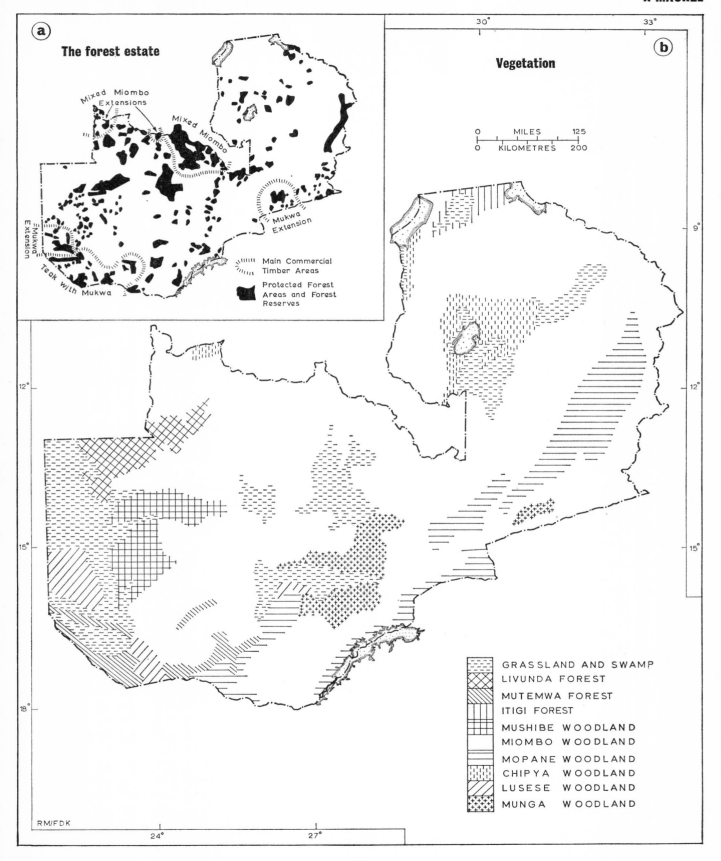

(a) The forest estate

Mixed Miombo Extensions

Mixed Miombo

Mukwa Extension

Mukwa Extension

Teak with Mukwa

⠿⠿ Main Commercial Timber Areas

■ Protected Forest Areas and Forest Reserves

(b) Vegetation

0 MILES 125
0 KILOMETRES 200

GRASSLAND AND SWAMP
LIVUNDA FOREST
MUTEMWA FOREST
ITIGI FOREST
MUSHIBE WOODLAND
MIOMBO WOODLAND
MOPANE WOODLAND
CHIPYA WOODLAND
LUSESE WOODLAND
MUNGA WOODLAND

RM/FDK

9 SOILS

Soil characteristics are mainly due to climatic factors, parent rock material and topography. The decisive climatic factor in Zambia is rainfall, which has affected the degree of soil weathering and leaching. In southern Zambia, where annual rainfall is under 40 inches (1000 mm.) per annum, these processes are slower than in the rainier north, with up to 50 inches (1250 mm.). The effects of increasing rainfall on the extent of leaching are modified by underlying parent rock material, which widely and closely influences soil texture, colour, structure and other morphological characteristics.

The eight soil groups mapped represent gross simplification imposed by scale and limited detailed knowledge: comments made below on soil potential are consequently equally generalized.

Fersiallitic soils occur mainly on parent rock materials rich in ferromagnesian minerals (dolomite, calcareous schist, etc.), but may even cover old alluvium—'Kafue basin alluvium'. They have a moderate base status (pH five to seven). Topsoil texture ranges from clay to sandy clay loams or sandy loams, while solum thickness varies from 50 to over 300 cm. Colour changes with drainage: red clays and reddish brown to yellowish red loams occur in well-drained environment, while grey brown or greyish soils indicate poor drainage. Fersiallitic soils are formed on uplands in Central Province (Lusaka, Mumbwa, Kabwe), in the Monze-Mazabuka Districts, and in Eastern Province (Petauke-Chipata), usually on nearly level to gently undulating topography, with slopes ranging from under one to over five per cent. Here average annual rainfall is under 40 inches (1000 mm.). The relatively wide soil variation is attributed to the proximity of parent materials. Fersiallitic soils are suitable for cultivation of a wide range of climatically adapted crops. They include the most fertile Zambian soils, now widely cultivated.

Ferrallitic soils derive from various parent rocks, including granite, gneiss, sandstone and schist. Covering half Zambia, they occur mainly on gently undulating uplands with slopes of up to three per cent or more. They fall into two groups: the northern ferrallitic soils of the higher rainfall area (over 1000 mm. per annum) and the southern ferrallitic soils. The latter vary from sandy loams to loamy sands. Usually clay content increases with depth: a sandy surface horizon occurs on loamy sand or sandy loam, underlain by sandy clay loam. Soil colour changes from yellowish red to yellowish brown in well drained areas, to greyish brown where poorly drained. The solum thickness extends to over 180 cm., but shallow soils, often with rock outcrops, are common associates. These soils, found in Southern, Eastern and Central Provinces are partly suitable for cultivation. However sandy soils particularly require careful management, while vast areas are best suited to permanent vegetative cover utilized through timber production, grazing, or wildlife. In contrast, the northern ferrallitic soils are more leached because of higher rainfall with lower base saturation (pH four to five). The clay content is generally higher: soil textures change from clays to sandy clays or sandy clay loams, showing gradually increasing

clay content from the coarse-grained surface soil to the subsoils. These deep friable soils, 180 cm. deep, show a colour range from dark reddish brown through red to yellowish red. They occur in Northwestern, Western, Northern and Luapula Provinces, and are widely used for chitimene cultivation (p. 58). They may be used for local crops under good soil management and for timber production or pasture grasses.

Barotse sands are deep, loose, structureless sands. They comprise wind and water-sorted quartzitic sands with very low clay and silt content throughout the soil profile, usually under five per cent clay plus silt. The solum thickness is generally over 180 cm. Normally whitish or grey where the surface is discoloured with organic matter or ash, they pass to golden or reddish colours where stained with iron oxide (most frequently on the Zambezi scarps). Their origin is controversial. One view is that they were transported by wind from the Kalahari Desert during late Tertiary times: another, that they are developed from underlying Karroo sandstone by a process of water transport and subsequent wind action. Vast areas of western Zambia are covered by Barotse sands, which extend as shallower lobes into Mwinilunga, Kasempa and Namwala Districts. They are best suited to permanent vegetation cover (woodland, grassland), utilizable through grazing, timber production or wildlife habitat.

Vertisols of the Kafue Flats consist of deep, calcareous cracking clays. They change in colour from black in the upper horizons to grey at depth. The surface pH ranges from 5·7 to 7·3, increasing to 8·5 in the subsoil. A characteristic calcium carbonate horizon generally occurs within 120 cm. of the surface. The Kafue vertisols are formed on the nearly level flood plains of the Kafue Flats. Of alluvial (lacustrine) origin they experience seasonal flooding. An estimated 1·7 million acres (7000 sq. km.) are covered by these soils between Iteshi Teshi and the Kafue Gorge (p. 119[d]), which may also be found as small bodies along other rivers and swamps. They may be utilized for grazing cattle and wildlife and, particularly in border zones, may produce crops adapted to wet habitats after adequate drainage management.

Vertisols of the river valleys cover the Luangwa and its tributary valleys, the Luapala, and parts of the Zambezi valley. They are believed to derive from Karroo sediments, largely by colluvial and alluvial processes. They comprise a mixed group of soils. The fluvial deposits have been variously sorted during transport: they may range from lighter coloured, freshly deposited sands of river beds and local older beds of darker sands, through dark brown sandy loams, to lighter greyish and darker greybrown clay loams of more cloddy tendency, and finally to dark grey clays similar to Kafue vertisols. In parts of the Luangwa valley, especially where drainage is poor, soils tend to be halomorphic due to salt accumulation. These are known as solonetzic grey clays to sandy loams.

Vertisols of flood plains are hydromorphic soils derived from siliceous parent material. They generally have a peaty organic horizon, ranging from under 25 to over 180 cm. thickness. The usually black topsoil horizon is underlain by quartz sands ranging in colour from dark greyish brown to pale grey. The peat horizon usually has a pH of 3·5 to 4·5, if not drained and cultivated. These soils are found in the flooded areas of the Zambesi and tributary rivers in Western Province, around major swamps (Lukanga, Bangweulu, Busanga) and in depressions of dambos. Parts may be used for grasslands or locally adapted crops if protected from flooding and adequately drained.

Lithosols are shallow to very shallow escarpment soils, often intermixed with outcrops and surface rocks ('rock and rubble'). They are frequently underlain by laterite crusts and/or quartz gravels or weathering rocks. Texture ranges from sand through loamy sand to sandy clay loam, rock material increasing with depth. The colour of the well-drained soils usually ranges from dark greyish brown to reddish brown. Lithosols are developed from granite, gneiss, schist or sandstone. They are best suited to a permanent vegetation cover utilizable for wildlife or a few woodland products (charcoal).

R MÄCKEL

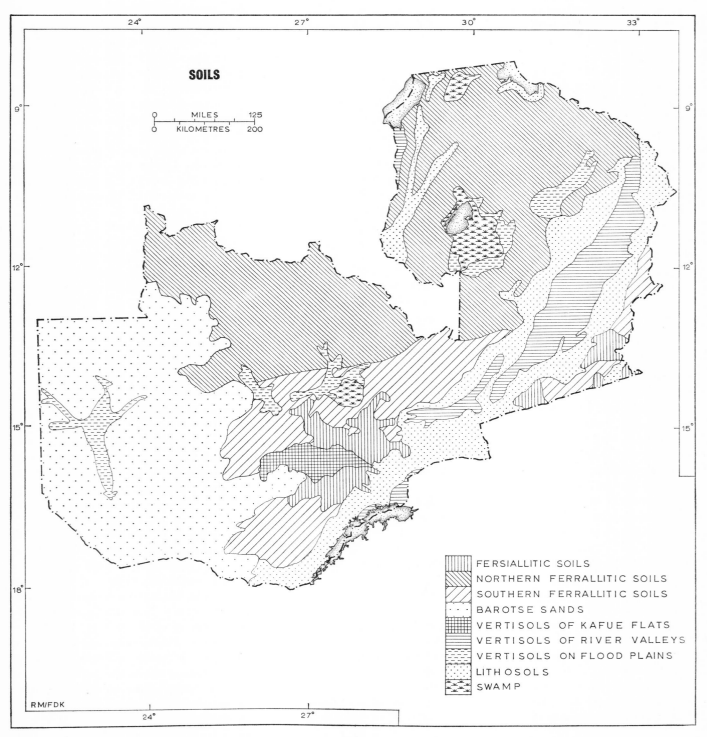

SOILS

MILES 0 — 125
KILOMETRES 0 — 200

||||| FERSIALLITIC SOILS
NORTHERN FERRALLITIC SOILS
SOUTHERN FERRALLITIC SOILS
BAROTSE SANDS
VERTISOLS OF KAFUE FLATS
VERTISOLS OF RIVER VALLEYS
VERTISOLS ON FLOOD PLAINS
LITHOSOLS
SWAMP

RM/FDK

Zambia lies mid-way between the two major areas of Africa, Tanzania and the Transvaal, where evidence has been recovered of the earliest stages of human development. So far, however, no sites which may be attributed incontrovertibly to this period, two million to half a million years ago, have been found in Zambia. Fig *a* therefore shows the distribution of sites attributed to the later, Acheulian, stage of the Early Stone Age. From this period onwards, Zambia's archaeological record is comparatively complete.

The Early Stone Age (fig. *a*)

The Zambian Early Stone Age was first intensively studied in the Livingstone-Victoria Falls area of the Zambezi valley where abundant artefacts occur but where the majority have been transported by the river some distance from their original place of deposition and are frequently mixed with later material in the process. Concentrations of artefacts occur in the gravels laid down by the Zambezi and its tributaries and subsequently left high and dry by the river's downcutting both upstream and downstream of the Victoria Falls. Comparatively undisturbed sites have occasionally been found farther from the main river channel. This material may be attributed to the past quarter million, and perhaps to the past one hundred thousand years.

Further information has recently been obtained at the Kalambo Falls near Mbala. Here the Kalambo River cuts through seventy feet (22 m.) of fluviatile deposits in which are preserved successive archaeological horizons dating from the Iron Age back to the final stages of the Early Stone Age. The earliest human settlements so far investigated at Kalambo Falls have been radiocarbon dated to about sixty thousand years ago. Still older material is known to occur below the present water level. The camp-sites were marked by rich concentrations of the characteristic stone artefacts of the period: fine bifacially flaked handaxes and cleavers as well as flake tools. Waterlogged conditions have ensured the preservation of wood and bark, including several probable artefacts. Fossil pollen has formed the basis for a reconstruction of the prehistoric environment.

The Early Stone Age people of Central Africa were hunters, gatherers of wild vegetable foods and, perhaps, fishermen. They led a wandering life, perhaps rarely settling in one spot for more than a few weeks at a time. When a large animal was killed, a camp would be made around the carcass until it was eaten, when the group would move on. No more elaborate shelters than temporary windbreaks of broken branches were constructed and the people slept in the open, sometimes in grass-lined hollows.

The physical type of the people responsible for the Central African Acheulian cultures is not well known, but skeletal remains from sites in Tanzania and in North Africa are attributed to *Homo erectus* and compared with the *Pithecanthropus pekinensis* fossils of the Far East. Much of the Old World was at this time occupied, albeit sparsely, by people at a comparable stage of cultural development.

Between sixty thousand and fifty thousand years ago began a slow process of cultural change, perhaps partly in response to environmental change and to an increase in human population. For the first time, our evidence is sufficiently complete for us to distinguish different socio-economic groupings within the archaeological record but we are not yet able to differentiate satisfactorily between chronological and geographical/environmental factors in this change.

The Middle Stone Age (fig. *b*)

The earliest of these post-Acheulian cultural stages has been termed 'Sangoan'. Stone artefact assemblages of this time are characterized by the presence of thick, heavy pick-like tools which contrast with the more finely finished handaxes. Flake tools tend to be larger, more abundant and more standardized into clearly defined types. Sangoan sites are more frequent than those of the Early Stone Age and often show signs of more prolonged occupation. The area of settlement was now beginning to spread from the major river valleys and lake basins to the smaller dambos of the plateau areas and many caves were first occupied at this time. This last development may be linked with the spread of the controlled use of fire. The Sangoan is generally regarded as the first phase of the Middle Stone Age, although it retains many features reminiscent of the earlier period and may have its origins far back in Early Stone Age times.

During the later phases of the Middle Stone Age, regional variation becomes still more clearly defined. In the Zambezi valley, near Livingstone and farther downstream, picks and other large tools are superseded by flakes struck from carefully prepared discoid cores and retouched into a variety of knife, scraper and spearpoint tools. In the Upper Zambezi region of western Zambia small handaxes and picks seem to have been retained and the local Middle Stone Age shares some features with that from Angola. At Kalambo Falls the artefacts are more closely comparable with the Lupemban industries of the Congo. In all areas we can detect a tendency towards a greater variety and specialization in man's cultural activities, although a hunting and gathering economy continues. Research has not yet reached a stage where we can even begin to comprehend the chronological and cultural inter-relationships of these regional variants. Throughout Zambia they can be demonstrated to succeed industries of Sangoan type but we cannot yet tell to what extent external stimuli were responsible for developments within the indigenous population.

The skull of *Homo rhodesiensis*, found on the Broken Hill Mine at Kabwe in 1921, almost certainly belongs to the Middle Stone Age and represents a physical type closely related to the Neanderthaloids of Europe and the Near East.

Fig *b* combines the distribution of Sangoan and later Middle Stone Age sites in Zambia. Comparison with fig *a* clearly demonstrates the increased frequency of Middle Stone Age sites and the greater area of the country settled at that time. By the end of the Middle Stone Age most of Zambia was subject to human occupation, with the exception of the Kalahari sand country of the far west where lack of stone must either have deterred human settlement or restricted tool-makers to the use of perishable materials.

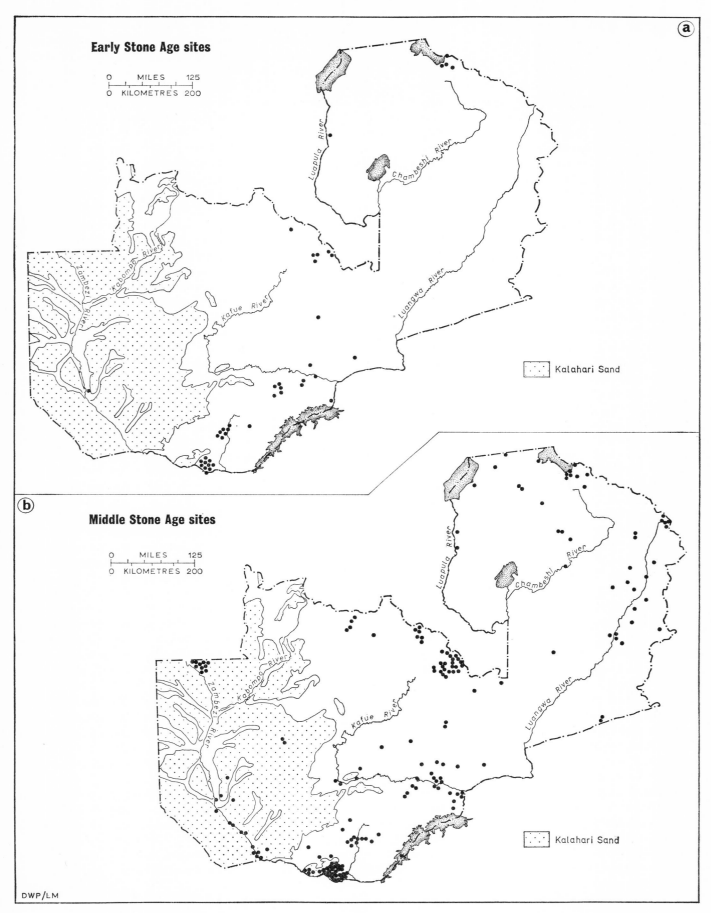

Early Stone Age sites

0 MILES 125
0 KILOMETRES 200

Luapula River

Chambeshi River

Zambezi River

Kabompo River

Kafue River

Luangwa River

⋯ Kalahari Sand

ⓐ

ⓑ

Middle Stone Age sites

0 MILES 125
0 KILOMETRES 200

Luapula River

Chambeshi River

Zambezi River

Kabompo River

Kafue River

Luangwa River

⋯ Kalahari Sand

DWP/LM

The Late Stone Age (fig. *b*)

Industries of Late Stone Age type were active in central Zambia by about fifteen thousand years ago. These are differentiated from the preceding Middle Stone Age by the introduction of cultural traits of paramount importance, but the degree of continuity between the two stages must not be underestimated. Even if, as there is some evidence to suggest, the original stimulus which led to the development of the Central African Late Stone Age industries came from some external source, it is now clear that many facets of Middle Stone Age culture survived into comparatively recent millennia, particularly in the Zambezi valley.

During the Late Stone Age we find for the first time numerous human settlements on the plateaux, where caves and rockshelters frequently show signs of prolonged occupation. River valley and lakeside open sites continued to be favoured, particularly in the south.

Characteristic stone artefacts of this period are very small in size and include scraping, cutting and boring tools, many of which were used hafted, as well as arrow points and barbs. The introduction of the bow and arrow at this time must have revolutionized hunting. Bone tools are frequently found while bone and shell beads and fragments of ochre indicate a liking for personal adornment.

Variations in stone tool types enable at least three regional groupings to be distinguished within the Zambian Late Stone Age. Those generally known as the Zambian Wilton and the Nachikufan, found respectively in the Southern Province and on the Central-Northern Province plateau, have been known for some years, while a third variant, named after the Makwe rockshelter, has recently been recognized in the Eastern Province. In each zone a typologically based succession of local development stages is indicated. It is at present impossible to say whether the boundaries of these regional types are definable within close geographical limits or whether the cultures as at present known are merely the best known modes of a relatively continuous range of variation. It is an open question whether this variation is dependent *per se* on the territorial boundaries of socio-political population units or on economic/behavioural factors subject to the local environment.

Human skeletal remains, notably the large and well-preserved series from Gwisho Hotsprings near Monze indicate that the Late Stone Age industries were, for the most part, the work of people of Khoisan physical type.

The Early Iron Age (fig. *b*)

It is against the backcloth of a widespread Late Stone Age population that we must view the appearance of the Zambian Early Iron Age people. Their way of life provides a complete contrast with that of the Late Stone Age; methods of food production, both agriculture and animal domestication, were introduced, as were the techniques of metallurgy, pottery and the construction of pole and dagga houses. Settled life in permanent or semi-permanent villages makes its first appearance on the Zambian scene. Although it is not yet known whether the introductions of these new techniques were precisely concurrent it is clear that their arrival was intimately connected with large-scale population movements and coincided with the arrival of negroid people who may have spoken Bantu languages. These events took place from about the second to the fourth century AD.

More than seventy Early Iron Age sites are now known in Zambia. These may be divided into five groups, recognizable by the typology of their associated pottery; the distributions of the groups are indicated on the map. They appear to have entered Zambia at roughly the same time from a primary or secondary centre of dispersal lying to the west of Lake Tanganyika or in the Katanga, and to have been discrete cultural entities prior to their establishment in Zambia.

In northern Zambia the Kalambo group Early Iron Age population appears to have been sparse; throughout the first millennium AD the majority of the people in the area probably retained their Late Stone Age mode of life. The Copperbelt, on the other hand, was much more densely populated by the farming peoples of the Chondwe group and exploitation of copper deposits dates from around the middle of the first millennium AD. The Kapwirimbwe group settlers of the Lusaka plateau were firmly established at an early date and from the beginning were smelting and forging iron on a substantial scale. It is only in the Southern Province that the Early Iron Age population appears to have been dense enough largely to displace the Late Stone Age hunters. The farmers of the Kalundu group on the plateau and the Dambwa group in the Zambezi valley founded villages which were occupied for many generations. In all other areas of Zambia the Late Stone Age people survived until a very few centuries ago.

The date at which the Early Iron Age folk were replaced by later arrivals differs in various parts of Zambia. In the north the Early Iron Age appears to have lasted for over a thousand years, while the Kalundu group in the south was superseded by the Kalomo culture by about AD 800–900.

Rock art (fig. *a*)

Rock paintings, widely distributed through Zambia wherever suitable rock surfaces exist, fall into two stylistic groups. The rare naturalistic paintings of animals, although of little artistic merit when compared with the 'Bushman paintings' of Southern Rhodesia, South Africa and Lesotho, may safely be attributed to the Late Stone Age hunters. The much more frequent schematic designs, on the other hand, now appear to have been the work of Iron Age peoples and to be associated with ritual and religious ceremonies.

Note

The archaeological distribution maps have been compiled from the records of the Zambia National Monuments Commission and include sites discovered up to May 1969.

The terms 'Early Stone Age', 'Middle Stone Age', etc. are used here in a cultural rather than a chronological sense and are in no way indicative of finite periods of time.

D W PHILLIPSON

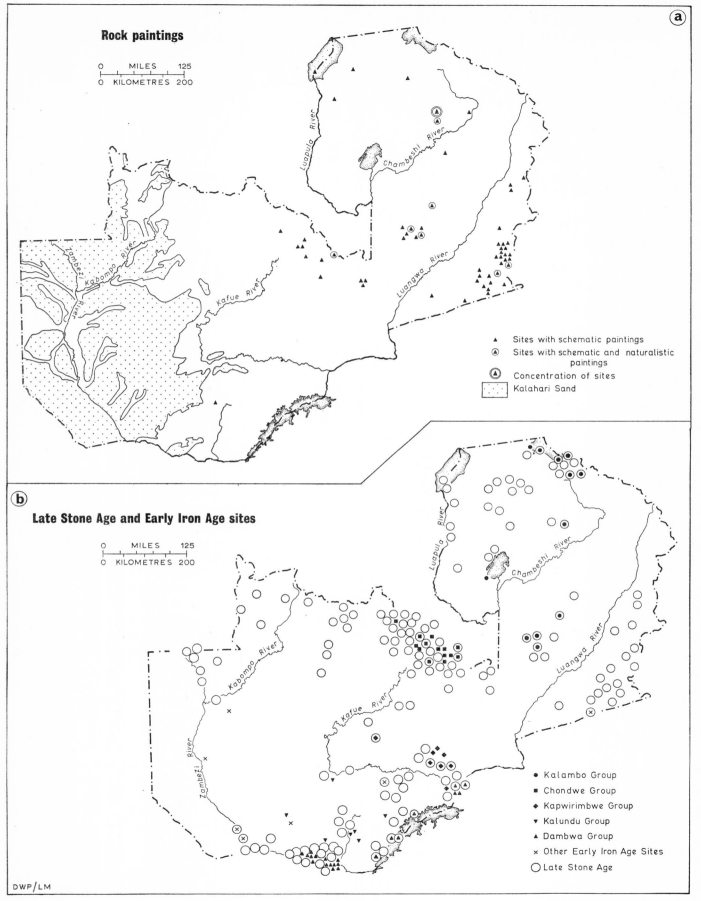

Rock paintings

0　MILES　125
0　KILOMETRES　200

▲ Sites with schematic paintings
⊕ Sites with schematic and naturalistic paintings
⊛ Concentration of sites
⬚ Kalahari Sand

Luapula River
Chambeshi River
Zambezi River
Kabompo River
Kafue River
Luangwa River

ⓐ

Late Stone Age and Early Iron Age sites

ⓑ

0　MILES　125
0　KILOMETRES　200

● Kalambo Group
■ Chondwe Group
◆ Kapwirimbwe Group
▼ Kalundu Group
▲ Dambwa Group
✕ Other Early Iron Age Sites
○ Late Stone Age

Luapula River
Chambeshi River
Kabompo River
Kafue River
Zambezi River
Luangwa River

DWP/LM

12 PRE-COLONIAL KINGDOMS AND TRIBAL MIGRATIONS, AD 1500-1900

The complex and shadowy history of pre-colonial kingdoms in Zambia and of the external influences that bore upon them can be illustrated only in rather cursory fashion on the maps opposite, which should be regarded as unavoidably highly diagrammatic. They do show, however, that both similarities and differences in movement and settlement patterns took place during three broad periods of Zambian history, beginning around AD 1500.

The little that is known concerning the inhabitants of Zambia before AD 1500 comes to us through the findings of archaeological research (p. 28) and through oral tradition relating to these peoples. It seems probable that large areas of present-day Zambia were then inhabited by various Bantu-speaking peoples, among whom moved scattered bands of nomadic Bushmen hunters. Some slight impression of the geographical patterns of settlement and culture in this early period may be obtained from the maps of major tribal and linguistic groups on p. 35.

From *AD 1500 to 1700* a number of migrations from the Luba and Lunda empires of Katanga introduced a new element into Zambian history. These new groups introduced chieftainship or kingship organization into Zambia and further stimulated the existing development of long distance trade. The various arrows that attempt to portray tribal migration should not, obviously, be interpreted literally as actual routes followed by the migratory tribes. They indicate rather the general directions of movement of groups that could rarely have been more substantial than a chief with a handful of his followers, who integrated with the existing population in their areas of settlement. These settlement areas of chiefs from Katanga—in some instances of a collection of related chiefs—are shown in a generalized way in fig *a*. In a few cases the settlement groupings can be regarded as small centralized kingships, but the solitary large scale political entity before 1700 was Undi's kingdom over some Chewa, Nsenga and other peoples. Undi's kingdom was known to the Portuguese as 'the Maravi (Malawi) Empire', although it was most certainly no empire. 'Maravi' refers to the Congolese ances-

try of the Chewa, it is likely that this is how modern Malawi and Lake Malawi got their names.

Fig *b*, covering the period *AD 1700 to 1800*, illustrates further migration of new groups of chiefs and peoples from Katanga, in a pattern continuing that of the preceding period. Additionally, new groups now emerged as offshoots of already established groups of chiefs. A number of sizeable kingdoms or empires also developed during the period, in some instances from mergers of peoples with previously separate political identities. One of the most important events during this period was the founding of the Eastern Lunda (Kazembe's) state on the Luapula, around 1740. This stratified conquest state contrasts with the loose incorporative system of the Bemba state, which also emerged during the late eighteenth century under the ritual headship of Chitimukula. This contrast may be explained largely on the grounds of the different ecologies of the Luapula valley and the Bemba plateau.

The various developments that took place from *AD 1800 to 1900* (fig. *c*) show significant differences from earlier patterns. Migration from Katanga had now ceased and had been replaced by a series of migrations from South Africa, notably the Ngoni invasion into eastern Zambia, which founded Mpeseni's and Mbelwa's states and the secondary Kalolo invasion which, in the eighteen-forties, transformed the Lozi state and gave it its language. Some empires continued to grow, while others declined. In this period, for the first time, factors other than tribal migrations can be seen influencing Zambian history from the outside. These are the raiding and trading by the Arabs and the Swahili through present-day Tanzania and Malawi and by the allies of the Portuguese—the Chikunda and Mambari (or Mbundu)—from Mozambique and Angola. To these influences may be added raiding by the Yeke from Katanga. Contributing to the wholesale disturbances caused by all these activities were widespread raiding activities by peoples already settled in Zambia, such as the Bemba, Lozi and Ngoni. Such raids are represented in a very generalized way by arrows radiating from the areas of settlement of the people concerned. Some states survived the attacks comparatively well, whereas others were overwhelmed and virtually ceased to exist. This is illustrated by the absence from Fig. *c* of certain states that are represented on the maps of earlier periods, such as the Chewa.

H W LANGWORTHY

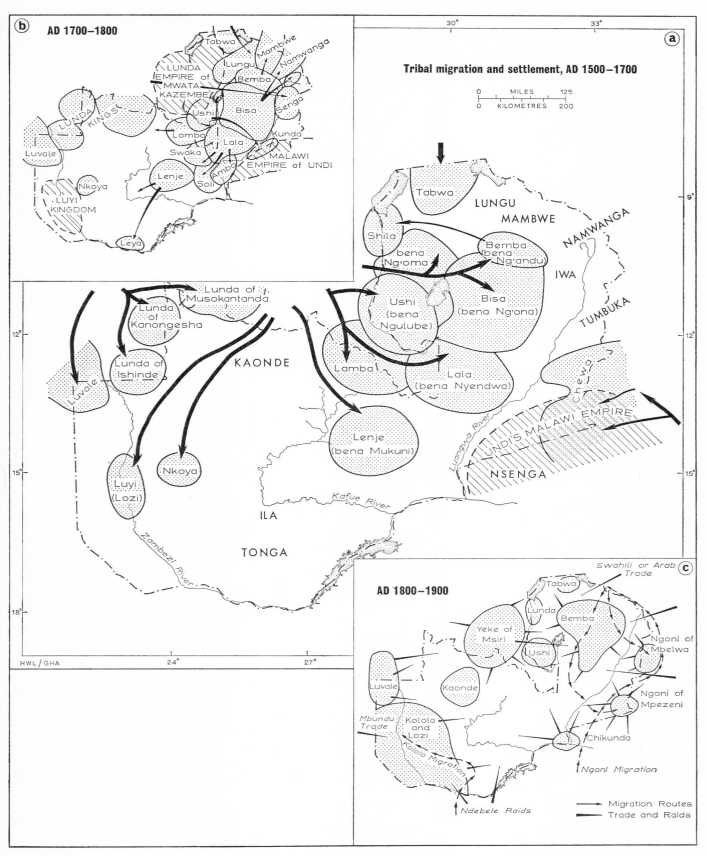

(b) AD 1700–1800

Tabwa
Mambwe
Namwanga
LUNDA EMPIRE of MWATA KAZEMBE
Lungu
Bemba
Senga
LUNDA KINGS
Ushi
Bisa
Luvale
Lamba
Lala
Kunda
Nkoya
Swaka
Amba
MALAWI EMPIRE of UNDI
LUYI KINGDOM
Lenje
Soli
Leya

(a)

30°   33°

Tribal migration and settlement, AD 1500–1700

MILES
0   125
KILOMETRES
0   200

Tabwa
LUNGU
MAMBWE
NAMWANGA
9°
Shila
bena Ng'oma
Bemba (bena Ng'andu)
IWA
TUMBUKA
Ushi (bena Ngulube)
Bisa (bena Ng'ona)
Lunda of Musokantanda
Lunda of Kanongesha
12°
KAONDE
Lamba
Lala (bena Nyendwa)
Chewa
Lunda of Ishinde
Luvale
Luangwa River
UNDI'S MALAWI EMPIRE
Nkoya
Lenje (bena Mukuni)
NSENGA
15°
Luyi (Lozi)
ILA
Kafue River
Zambezi River
TONGA

(c) AD 1800–1900

Swahili or Arab Trade
Tabwa
Lunda
Bemba
Yeke of Msiri
Ushi
Ngoni of Mbelwa
Luvale
Kaonde
Ngoni of Mpezeni
Mbundu Trade
Kololo and Lozi
Chikunda
Kololo Migration
Ngoni Migration
Ndebele Raids

→ Migration Routes
▬ Trade and Raids

HWL / GHA   24°   27°

Z.M.—3   33

13 LANGUAGES AND TRIBES

During 1970 the results of an official census on 'mother tongue' in Zambia were expected to be available, while an intensive linguistic survey under the auspices of the East African Language Survey was under way. For the present, however, insufficient data are available to enable the shadowy threads of language distribution to be unravelled, let alone mapped, with any degree of confidence. Fig. *a* (like similar language maps published elsewhere) should therefore be regarded as a sketchmap. It is also intended merely as an historical statement, concerned with linguistic origins and basic rural distributions. Thus, for example, Luyana is the archaic language of pre-Kololo Barotse, of great scholarly interest but spoken by only a small number of people today. In the absence of precise data the map shows nothing of the polyglot situation in the fast-growing towns (p. 80), where roughly thirty per cent of all Zambians, drawn from many tribal and linguistic backgrounds, live in conditions of social and cultural intermixture. Thus, perhaps 200 000 people speak Nyanja in the capital, Lusaka, which on the map falls within the Bantu-Botatwe group area (including Tonga).

The map depicts only first or home language distribution. In fact, a three-tier linguistic system exists today, although this cannot yet be meaningfully portrayed. English is to date the sole official language of the country: the language of documentation, of political pronouncements at national level, of business and technology, and of all education above lower primary level. A second tier comprises some of the nine major language groups that are widely enough spoken to serve as partial *linguae francae*: these include Bemba, Nyanja, Lozi and Tonga. The bottom tier comprises truly localized languages. This multiple structure provides the means of communication in present-day Zambia, depending as much on a major foreign language—English—as upon the indigenous tongues indicated on the map. This picture is considerably simplified, however, in that many more distinct languages and dialects are recognized in the country.

The map indicates a very generalized linguistic pattern. Localities in which there is a great deal of admixture of languages are shown by over-lapping shading divisions. Within some major groups, indicated by the larger print, there are distinct yet closely related languages as, for example, Lala (fig. *b*) within the Bemba group. Something of this can be deduced by comparing the two maps. However, languages falling within a broad grouping are not necessarily mutually understood.

The overall distribution of languages, as depicted, may well indicate cultural and linguistic patterns existing partly before the arrival of chiefs and kings from about AD 1500 (p. 32). However, some minor language groups certainly indicate much more recent and small-scale migrations into Zambia—such as those of the Shona, Nyika and Chokwe—or the mixing of two different neighbouring languages to produce a new language, such as Nsenga.

The map of tribal divisions is also generalized and historical in character. Within the limits of available data it is regarded as reasonably accurate for the rural areas, but gives no indication of the mixture of tribes living together in the towns.

Tribal differences are based on even less obvious and more complex criteria than are linguistic differences. Languages, material culture, shared historical experience, the character of rulers and colonial administration—all are relevant factors. It is possible for people to be considered as belonging to more than one tribe, with traditional chiefs belonging to yet another, for example, the Soli. Other groups, such as the Lala, Swaka and Ambo, or the Chishinga, Ng'umbo, Mukulu and Unga each have common cultural patterns and related chiefs, but largely because of geographical and administrative factors they have developed into more or less distinct tribal entities. On the map such tribal distinctions are indicated by dotted line boundaries, whereas more distinct divisions are indicated by solid lines.

The basic criteria used in showing ethnic or tribal boundaries for most parts of Zambia have been the origins and identities of traditional chiefs. In general, chiefs and their peoples have developed, over time, a common identity in most parts of Zambia. However, it is a frequent occurrence to find that some of the people in an area maintain a separate identity from that of the chief and some of his people, different languages and cultures usually being involved. For example, in eastern Zambia Kunda chiefs have Chewa people, or Chewa chiefs have Tumbuka or Bisa people.

In western Zambia tribal and linguistic admixtures are very complex, largely as a result of the history of the past 130 years. About 1840 a new language, Sotho, was introduced from South Africa by the Kololo conquerors of the Lozi. The admixture of this with local languages to form Lozi largely replaced the Luyana language and has continued to be the *lingua franca* of the various peoples of the Lozi sphere of Western Province. The political and social system was such that although Lozi chiefs ruled the whole area, subject peoples maintained a distinct identity. Many of the smaller languages and tribal groups in the area are the result of comparatively recent migrations. The Mbunda arrived before AD 1800, but the Luvale, Nkoya and others came in as traders or as refugees from wars during the nineteenth century. During the present century large numbers of Chokwe and Luchanzi have settled in more sparsely populated areas.

Group names printed in lower case on the map, mostly in western Zambia, refer generally to sub-tribal groups of people. The Kwandi and Simaa are Lozi people traditionally ruled by Lozi chiefs. They generally speak the earlier Luyana language and the newer Lozi language.

An interesting tribal group, the Twa, are mostly found in the Kafue Flats and the Lukanga and Bangweulu swamplands in central and northern Zambia. Genetically they are regarded as being between Bushmen and Pygmy in characteristics, having retreated to these remote areas before the advance of Bantu-speaking peoples. Today the Twa speak Bantu dialects strongly influenced by the languages of their nearest neighbours, with whom they may share the swamp fishing grounds.

H W LANGWORTHY

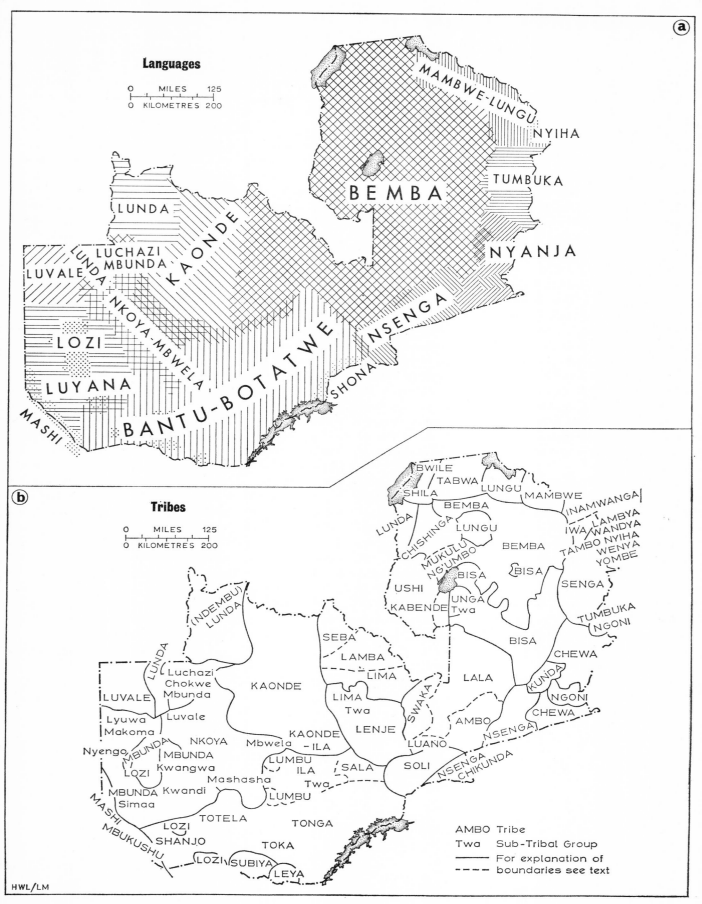

14 EUROPEAN EXPLORATION BEFORE 1895

During the century before present-day Zambia came under white rule, a handful of intrepid and highly individualistic Europeans, with their African retainers, undertook long and hazardous journeys across this large and unknown land. They came for a variety of reasons. The earliest Portuguese travellers and their Chikunda agents were motivated, at least in part, by the desire to establish trading contacts, particularly with the more powerful kings such as Mwata Kazembe along the Luapula. To this end the remote trading station of Feira had been established at the confluence of the Zambezi and its tributary the Luangwa, by about 1720, to be followed in 1826 by a second trading station at Macombo on the upper Luangwa. Expeditions such as those of Lacerda in 1798 and Monteiro and Gamitto in 1831–32 had political as well as commercial motives. These early Portuguese expeditions are shown in fig. a.

The main stimulus to pre-colonial European enterprise in Zambia was provided by David Livingstone. From 1850 to 1873 the great explorer tramped over much of the country, spurred on by burning geographical curiosity but always with the ultimate goal of introducing Christianity and the material benefits of civilization through commerce. Contemporaneously with one of Livingstone's early journeys, the Portuguese slave and ivory trader Silva Porto (fig. a) penetrated from Angola to establish commercial relationships in Barotseland (now Western Province). The routes of Livingstone's Zambian journeys are shown in fig. b.

After Livingstone's death at Chitambo near Lake Bangweulu, in 1873, a number of European traders undertook journeys, most of them from the south or from mission settlements already established in Malawi. Most prominent among these were Westbeech in Barotseland and the Moir brothers, representing the African Lakes Company, in what are now the Eastern and Northern Provinces. It is probable that many more individual traders came into the area before 1895; if so, however, they have left no known accounts of their journeys.

Most of the European travellers of the later nineteenth century, however, were British missionaries following Livingstone's example and struggling to implement his ideals (p. 38). After a solo attempt by Arnot (Plymouth Brethren) to evangelize the Lozi at Lealui, 1882–84, the first mission stations in Barotseland were opened by the Paris Missionary Society, under the leadership of Coillard, at Sesheke in 1885 and Sefula in 1886. Gradually the Zambezi River above the Victoria Falls became a recognized routeway for Europeans travelling to the court of the Lozi king Lewanika at Lealui. In figs. c and d only the tracks of travellers who left this general route into Barotseland have been separately indicated. The various 'tourists' who visited the Victoria Falls during this period are not noted. Other significant travellers in western and southern Zambia before 1895 were the Portuguese explorers Capello and Ivens in 1884; the Czech doctor, Emil Holub; Selous, the British hunter and explorer; and Baldwin and Buckenham, the Primitive Methodist missionaries who opened Nkala mission in 1893.

In the years following the death of David Livingstone a number of missionaries and traders also entered the northern and eastern parts of what is present-day Zambia. This resulted in the emergence of another major routeway, the 'Stevenson Road' from Karonga on Lake Nyasa (now Lake Malawi) to the southern end of Lake Tanganyika. In figs. c and d it has not been possible to distinguish the routes of individual travellers along this routeway. By 1895 the London Missionary Society had established Fwambo mission, the White Fathers had opened Mambwe and the African Lakes Company had set up trading stations at Abercorn (now Mbala) and Fife. Before 1889 perhaps the only Europeans travelling in other parts of eastern Zambia were the French journalist Giraud during 1884 and the German trader Karl Wiese, who undertook an expedition to Mpezeni in 1889 on behalf of the Portuguese government (fig. d.). In addition to continuing missionary and trader activity, a number of journeys were undertaken between 1890 and 1895 by such treaty and concession seekers as Alfred Sharpe and Thomson and also by Wiese (fig. d). During this period the first small administrative centres were established at Abercorn and on Lake Mweru at Chiengi and Kalungwishi.

These developments in the eighteen-nineties marked the end of the period of exploration and the beginnings of formal European political control of the area, achieved through Cecil John Rhodes's British South Africa Company.

H W LANGWORTHY

EUROPEAN EXPLORATIONS

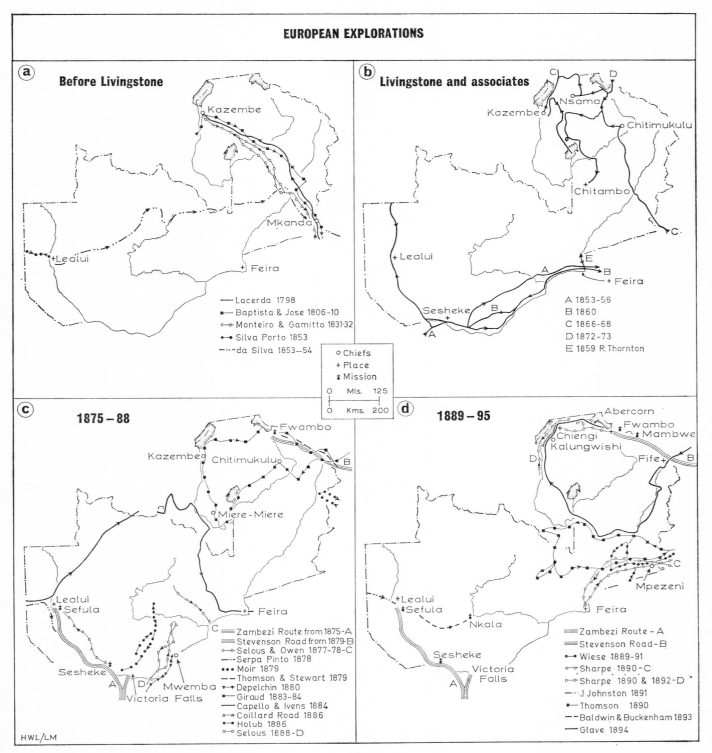

(a) Before Livingstone

Kazembe

Mkando

+Lealui

+ Feira

——— Lacerda 1798
■■■ Baptista & Jose 1806-10
○—○ Monteiro & Gamitto 1831-32
●—● Silva Porto 1853
—··— da Silva 1853—54

(b) Livingstone and associates

C   D
Nsama
Kazembe   Chitimukulu

Chitambo

+Lealui

A   E
   B
+ Feira

Sesheke
B

A

A 1853-56
B 1860
C 1866-68
D 1872-73
E 1859 R.Thornton

○ Chiefs
+ Place
⚑ Mission

0   Mls.   125
0   Kms.   200

(c) 1875 – 88

Fwambo

Kazembe   Chitimukulu
B

Miere-Miere

Lealui
Sefula

+ Feira

C

Sesheke

A   D
  Mwemba
Victoria Falls

≡≡≡ Zambezi Route from 1875-A
≡≡≡ Stevenson Road from 1879-B
○—○ Selous & Owen 1877-78-C
—··— Serpa Pinto 1878
●●● Moir 1879
— — Thomson & Stewart 1879
▶—▶ Depelchin 1880
+—+ Giraud 1883-84
——— Capello & Ivens 1884
▲—▲ Coillard Road 1886
●—● Holub 1886
○—○ Selous 1888-D

(d) 1889 – 95

Abercorn
Fwambo
Chiengi   Mambwe
Kalungwishi
D   Fife+   B

Mpezeni

C

+Lealui
⚑Sefula

+ Feira

Nkala

Sesheke
Victoria Falls

A

≡≡≡ Zambezi Route – A
≡≡≡ Stevenson Road-B
●—● Wiese 1889-91
○—○ Sharpe 1890-C
○—○ Sharpe 1890 & 1892-D
—··— J Johnston 1891
■—■ Thomson 1890
— — Baldwin & Buckenham 1893
——— Glave 1894

HWL/LM

15 MISSIONS

Christian missions drawn from a wide variety of sects and denominations have been vitally involved in the development of Zambia and continue to play a prominent role in the spiritual, educational and medical life of the country. The main map (fig. *b*) illustrates their contemporary distribution, but does not show independent missions, nor churches and administrative centres in the major towns.

It was the work of David Livingstone, the missionary explorer, which first brought Central Africa to public notice in Britain and Europe (p. 36). His reports of heathen peoples cruelly ravaged by the slave trade awakened the humanitarian conscience and kindled evangelistic zeal. Following his death in 1873, several missionary societies made plans to carry the Gospel into the lands north of the Zambezi.

With great courage and determination, small parties made their way slowly inland from various points on the African coast. However, the early years were full of difficulty: disease and death, tribal wars and tenuous lines of communication left little opportunity for direct evangelism. Much time was also spent winning the confidence of the local people and learning their language.

These missionary pioneers arrived well before the establishment of colonial administration and despite their small numbers they soon exercised a powerful influence on local affairs. South of Lake Tanganyika, in the London Missionary Society's area, the slave trade had so weakened the social fabric that the missionary tended to acquire far-reaching powers as protector, administrator and judge. Conversely, where tribal organization was strong, as in Western Province (formerly named Barotseland), the missionary's role as an adviser was more indirect, but no less effective.

Most missions, wanting settled conditions in which their work could flourish, were anxious to see the territory brought under some form of European control. In 1890 François Coillard, leader of the Paris Missionary Society, played a crucial role in persuading the Barotse to grant the Lochner Concession. This gave the British South Africa Company mineral rights over a vast area of western Zambia, which was thereby brought within the British sphere of influence. In other areas too, the missionary presence eased the transition to foreign rule.

Until well into the twentieth century there existed a clear pattern of regional specialization in the work of the missions— of which fig. *a* gives some indication. Most societies had small financial and manpower resources, which were best utilized in a series of stations reasonably accessible to one another. Language divides also tended to confine fields of operation to one particular tribe or linguistic group. Thus the Paris Missionary Society became closely associated with the Lozi (Barotse), the White Fathers with the Bemba, and the Dutch Reformed Church with the Nyanja speakers of the south-east. Other missions also restricted themselves to a particular area. The United Free Church of Scotland extended its work westwards on a broad front from its main base in Nyasaland. In a similar manner the

Jesuits and Seventh Day Adventists came from Rhodesia, and developed work among the Tonga people just across the Zambezi valley. The Universities' Mission to Central Africa, an Anglican body, located its posts very widely, thus creating for itself considerable problems.

Although their primary aim was spreading the Christian faith, the missionaries inevitably passed on other features of their culture and ideology, and in doing so were as much agents of social as religious change. They introduced new values, demonstrated the achievements of advanced technology, and encouraged individualism at the expense of tribal collectivism. They turned local languages and dialects into written forms, taught basic literacy, introduced new crafts (carpentry, building) and thus fitted their people to participate in the modern exchange economy.

During the inter-war years evangelistic work saw considerable expansion. New societies arrived and the old pattern of regional specialization was modified, becoming gradually less exclusive.

The rapid industrialization of the Copperbelt took the missions, hitherto accustomed to rural work, rather by surprise. While working on the mines, African Christians from various Protestant mission areas established their own inter-denominational 'Union Church', and only in the early nineteen-thirties did the missions seriously commence work there. Several Protestant groups followed the African example and co-operated in forming the United Missions in the Copperbelt, which based their activities at Mindolo, near Kitwe, and operated in each of the mining towns.

In the period after 1945 mission commitment to medical and educational work greatly increased (fig. *c*). Many societies handed over their primary schools completely to Government and turned their attention to secondary education. In 1969 there were forty secondary schools, more than ten seminaries and five teacher training colleges run by Christian bodies. According to a survey sponsored by the World Council of Churches in 1968, of a national total of 76 hospitals, 41 were run by missions who, in addition, were responsible for 47 rural health centres—some quite large—and 17 leprosaria (cf. p. 100).

Since the General Missionary Conference of Northern Rhodesia, which was first called in 1914, various churches, other than the Roman Catholic, have sought to work closer with one another. The Christian Council, which replaced the Conference in 1944, at present represents over twenty churches, missions and Christian organizations. Between 1945 and 1965 various steps towards church union were taken, culminating in the establishment of the United Church of Zambia, incorporating the work of the London Missionary Society, the Church of Scotland, the former Union Church, the former European Copperbelt Free Church Council, the Methodists, and the Church of Barotseland (Paris Missionary Society).

In recent years, but especially since independence, there has been a growing awareness that the distinction between the foreign mission and the local church must disappear. It has also been recognized that the age of the expatriate missionary is drawing to a close, and that the future of the Church rightly and inevitably rests with Zambian Christians.

J E GARDINER

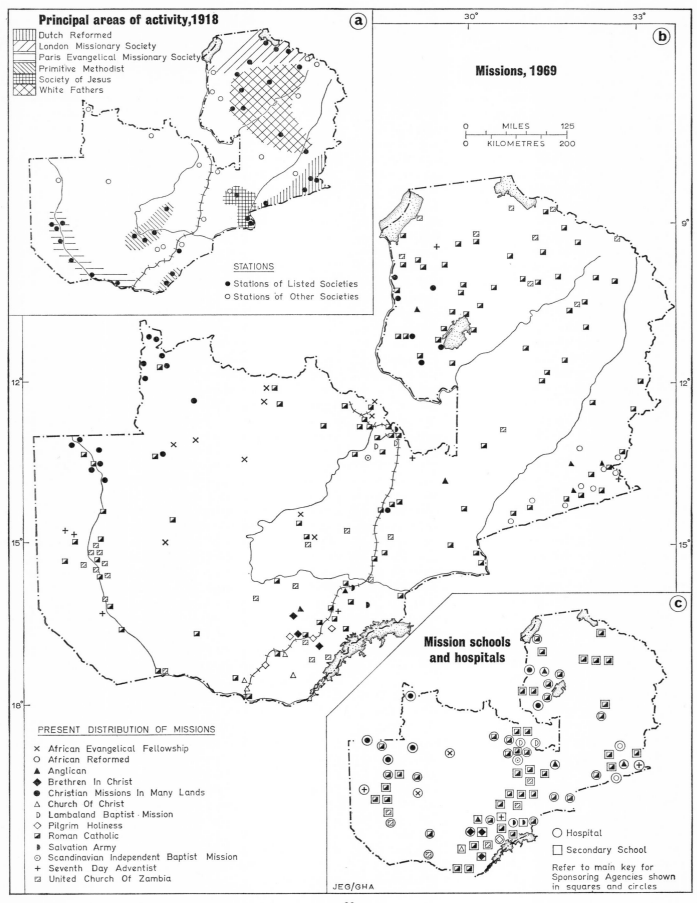

Principal areas of activity, 1918

- ||||| Dutch Reformed
- ///// London Missionary Society
- ===== Paris Evangelical Missionary Society
- \\\\\ Primitive Methodist
- ##### Society of Jesus
- ⊠⊠⊠⊠ White Fathers

STATIONS
- ● Stations of Listed Societies
- ○ Stations of Other Societies

(a)

(b)

Missions, 1969

```
0        MILES      125
0      KILOMETRES   200
```

30°   33°

9°

12°

15°

PRESENT DISTRIBUTION OF MISSIONS

- × African Evangelical Fellowship
- ○ African Reformed
- ▲ Anglican
- ◆ Brethren In Christ
- ● Christian Missions In Many Lands
- △ Church Of Christ
- D Lambaland Baptist Mission
- ◇ Pilgrim Holiness
- ◪ Roman Catholic
- ◗ Salvation Army
- ⊙ Scandinavian Independent Baptist Mission
- + Seventh Day Adventist
- ⊠ United Church Of Zambia

(c)

Mission schools and hospitals

- ○ Hospital
- □ Secondary School

Refer to main key for
Sponsoring Agencies shown
in squares and circles

JEG/GHA

39

16 ECONOMIC HISTORY

Trade and industry in Zambia have been traced by historians back to the early Iron Age, with evidence of iron smelting dating back to about AD 100 (p. 30). The local trade in iron and copper goods and in salt flourished throughout the subsequent centuries, while abundant evidence for long distance trade with the east coast has been found at Ingombe Ilede, near the confluence of the Zambezi and Kafue, which around AD 1400 appears to have been an important centre of trade in iron, gold, copper and ivory.

The trade in slaves, which probably constituted some part of long distance trade, accelerated in the nineteenth century after the closure of the Atlantic slave trade. The Arabs, working from bases on the east coast, were the largest operators. By disturbing local balances of power through their trade in guns, they maintained a situation of perpetual strife and ensured a steady supply of captives and slaves. Mbundu and Chikunda slavers similarly sought labour for the neighbouring Portuguese colonies of Angola and Mozambique.

Under such disturbing conditions the delicately balanced subsistence economies suffered disastrously. Crops were neglected or destroyed and resulting food shortages stimulated further rounds of plunder of more fortunate neighbours.

During the closing years of the century, the slavers retreated before the advance of the Christian missions who served as the vanguard of European penetration, which led to the formal extension of administrative control (p. 38).

At this time interest was stimulated in the mineral possibilities of the territory north of the Zambezi. Prospecting parties located deposits at Kansanshi (1899), at Broken Hill (1902), in the Hook of Kafue, and in the area of the present Copperbelt. Largely on the strength of these discoveries, which were mostly on the sites of African workings, the British South Africa (BSA) Company accepted administrative responsibility for Northern Rhodesia in return for its mineral rights. However, these finds proved initially disappointing, especially when compared with the remarkably rich copper ores discovered in Katanga.

The BSA Company's greatest contribution to local economic development in the territory was the construction of the railway, which determined the geographical pattern of development that persists to this day.

The few European farmers who settled in Northern Rhodesia faced tremendous physical and economic hazards. Nevertheless maize and cattle were produced along the railway, which reached the Katanga markets in 1909. Around Fort Jameson in the east, experiments were made with cattle, cotton and, most successfully, with tobacco.

Except for a desultory trade in cattle and maize in the south-western part of the country, the indigenous people at first took little part in the modern exchange economy. With the introduction of the hut tax, however, young men were forced to migrate for wage labour to the farms, mines and factories of Southern Rhodesia and South Africa, leaving the rural areas to stagnate. Thus the Company created a typically colonial dual economy comprising a relatively developed sector under European control, and an underdeveloped rural sector whose role was to provide labour, and to bear most of its social costs.

Obstacles to economic development during the years of Company rule were formidable. Distances were great and communications painfully slow. Before 1911 the western and eastern portions of the territory were administered separately from Livingstone (and previously Kalomo) and Fort Jameson respectively. Isolated within the heart of the continent, miners and farmers had either to rely on tiny local markets or produce goods of sufficient value to withstand crippling transport charges incurred in moving them to the coast.

When the Colonial Office assumed direct responsibility for Northern Rhodesia in 1924, it was one of the poorest of British possessions. Yet at this time high copper prices were forcing a re-evaluation of the Copperbelt. Further prospecting revealed that beneath the lean surface oxides lay immense reserves of sulphide ores which had only recently become workable with the introduction of the flotation technique of separation (p. 92).

The late nineteen-twenties were years of great optimism: here at last was the long-hoped-for bonanza. A high investment was made in mines and supporting services. With the influx of miners and technicians, the European population jumped from 3634 in 1921 to 13 846 in 1931. For the first time the internal labour market assumed sizeable proportions. In 1930 some 30 000 Africans were employed on the Copperbelt. New towns housed a growing industrial labour force that was to become slowly more urbanized as time went on and lengths of stay became longer (p. 82). Government responded to the prevailing euphoria by planning a new and grander territorial capital at Lusaka, nearer to the new focus of economic activity (p. 86).

Just as the first mines were coming into production copper prices plummeted during the depression, development work ceased and thousands of employees were dismissed. Many Europeans left the country for good. After 1932, conditions improved and the Northern Rhodesia copper industry, as a low cost producer, recovered more quickly than most. Rearmament, an insatiable war-time demand, and the 1947 devaluation of sterling formed the sequence of events that brought the industry from the verge of collapse to the high prosperity of the nineteen-fifties.

A quickening rate of European immigration became evident after the war, reaching a peak in the mid nineteen-fifties. Many new arrivals farmed along the line of rail, maize production expanded rapidly and virginia tobacco, hitherto exclusive to the Fort Jameson area, became an important export crop.

The creation of the Central African Federation in 1953 further strengthened Northern Rhodesia's economic links with southern Africa. However, Federation gave the territory a poor deal. Copper earnings subsidized development in the other member territories, especially Southern Rhodesia, where manufacturing industry and its accompanying commercial and financial infrastructure rapidly expanded.

Since independence Britain and decreasingly South Africa remain Zambia's major trading partners (p. 114), but coal and electricity, important though they be, are now virtually the only imports from Rhodesia. Strenuous efforts are being made to produce power, basic raw materials and manufactured goods locally or, where this is not possible, to find alternative suppliers. Communications are being improved with East Africa, with whom Zambia has much in common, politically and economically. The oil pipeline, the up-grading of the Great North Road, and the projected rail link with Dar es Salaam are but the first and most obvious indications of this new alignment (p. 106 and 110).

The principal problems of Zambian economic geography—the vulnerability and high cost of external trade routes and pronounced disparities in regional development—are of long standing. Yet the pattern established over six decades of colonial rule cannot be redrawn overnight, and it would seem that Zambia will be living through a difficult period of economic reconstruction for some years to come.

J E GARDINER

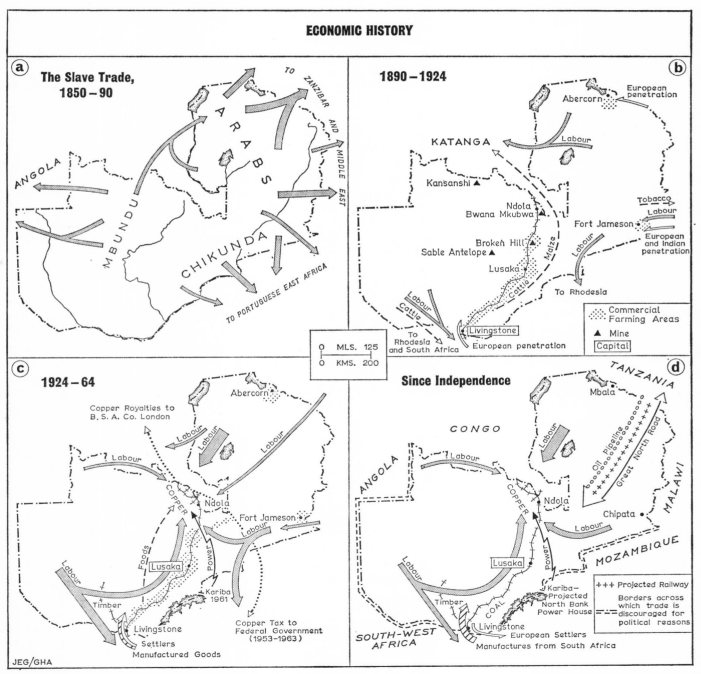

ECONOMIC HISTORY

a The Slave Trade, 1850 – 90

b 1890 – 1924

c 1924 – 64

d Since Independence

17 POPULATION DISTRIBUTION AND DENSITY 1

Until 1969, the only representative population census of Zambia was the 1963 Census of Africans, which, combined with the Federal Census of Population and Employees (European) of 1961, provided the basis for Kay's (1967) distribution and density maps. The present maps are based on preliminary returns of the National Census taken in August 1969 (kindly made available by the Central Statistical Office), the first full census in the country's history. At the time of writing (early 1970) only the crude totals have emerged; consequently, only distribution and density maps are presented, based on provisional data, while comments are necessarily tentative.[1]

For the 1969 Census Zambia's (then) 44 administrative districts (p. 50) were divided into over 1600 'supervisors' areas'. In each of these the census supervisor was given from two to nine enumerators. The latters' areas cannot be geographically identified and consequently supervisors' areas, which can, have been used in constructing both maps. Averaging approximately 180 sq. miles (466 sq. km.), these provide a sufficiently close network, certainly better than was available for the 1963 data: nevertheless, in sparsely peopled regions some are distinctly large—the largest covering 4189 sq. miles (10 850 sq. km.). In the density map, contiguous areas in the same categories are grouped for shading purposes.

For the distribution map the same dot value (500) was chosen as for Kay's earlier map, to allow rough visual comparison: because of inevitable subjectivity in the actual placing of dots, however, and because census areas have changed in the interim, such comparison should be made with caution. Kay's technique of constructing his density map via a dot count within a grid framework has not been followed here, since subjective differences in dot placement would be compounded by basing density calculations on the dots, rendering density comparisons misleading. In any case, the 1969 census areas are adequate for the conventional choropleth technique adopted.

The 1969 preliminary returns give a national population of 4 054 000;[2] the Central Statistical Office estimates that 95 000 of these are non-Africans (cf. 74 460 Europeans and 7790 Asians in 1961). With a total land surface of 290 586 sq. miles (752 618 sq. km.) this gives the low overall density of 13.9 to the sq. mile (5.4 per sq. km.). Population growth (previously estimated at 3.2 per cent) is calculated at 2.5 per cent per annum: total increase since June 1963 has been 16.2 per cent.

The density and distribution maps can conveniently be discussed together. The most striking feature of both maps is the linear concentration along the spinal line of rail. Over 40 per cent of Zambians live within 25 miles of the railway, an area including all sizeable urban centres. Large variations in overall

density are also noticeable. The highest density category, over 500 per sq. mile, covers only 344 sq. miles (891 sq. km.), or 0.12 per cent of the national area, but accounts for 1 131 496 people, or 28 per cent of the population. In marked contrast, the lowest density category, with under 5 to the sq. mile (1.9 per sq. km.), occupies 57 per cent of the national area but has only 9 per cent of the population.

The small areas with the highest population densities are mostly urbanized localities along the line of rail, together with others associated with provincial and district capitals. Town distribution, discussed separately (p. 80), is not considered further here. Excluding urbanized supervisors' areas, the average density over the remainder of Zambia is only 10 per sq. mile (3.9 per sq. km.), a figure taken as the average in considering the rural areas.

Rural population

The large expanses with *very sparse population* (under 5 per sq. mile, or 1.9 per sq. km.) occur in two main regions, the middle Kafue valley and the Luangwa valley. Both regions separate more densely peopled peripheral areas from the line of rail. Both lack resource potential for close settlement and are infested with tsetse-fly (p. 57[a]), with its negative effects on settlement. Consequently they include the major game reserves of the country—the Kafue National Park and the Luangwa Valley Reserve (p. 109[b]). Virtually uninhabited land in these reserves forms core areas from which lobes of sparser population extend outward. Other sparsely peopled areas include Forest Reserves and Protected Forest Areas (PFA's), where cultivation and settlement are actively discouraged. Small unpopulated areas visible on the Copperbelt (distribution map) are, in fact, Protected Forest Areas.

Denser rural population (over 25 per sq. mile, or 9.6 per sq. km.) occurs in four main regions, each containing minor nodes: the line of rail; within Eastern Province; the upper Zambezi valley; and within Northern and Luapula Provinces. Denser rural population along the line of rail occurs particularly in three localities—the Copperbelt, the Lusaka–Mumbwa area, and a belt from Kalomo northward to the Kafue River, with smaller concentrations around Kabwe and Livingstone. These growing concentrations reflect the pull of the urban centres. The line of rail is a pioneer zone of development, characterized by relatively advanced farming with both livestock and crops, maize being the staple. Flanking it, colonial 'native reserves' were established that attracted many people, some effectively dispossessed of customary land by its alienation to Europeans and others seeking employment on the nearby commercial farms, thus raising population densities (p. 48). The Eastern Province area extends from Chipata to Petauke, with an outlier around Lundazi. Here, too, is good land with some history of European and African commerical farming, producing maize as a staple, groundnuts and cattle. The upper Zambezi plain has its main concentration around Kalabo, Mongu and Senanga, with smaller nodes around Balovale and Chavuma, Sesheke and Mulobezi, and Mankoya. The virtually subsistence economy includes fishing, livestock and a variety of staples—mainly maize, cassava, and bulrush millet. In northern Zambia several areas have denser rural

---

[1] Continuing studies of distributional aspects of the new census form part of the research programme of the Cartographic and Location Analysis Unit of the Zambian National Council for Scientific Research. Publication of the first of a series of map sheets and texts is expected early in 1971.

[2] Subsequently adjusted to 4056 995 Central Statistical Office, Lusaka, 1970).

populations. The lower Luapula valley and the shore of Lake Mweru, the Bangweulu lake and swamp depression and the Mbala–Mpulungu area all have fishing central to their economies, including commercial sales to the Copperbelt. As with the upper Zambezi, their population fluctuates seasonally as fishermen move to temporary camps with low water (the census month, August, being a low-water period). In fishing areas, settlement forms marked linear distributions along riverbanks, lake shores and swamp edges. Other areas of denser rural population are found on plateau country around Kasama, the capital of Northern Province, and along the high borderland with Tanzania. Here, as in lake and river areas in the north, the staple crop is commonly cassava.

Population distribution reflects complex inter-related factors impossible to consider here: however, some general points may be noted. All areas of denser rural population have a comparatively broad-based economy with crops and either fishing or the keeping of livestock, and not the simplest, millet-based bush rotation economy that supports only lower densities. Secondly, all (except the remote upper Zambezi) produce some surpluses of saleable primary produce. Thirdly, rural population concentrations often reflect the location of major pre-colonial political groupings (cf. p. 32). It is of interest to note that the Luapula valley is the only area of denser rural population which has tsetse-fly. Here the attraction of fishing (plus historical factors) has overcome the usually negative effects of tsetse infestation.

Finally, there are areas of *intermediate rural population density* (5 to 25 per sq. mile), usually surrounding higher density areas. One such area links the Bangweulu and the Luapula–Mweru population concentrations; a second extends between the

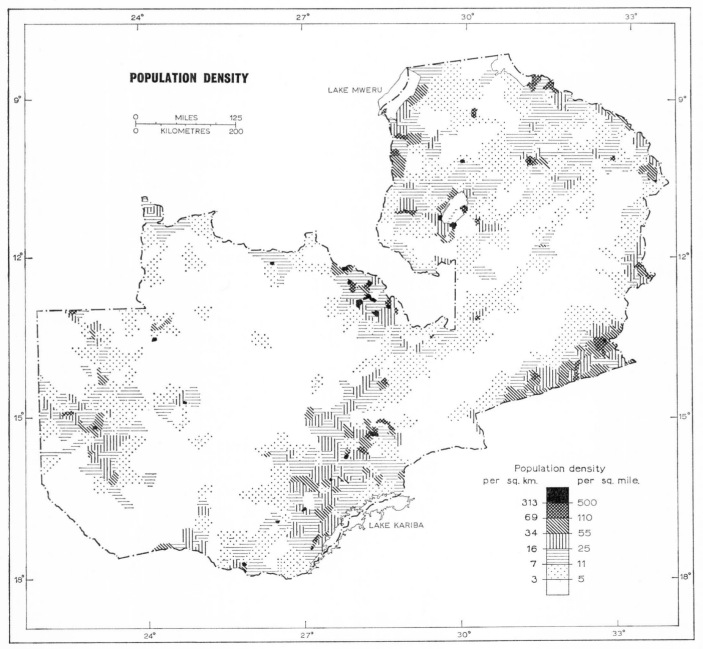

18 POPULATION DISTRIBUTION AND DENSITY 2

Kasama concentration and the Mbala–Mpulungu and Tanzania border areas; a third clearly follows the watershed between the Luangwa and Chambeshi valleys along the route of the Great North Road; and a fourth flanks the north-western border west of the Copperbelt. Each of these is a plateau or watershed area where a fairly even population scatter is associated with chitemene (slash and burn) cultivation (p. 58), and where little or no saleable agricultural surplus is produced.

Province and District	Population 1969	1963	Intercensal change
	(000)		(per cent)
CENTRAL			
Lusaka urban	238	109	219·2
Lusaka rural	97	76	26·7
Feira	8	9·5	—15·7
Mkushi	59	54	7·3
Mumbwa	61	54	13·0
Serenje	54	56	—5·3
Kabwe urban	86	58	48·3
Kabwe rural	105	86	22·1
TOTAL	708	505	40·2
COPPERBELT			
Chililabombwe	47	34	38·2
Chingola	105	59	78·0
Kalulushi	34	22	54·5
Kitwe	195	123	58·5
Mufulira	107	80	33·8
Luanshya	98	75	30·7
Ndola urban	159	94	69·1
Ndola rural	70	57	22·8
TOTAL	815	544	49·8
EASTERN			
Chipata	260	239	8·8
Lundazi	124	123	0·8
Petauke	125	118	5·9
TOTAL	509	480	6·0
LUAPULA			
Kawambwa	165	172	—4·1
Mansa	81	87	—7·0
Samfya	92	98	—6·1
TOTAL	338	357	—5·3
NORTH WESTERN			
Balovale	56	53	5·7
Kabompo	32	33	—3·0
Kasempa	33	34	—2·9
Mwinilunga	53	46	15·2
Solwezi	53	45	18·0
TOTAL	227	211	7·6

Province and District	Population 1969	1963	Intercensal change
	(000)		(per cent)
NORTHERN			
Chinsali	57	71	—19·7
Isoka	78	82	—4·9
Kasama	108	114	—5·3
Luwingu	78	81	—3·7
Mbala	94	91	3·3
Mpika	58	60	—3·3
Mporokoso	68	65	4·6
TOTAL	541	564	—4·1
SOUTHERN			
Choma	99	97	2·1
Gwembe	76	69	10·1
Kalomo	77	75	2·7
Livingstone	51	38	34·2
Mazabuka	161	154	4·5
Namwala	35	33	6·1
TOTAL	499	466	7·1
WESTERN			
Kalabo	107	96	11·5
Mankoya	57	47	21·3
Mongu	113	105	7·6
Senanga	91	72	26·4
Sesheke	49	43	14·0
TOTAL	417	363	14·9
ZAMBIA TOTAL	4054	3490	16·2

Distributional changes 1963–69

Comparison of the available 1963 and 1969 statistics (see Table) and maps shows that the overall population increase since 1963 (16·2 per cent) is most unevenly distributed, due mainly to the increasing concentration of people into small nodal areas at the expense of vast, sparsely peopled hinterlands.

The table is crude since changed delimitation of census areas permits only district figures to be directly compared, but it shows that all Luapula, most of Northern and parts of North-western provinces have experienced population decreases, the greatest loss being 19·7 per cent in Chinsali District. Definitive reasons for this must rest upon an analysis of more detailed returns, but the Copperbelt urban/industrial region clearly continues to act as a magnet (p. 82). Much of eastern and southern, and parts of western and north-western Zambia have had less than average population increases and may also be areas of net out-migration. Only Lusaka, Kabwe, Livingstone and the Copperbelt districts (all urbanized) plus six rural districts, have had above-average increases. Since rural districts in this group have increases only slightly above the national average, large population increases, implying significant in-migration, as well as natural increases, have been confined to urbanized districts, which record from a 30 to 219 per cent gain over the period. The popular impression of 'urban drift' in Zambia thus appears confirmed by the preliminary returns. A secondary factor is that most capitals of rural districts losing population have themselves grown, leaving their hinterlands with even greater losses than the figures indicate. This suggests that population movement to certain provincial and district capitals may form a stage in the movement to larger towns. The age structure of the rural population must surely be adversely affected (p. 46), for towns particularly attract young men, so that many rural districts report serious losses of men of working age.

Some isolated instances of population change are due to local factors that cannot be considered here. Two examples are the movements of people to the Maamba coalfield near Lake Kariba (p. 90) and to the new town at Kafue, now under construction (p. 88).

In general, movement toward central places offering hope of employment and modest urban amenities is marked, and the truly rural population is widely declining. Nevertheless in 1969 the process was at an early stage, and almost 70 per cent of Zambians are still rural dwellers.

M E JACKMAN

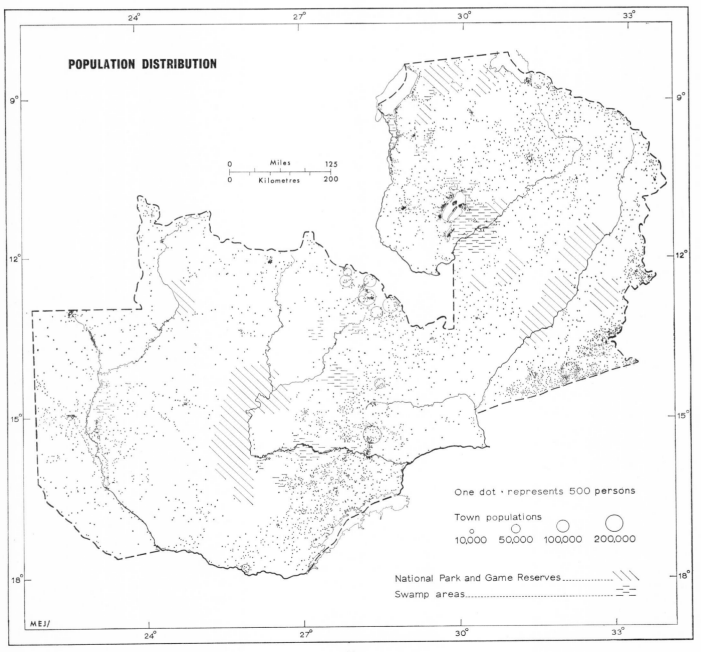

POPULATION DISTRIBUTION

One dot · represents 500 persons

Town populations
10,000 50,000 100,000 200,000

National Park and Game Reserves ....

Swamp areas ....

MEJ/

19 AGE-STRUCTURE, SEX RATIO AND MIGRATIONS (1963)[1]

The 1963 census divided the African population into three age groups: under 21 years, 55·4 per cent; 21–45 years, 33·2 per cent; and over 45 years, 11·4 per cent. Clearly the economically most active group is relatively small and the burden of young dependants is considerable. Regional variations in age structure are not great (fig. *b*). The population of the towns and European farming areas includes only 4·5 per cent over the age of 45 but 39·4 per cent between 21 and 45 years because of selective effects of rural-urban migration, which involves few elderly persons. Implications for the age structure of areas supplying migrants are mostly self-evident. Throughout most of north-eastern Zambia persons aged 21–45 constitute a particularly small proportion and young persons an exceptionally high proportion of the total. However, children and young persons comprise a small proportion of the population in north-western and western regions (e.g. Kabompo, 37 per cent; Balovale, 38 per cent, and in some of these areas elderly persons (over 45 years) are particularly numerous (Mankoya, 23 per cent; Mongu-Lealui, 22 per cent). These structures may be explained by factors affecting natural increase as much as by effects of migration.

The sex ratio exhibits greater regional diversity (fig. *c*). In 1963 the national figure was 97·5 men per 100 women. In towns and European farming areas, for every 100 women there were 179 and 162 men respectively and in (African) rural areas generally there were only 81 men per 100 women. Clearly far more men than women migrate from rural areas. However, within rural areas a significant sequence of sex ratios is discernible relative to distance from and difficulty of access to the main areas of employment. Rural areas close to major employment centres, such as those of Ndola, Kabwe, Mansa and Mkushi Districts, have relatively numerous adult males; in some cases more than women. As distance from main areas of employment increases the sex ratio generally widens, and over much of Zambia there are between 70 and 90 men per 100 women. Three large areas, all remote and relatively isolated, have extraordinarily ill-balanced populations. Western Province is 500 miles from the Copperbelt and internal communications there are poor; the Gwembe valley was effectively isolated until recently by rugged 'escarpment hills'; and the Luangwa valley and Lundazi areas also are remote, with poor communications. Such regional differences in the sex ratio may be explained in terms of rural-urban migrations.

Labour and population statistics for 1962 permit calculation of a rate of 'absenteeism' for each Chief's Area in terms of taxable males living away from their *de jure* rural homes (fig. *a*). All rural areas suffer heavy losses of able-bodied men, but there are marked regional differences in intensity of rural depopulation. Lack of balance between the sexes in both rural and urban areas is commonly explained by the predominance of men in rural-urban migrations, but comparison of figs *a* and *c* invites

[1] Relevant 1969 census figures were not available at the time of writing.

consideration of regional differences in the exodus of women from rural areas. In extensive areas near major employment centres there is a narrow sex ratio or even an excess of males, despite a considerable exodus of men. Movement of males into areas peripheral to employment centres could compensate for loss of local men, although only partly. Probably more significant is a very considerable exodus of women as well as men from these areas. This hypothesis is supported by studies of the tribal composition of urban populations which show that women of local tribes constitute a large proportion of the adult female population. Apparently as distance, difficulty and cost of travel increase so rural-urban migration of women decreases. Few women seem to migrate from the three particularly remote or inaccessible areas and therefore, although male exodus is not particularly high, the sex ratio is wide. Perhaps extreme conservatism is also responsible for low rates of migration from these areas.

Minor features on fig. *c* apparently do not accord with this general hypothesis. In the lower Luapula valley, the Bangweulu Swamps and the Kafue Flats the sex ratio is narrow, and it seems likely that major commercial fisheries in these areas attract male immigrants. Relative ease of transport by 'fish lorries' may also facilitate emigration of women. In small areas around townships such as Mongu, Kawambwa, Sesheke, and Katima Mulilo and along the Livingstone to Kataba railway the sex ratio is narrow. Again economic opportunities have probably attracted male immigrants; and possibly there is a movement of women from these rural areas *into* local townships. Finally, a small area in Eastern Province has more than 90 men per 100 women. This is a resettlement area for Ngoni peoples from overcrowded lands. Most households moving into it have a male head and a considerable male labour force was still working there in 1963. Thus, on the whole, the minor features on fig. *c* do not conflict with the general hypothesis stated above.

Finally, some recent trends may be of interest. The population of major towns is growing more rapidly than that of the country at large. Thus, in the two years 1963 to 1965 the national population increased by 6·1 per cent while conservative official estimates show that the ten main town populations grew by 12·8 per cent. If most of this influx were of women, a movement towards a more balanced population would be indicated, but evidence suggests that this is not so. Urban growth, in fact, seems to have been temporarily outstripped by expansion of employment, which rose by 18·5 per cent between 1963 and 1965. This increase is almost entirely in the urban sector and involves a predominantly male labour force. Moreover, there is evidence that the number of unemployed males in urban areas has increased markedly in recent years. It thus seems that since independence there has been a large, predominantly male, influx of population in the urban areas. General implications for the sex ratio and, to a lesser extent, for the age structure of the various rural and the urban sectors of the population are fairly self-evident. Problems associated with imbalance have, temporaily at least, been intensified and the task of creating a reasonably balanced and stable structure throughout Zambia made the more arduous.

G KAY

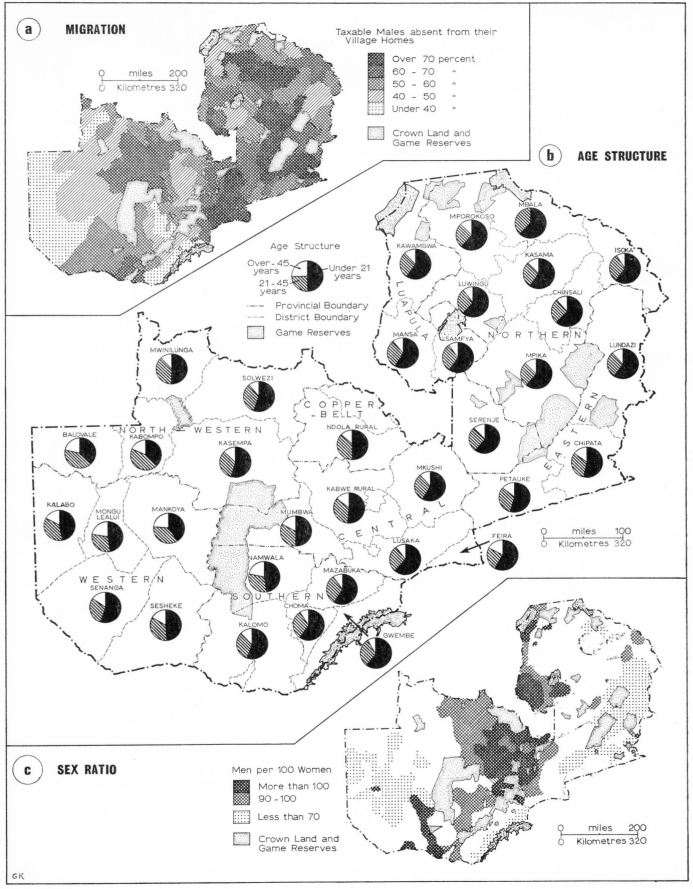

COLONIAL LAND RIGHTS

The system of land rights established during the colonial period, while ill-defined, still clearly reflected the differences between European settlers and miners, who wished to impose a set of well-delimited territorial divisions, and the indigenous shifting cultivators and pastoralists, whose attitudes to land demarcation were inevitably more ambiguous. Lands acquired for exploitation by Europeans were of four main types: land alienated for mineral exploitation, land alienated for farm settlement on both freehold and leasehold basis, land suitable for expansion in these sectors, and land designated as forest and game reserves. At the same time there were three types of African land holding: the native reserves, the native trust territories and the Protectorate of Barotseland (now Western Province).

Boundaries between 'African' and Crown (basically European) territories were established by a series of pragmatic acquisitions and subsequent legal consolidations. In the early years of colonization, before the establishment of the government of Northern Rhodesia in 1924, land apportionment was in the hands of two private trading organizations, the British South Africa Company and the North Charterlands Exploration Company. Both companies negotiated with local chiefs for land which they considered suitable for European settlement or mineral exploitation on the basis of the Lawley Lewanika Concessions (1898–1900) and the Thompson Sharpe Treaties (1890–91). However, actual farming alienations often proceeded on a *de facto* basis: individuals established claims and then informed the relevant concessionary company. These farms were concentrated in two areas, namely, along the railway line from Livingstone to Broken Hill (Kabwe), and on the good tobacco and maize soils of the Eastern Province around Fort Jameson (Chipata). Some lands were also opened up near Abercorn (Mbala) on the southern shore of Lake Tanganyika.

After 1924 all these *de facto* alienations were granted legal status and the two concessionary companies were allowed to retain 15 000 sq. miles of territory for possible expansion, mainly in the Eastern and Northern Provinces. In 1928–29 some attempt was made to safeguard African lands against further European expansion by official recognition of the rather informally established *Reserves* along the perimeters of alienated farmlands, though these Reserves were still given no firm legality. With the exception of Barotseland (which gained pseudo-independent status in 1890–1900 and was subsequently immune from European encroachment), the territory outside the alienated land and the Reserves, occupying almost 60 per cent of the area of Northern Rhodesia, was given over to the Crown. Here the rights of both African and European remained vague until 1947, when the government of the day (while recognizing the land alienated for settlement) designated the rest of the territory as *Native Trust Land* to be held under customary law, making it

ineligible for further expatriate development 'unless it was in the interest of all races'.

In this way three types of African land right were established, each representing a different degree of association with the ruling power. At one extreme, Barotseland retained its feudal semi-independent protectorate status, until independence in 1964. At the other, the Native Reserves became mere appendages to the alienated farmlands of the European settlers. Designed to preserve African lands from further settler encroachment, many of the Reserves became little more than rural ghettoes. Suffering an influx of the dispossessed from the alienated lands and of dependants of farm workers from the trust territories, the lands of the Reserves were soon over-populated, with densities sometimes reaching over 100 per sq. mile, twelve times greater than the safe ecological limit. Despite periodic attempts by the colonial administration to resettle surplus populations on unoccupied Crown Lands and to improve African agriculture, these Reserves are still over-grazed and over-cultivated and the soil exhaustion in some areas is severe. Between the extremes stood the *Native Trust Territories*, with ill-defined rights under customary law where European influence was usually restricted to administration and to missionary endeavour.

Following independence, the Zambian Government has become increasingly aware of the indeterminate nature of traditional land rights (under customary law) which clearly inhibit permanent settlement and agricultural improvement. It has also been embarrassed both by the pressure on resources in the old Reserves and the inequalities written into the new constitution at independence in order to safeguard the more precisely defined European land rights. Since 1964 the problems caused by these constitutional discrepancies have been exacerbated by the exodus of European farmers, many of whom were unable to sell their properties for what they regarded as a reasonable price. These absentee landowners retain a 'paper occupancy' over more than half the available farmland in the line of rail and over most of the alienated land in the Eastern Province, where few, if any, European farms are still in use. Naturally, 'squatters' have begun to move from the Reserves on to the unoccupied farms. In August 1969 a National Referendum granted the National Assembly the power to change the constitution and the opportunity to make a radical revision of land rights and impose compulsory purchase and compensation levels.

The problem of the next decade will be to reconcile European farming claims with the need to evolve and establish a new and distinctively African system of land rights that can replace the indeterminacy of the old subsistence values. In view of the fluidity of customary rights and laws of inheritance, the complexities of squatter occupation of State Land clearly suitable for more intensive occupation, and the interests of the residual but extremely important European farming element, the task of meeting the differing levels of expectancy will not be an easy one.

D J SIDDLE

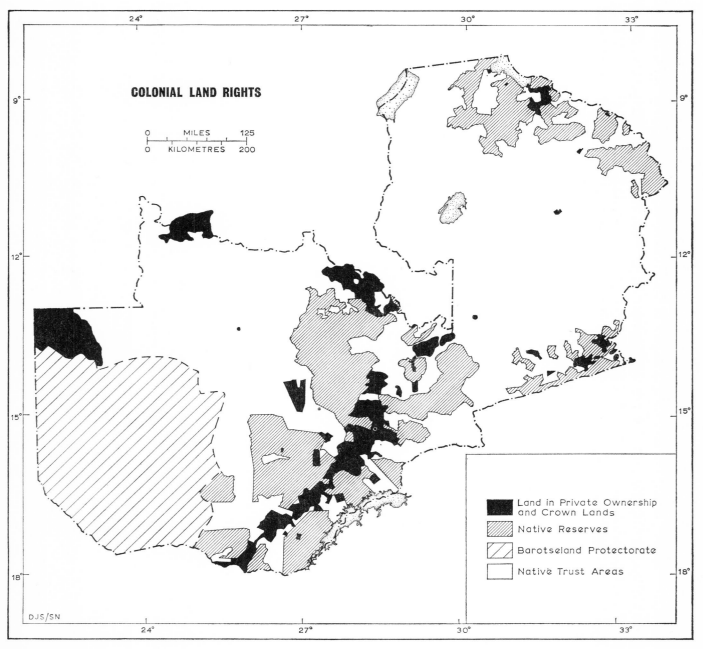

COLONIAL LAND RIGHTS

0   MILES   125
0   KILOMETRES   200

	Land in Private Ownership and Crown Lands
	Native Reserves
	Barotseland Protectorate
	Native Trust Areas

DJS/SN

21 ADMINISTRATIVE DIVISIONS

There have been six main types of administrative division in Zambia during the last fifty years: *court areas*; *provinces*; *districts*; *native authority areas*; *chiefs' areas*; and *parishes*. Of these, only native authority and chiefs' areas were distinctively indigenous.

With the exception of Barotseland (now Western Province), which acquired semi-independent status in 1890–1900, the country's first administrative boundaries (*court areas*) were established by the British South Africa Company in 1911 to demarcate the areas of jurisdiction of the magistrates' courts. There were ten such areas in the territory (Tanganyika, East Luangwa, Luangwa, Luapula, Mweru, Awemba, Serenje, Kafue, Batoka, Barotse-Kasempa) each serving up to four court centres depending on the size of the unit. While paying some cursory attention to tribal territories, the boundaries of the court areas were usually defined by a fairly arbitrary selection of astronomical lines and by rivers, watersheds and other convenient physical features. These court areas were eventually rationalized into seven *provinces* in 1937, although the only radical re-alignment of boundaries was in the Northern and Central Provinces. It must be stressed, therefore, that the fairly arbitrary divisions of 1911 provided the spatial framework of the Northern Rhodesian provincial administration which, with minor modifications, was inherited by the independent government of Zambia in 1964.

When the seven new provinces were established in the reorganization of 1937, they were divided into thirty-four rural districts and ten urban districts. District Officers assumed responsibility for the rural districts, assisted by local courts operating the system of customary law under the chiefs and local officials in the chiefs' areas. Urban units were run by town councils in the British manner. At various times after the Second World War attempts were made to establish rural *parishes*, mainly to define 'village' areas and to circumscribe settlement migration. These units were seldom precisely defined, were unpopular and rarely effective, and were abandoned even before independence. Since independence *chiefs' areas* have also been abandoned together with the *tribal authority areas* through which they operated, as part of an attempt to diminish the divisive elements of tribalism that afflict Zambia in common with most new African states. Today the country is administered through its structure of eight provinces (Barotseland became a province in 1964 and was re-named Western Province in 1969) and thirty rural districts. Since the map was drawn the number of administrative districts has been increased. Some use is still made of the old chiefs' areas as the basis for census data collection.

Provinces diverge widely in character and size. They range from the pastoral, still largely undeveloped Western Province, to the commercial farming provinces of the centre and south; from the small and relatively highly urbanized Copperbelt Province with a population of 815 000 (1969) to the large and empty territory of Northwestern Province with population densities of between three and eight persons per sq. mile in an area the size of Malawi.

The size of even the smallest province reflects the vastness of Zambia compared with some other African states. Western Province is larger than six of Africa's countries (Lesotho, Burundi, Equatorial Guinea, French Somaliland, Rwanda and Swaziland) and almost three times the size of the Gambia. Northern, Northwestern, Western and Central Provinces are all larger than Liberia, Malawi, Tunisia and Dahomey and over half as large again as Sierra Leone. Even some of the rural districts are of 'national' size. Kasempa, in the Western Province, for example, with a mean population of a little over two per square mile, is three times the size of Swaziland. Indeed, most of the districts (with an overall mean size of more than 8000 sq. miles) are larger than several independent African states, and only three (Choma, Samfya and Feira) are smaller than, for example, the Gambia.

There are considerable problems in administering provinces of this size and number, especially when most of them have mean densities of population of less than ten per sq. mile (p. 42), a shifting form of settlement based on 'slash-and-burn' agriculture (p. 58) or pastoralism, and poor communications. Until recently, most administrative decisions had to be taken either in the provincial headquarters or in Lusaka and there were weeks and even months of delay in communicating these decisions to village level.

The pragmatic and piecemeal manner in which these provincial and district boundaries were fixed has also meant that a good deal of time and energy has been spent in attempting to reconcile the frequently disparate social and economic interests and demands of those confined within these arbitrary administrative limits. It is significant to note in this context that recent development surveys (e.g. the Kafue Basin Survey, the Luangwa Valley Survey and the Catchment Basin schemes) have ignored provincial and district boundaries that bear little relation to rational regional planning. On the other hand, the fact that available data was based on existing administrative divisions forced the government to use these divisions as 'planning regions' in the First National Development Plan of 1966–70.

Current moves by the Zambian Government to decentralize the administration may go some way towards solving problems of the slow communication of ideas and should be welcomed as long overdue. However, rationalization of administrative boundaries on coherent regional lines should take place *before* the emergence of clearly identifiable regional (i.e. provincial) planning policies, for these will inevitably make subsequent changes more difficult.

D J SIDDLE

ADMINISTRATIVE DIVISIONS

MILES 0 — 125
KILOMETRES 0 — 200

MBALA

MPOROKOSO

KAWAMBWA

KASAMA

ISOKA

NORTHERN

LUWINGU

CHINSALI

MWINILUNGA

MANSA

SAMFYA

LUAPULA

MPIKA

LUNDAZI

SOLWEZI

NDOLA (RURAL)

NORTH-

COPPER —BELT

SERENJE

CHIPATA

WESTERN

KABOMPO

BALOVALE

KASEMPA

MKUSHI

EASTERN

KALABO

KABWE (RURAL)

MONGU LEALUI

MANKOYA

MUMBWA

CENTRAL

LUSAKA (RURAL)

PETAUKE

WESTERN

FEIRA

SENANGA

NAMWALA

MAZABUKA

URBAN DISTRICTS

SESHEKE

CHOMA GWEMBE

SOUTHERN

KALOMO

1. Chililabombwe
2. Chingola
3. Mufulira
4. Kalulushi
5. Kitwe
6. Luanshya
7. Ndola
8. Kabwe
9. Lusaka
10. Livingstone

BOUNDARIES

--- Provincial

········ Rural and Urban District

DJS/LM

51

Upon achieving independence on 24 October 1964, Zambia became a republic within the Commonwealth. Its constitution establishes a presidential system of government, though one which incorporates numerous features from British practice. With the powers accruing from its dual roles as Head of State and Head of Government, the Presidency is constitutionally an imposing office. Zambia's first President, Dr Kenneth Kaunda, leader of the ruling United National Independence Party (UNIP), won a second term by a commanding majority at the December 1968 General Elections.

The Executive also includes a Cabinet, comprising a Vice-President and up to 19 Ministers. While the President cannot belong to the legislature, his Cabinet team is drawn from this source. Formally, the Cabinet has an advisory role; its members remain responsible to the President and among them only the Vice-President has any constitutional stature. The National Assembly consists of 105 elected members and up to 5 more nominated by the President; there is also a House of Chiefs, a deliberative body.

The President's term of office coincides with the Assembly's (normally five years) and both are elected by the same mechanism: all parliamentary candidates having pledged their support for a presidential nominee, the ballots in the Assembly elections are automatically recorded in the presidential contest (in unopposed constituencies, the appropriate candidate receives all registered votes); a plurality suffices to win. Dr Kaunda's contender in the 1968 elections was Mr Harry Nkumbula, Leader of the Opposition in the Assembly and African National Congress (ANC) president since 1951.

The closing years of the colonial era were marked by uncertainty over Northern Rhodesia's future status, though the 1964 Constitution—then the fourth in under six years—has since provided a stable governmental order. Before 1950, colonial development had left unsettled any viable reconciliation of interests between the African populace and the European settler community (in 1954, approximately two per cent of the population), and the territory's inclusion in the Federation of Rhodesia and Nyasaland (1953–63) led to political impasse, broken only by the 1962 territorial elections which brought to power the first African government.

Current party divisions date from a fissure in ANC late in 1958. This was a consequence of long-standing disagreements over the anti-Federation campaign, though precipitated by British proposals concerning African political advancement. UNIP was formed in August, 1959 after an unsettled period which saw the banning of a predecessor. While the initial cleavage was between militants and moderates, subsequent shrinkage of ANC's popular support reduced that party, by the January 1964 elections, to a sectional grouping confined largely to Southern and parts of Central Provinces. ANC's capture of only 10 of the 75 seats engendered confidence in UNIP leaders that a one-party state would be achieved through the ballot box.

African party development bore directly on suffrage expansion and, until independence, franchise extensions followed rather than preceded African political organization. A qualified franchise had underpinned European electoral dominance prior to 1959, when constitutional reforms introduced two voting rolls and racially-allocated constituencies—an arrangement surviving independence in the 10 Reserved (European) and the 65 Main Roll (African) seats. The 1964 elections were the first based on universal adult suffrage. From 11 in 1958, the African electorate expanded to 7600 in 1959 and to nearly 1 380 000 by 1964. The registered vote stood at 1 587 966 in December 1968.

The 1968 constituency delimitation was occasioned by the Assembly's enlargement to 105 members and was among several changes made in anticipation of elections. The suffrage was limited to citizens; the Reserved seats were abolished; the voting age was lowered to 18; and voting altered to a marked-ballot, single-box system—thus ensuring secrecy, but, with illiteracy widespread, posing complications for election and party officials. Electoral administration was also extended, with 369 new polling districts bringing the total to 1622.

The delimitation itself was based on population rather than the voters' register, as previously. Constituencies were made as nearly equal as possible, allowing for terrain, communications and population density; 'sympathetic consideration' was given to rural areas. The last census having occurred in 1963, the Electoral Commission relied upon current population estimates. The 'population quota' (the quotient of the national total divided by 105) was 37 960. When possible, the Commission utilized existing administrative divisions: constituencies were grouped by provinces, then by districts, seldom crossing district lines (cf. p. 51 and 53). In districts with multiple constituencies, boundaries corresponded with chiefs' areas (Appendix 1, p. 126).

Of forty new constituencies, Northwestern Province received one; Eastern, Luapula and Western four each; Southern six; and Central, Copperbelt and Northern seven apiece. Proportional changes between 1963 and 1968 were not substantial. The two provinces losing most—Eastern and Northwestern—saw their combined share of seats fall by 4 per cent, to 19 per cent; the three gaining most—Central, Northern and Southern—experienced a combined increase of under 4 per cent, to 43·7 per cent. Discrepancy seemed likely, however, regarding the urban centres: although their growth was reflected in seven new seats, raising their total to twenty-one, the urban share of all seats actually dropped slightly (the 1969 census subsequently confirmed significant urban under-representation).

At 2767·4 sq. miles (7168 sq. km.), the average constituency approaches the Copperbelt in area. Smaller than Tanzania's, it is substantially larger than in Kenya, Uganda, Malawi, or Ghana and Sierra Leone, and could easily contain eighteen British constituencies. Complicating any reduction in areal size is the relative sparseness of Zambia's population and its uneven distribution (p. 42); an average of 15 123 registered voted contrasts with the 1966 UK average of 57 087. Compared with those above, Zambia's constituencies represent smaller populations in every instance except Sierra Leone's.

Approximately 40 per cent of the total population registered to vote in the 1968 elections—a figure similar to that for 1964 and comparing favourably with other African countries. Regarding constituency variations, seventy-four of the 105 did not deviate greatly from the average (15 123), falling within a range of 25 per cent above and below the mean. Of thirty-one cases showing appreciable deviation, eighteen were in excess, some considerably so: with over 25 000 registrants, Lusaka City Central, Lusaka City West, and Kabwe were more than 60 per cent above average. Fourteen of the eighteen were on the line of rail. Below average deviations were smaller, none being over 50 per cent from the mean.

The 1968 elections developed into a straight fight between UNIP and ANC. The National Progress Party, the renamed territorial branch of the old United Federal Party and winner of the ten Reserved seats in 1964, had dissolved itself. Another group, the United Party, was banned in August following inter-party violence. Led by an ex-UNIP minister, the UP was based on Western Province, although it was also active on the line of rail.

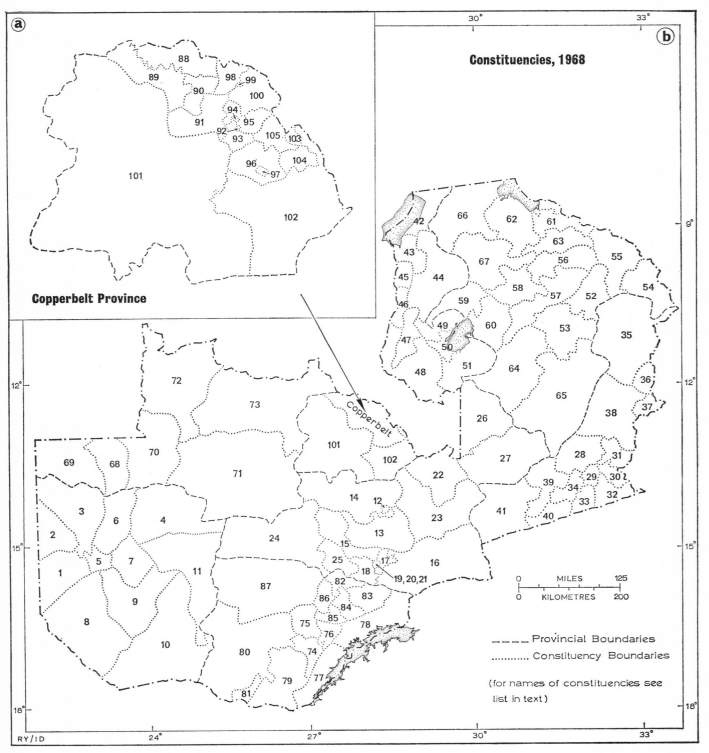

ANC absorbed many UP activists, including its leader, who won Libonda while still under restriction. Independent candidates declined from ten in 1964 to three in 1968. Two of these, both former NPP parliamentarians, ran in loose alliance with ANC.

Passing verdict after fifty months of independence, the electorate delivered an unmistakable endorsement of the ruling party's performance (see map and Appendix 1, p. 126). In a heavy poll, UNIP won fifty-one of seventy-five contested constituencies and 73 per cent of the valid votes. Dr Kaunda achieved 82 per cent of the presidential ballot, his 1 079 972 votes including over 421 000 from thirty unopposed seats. Enjoying a 4 per cent swing nationally, UNIP made more substantial gains in four provinces, including Southern. (Subsequently, granting ANC petitions, the High Court invalidated fifteen of the uncontested elections. At by-elections in July 1969, however, ANC candidates stood only for three Chipata seats, where their support proved weak. As had already been indicated by a national Referendum, held shortly before to amend the Constitution, the unopposed constituencies, with perhaps two exceptions, were 'safe' UNIP).

The ANC took twenty-three seats, while a twenty-fourth, Gwembe North (Number seventy-eight), was garnered by an independent pledged to Mr Nkumbula's presidential candidature. ANC was defeated in its Northwestern outpost of Mwinilunga (where 1964's victor lost his deposit) but regained Mazabuka, taken by UNIP in a by-election. ANC held its position in Central, but again failed to carry Livingstone or to penetrate Lusaka or Mufulira. Its following in Eastern Province had dwindled and nearly vanished at the 1969 Referendum. Although ANC won thirteen Southern Province seats, the 8·2 per cent swing to UNIP may understate ANC's loss there, since turnout was lower: in 1964, ANC received 79 per cent of the registered vote, in 1968 55·8 per cent. Its Mufulira showing apart, ANC made almost no electoral impression in five provinces; its support was confined to three and effectively deployed only in two.

ANC's surprise capture of eight seats in Western Province—defeating six ministers and junior ministers—thus presented a reversal of fortunes and the election's most dramatic turn. While linked to UP activities, the Lozi community's defection from UNIP had more complex roots. These included discontent over the pace of development there; the government's proscription of recruitment to South Africa, previously a prime outlet for Lozi migrant labour; the party's failure to articulate local grievances; and the 1967 UNIP Central Committee elections, when three of four senior Lozi politicians lost bids for top posts. Yet the size of the revolt remained uncertain. At 62·1 per cent, turnout was relatively low, while rejected ballots were over 10 per cent of those cast. ANC's provincial strength was unevenly spread and UNIP carried Mankoya (now Kaoma) District. In the Referendum, while turnout sagged, the voting did confirm December's results, suggesting the province's shift is for the longer term.

The broad patterns of intersectional cleavage, apparent from the elections map, correspond only partially with provincial boundaries. Defined by strength and direction of partisan support, electoral regions more closely approximate language areas (p. 35[a]), although with sufficient exceptions to indicate significant diversity among the forces affecting voter choices. As striking as the spatial arrangement of partisan alignments is the manner in which they divide the country into two single-party areas.

The elections may well have enhanced the competitiveness of Zambian political life by bringing a politics of choice to more voters. In 1964, five of every eight seats were contested; in 1968, five of every seven. Yet electoral competition retained a one-sided nature, for UNIP was far more likely to reach voters with its message and to be heard sympathetically. Thus of forty-one forfeited deposits, thirty-seven were ANC's. Even when losing, UNIP could average 2128 votes: its lowest poll was 481, in Mumbwa East and Monze West. By contrast, in its ten heaviest defeats, ANC's aggregate poll was 523. Moreover, apart from UNIP's loss of the eight in Western Province, few constituencies have changed hands since 1964 and, including the Referendum, only Mazabuka has shifted more than once. In only twelve seats did the losing party's votes amount to 30 per cent of those cast in 1968; six contests produced an opposition of 40 per cent or more.

Despite tendencies towards partisan stability, with competition occurring between rather than within party 'heartlands', indications of electoral flux exist. Admittedly some apparent shifts of allegiance were magnified extraneously—as in Eastern Province, where the swing to UNIP may partially have depended upon Chipata's constituencies going unopposed, or Central, where UNIP's swing was boosted by returns from rural strongholds uncontested in 1964. Where change was evident, three patterns were distinguishable.

Firstly, there was large-scale partisan conversion, notably in Western Province and Mwinilunga, but also apparent elsewhere. The augmenting of UNIP support in Southern Province probably had such a basis, the bulk of its added vote coming not from Livingstone but Mazabuka and Choma Districts. In Eastern Province's contested seats it was clear that ANC support had waned. Secondly, there was the impact of migration, as exemplified by Lusaka District, where ANC strength was diluted by the increased vote, pro-UNIP by five to one. To which category Copperbelt belonged remains uncertain: ANC's Mufulira support held steady in 1968 yet, with an expanded electorate, its percentage poll declined. A stronger Copperbelt swing to UNIP was only prevented by ANC growth outside Mufulira.

A third pattern was revealed by the turnout, down significantly on the 1964 mark of nearly 95 per cent, although still impressively high. Slackening popular involvement was a likely aftermath to independence, and 1968's figure (82·5 per cent) actually rises if ANC areas are excluded. Yet some decline was evident even in UNIP's poll: the party's share of the registered vote dropped from 65 per cent in 1964 to 56·4 per cent (and in the same seventy-five constituencies slipped further at the Referendum). The diverging of rural and urban turnout rates, a pattern absent in 1964, suggested the probability that political participation is becoming more a town than a country activity.

R A YOUNG

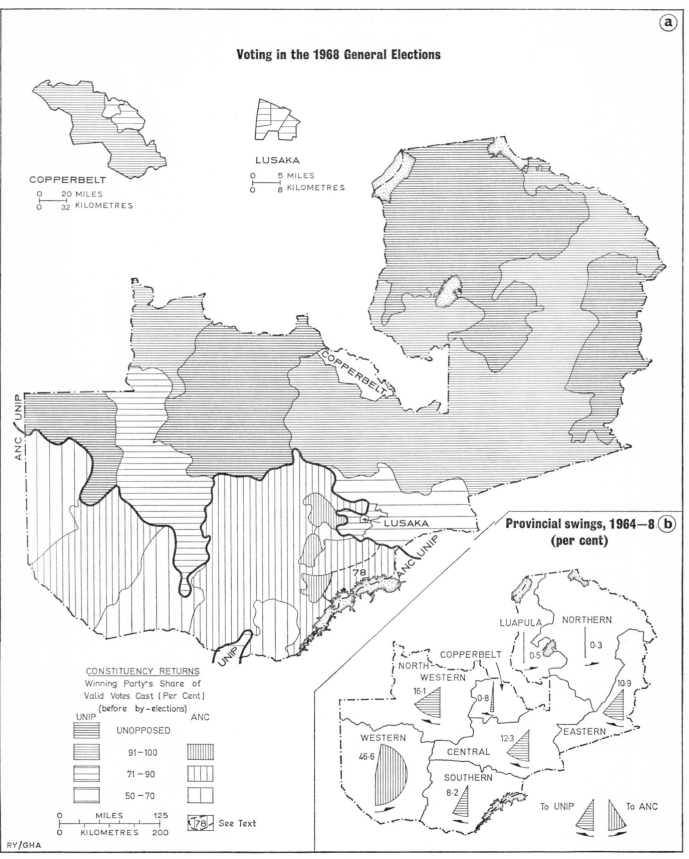

Voting in the 1968 General Elections

COPPERBELT

0   20 MILES
0   32 KILOMETRES

LUSAKA

0   5 MILES
0   8 KILOMETRES

ANC UNIP

COPPERBELT

LUSAKA

ANC UNIP

78

UNIP

CONSTITUENCY RETURNS
Winning Party's Share of
Valid Votes Cast (Per Cent)
(before by-elections)

UNIP   ANC
        UNOPPOSED
        91 – 100
        71 – 90
        50 – 70

0   MILES   125
0   KILOMETRES   200

78   See Text

Provincial swings, 1964—8 (b)
(per cent)

LUAPULA   NORTHERN
              0·3
NORTH-   COPPERBELT   0·5
WESTERN
16·1   0·8
                              10·9
WESTERN   CENTRAL   EASTERN
46·6   12·3
        SOUTHERN
        8·2

To UNIP   To ANC

RY/GHA

55

The maps show the distribution of the four main stock diseases in Zambia.

Trypanosomiasis. Several species of unicellular protozoal organisms of the family *trypanosoma* cause nagana in animals, while three species also cause sleeping sickness in man. Trypanosomes are transmitted by glossina species of the tsetse-fly family, infected persons, domestic stock or wild animals acting as trypanosome reservoirs. The latter suffer little from clinical trypanosomiasis.

This disease has been a major scourge, and it still causes high mortality in much of inter-tropical Africa and widely prevents stock-keeping. Historically, trypanosomiasis prevented the use of animals for draught purposes, thus indirectly necessitating human porterage until steam and motor engines reached inland Africa. Today the tsetse contributes to human malnutrition by its effects, especially on beef and dairy cattle raising. The trypanosomes cause chronic fever leading to wasting—rapid in animals but slower in man—and eventual death. Somnolence is a classical symptom in man following eventual invasion of the brain by the trypanosomes.

Control measures have aimed at clinical treatment of infected humans and livestock with modern therapeutic and prophylactic drugs, some 300 000 livestock being treated annually in Zambia at present. Large-scale control measures have been adopted against the tsetse vector of the disease.

Of the two most common flies, *Glossina pallidipes* prefers shady, humid, riverine conditions while *G. morsitans* prefers more open savanna country. Larvae are laid when ready to pupate and the pupae immediately burrow into soft damp soil or sand. Bush-clearing along river valleys has achieved some success against *G. pallidipes* while game exclusion from livestock areas controls *G. morsitans*. Tsetse-flies have an operational range of two miles from their breeding areas.

Latest techniques include the application of long-acting residual insecticides to tsetse resting sites. Success requires close knowledge of the habits of each species.

Of three major tsetse-fly areas in Zambia, two include the Kafue and Luangwa Valley Game Reserves. Here infestation is acceptable and control measures concentrate on preventing outward spread of the fly. The third area, the Luapula valley, has a dense riverine human population: here restrictions on human nutrition imposed by tsetse infestation is most serious.

African swine fever is a highly infectious virus disease of porcine animals, wholly confined to Africa until its recent spread to some European countries. In Zambia it is so far confined to Eastern Province, where it is regarded as endemic and is adjacent to similar endemic areas in Malawi and Mozambique.

The highly stable causal virus is present in all body fluids, secretions, excretions and tissues of infected animals. Infection is commonly spread by ingestion of infected materials. Warthogs and bushpigs, themselves highly resistant, serve as carriers. Disease outbreaks are usually sporadic and of an acute or subacute form. Occasionally the disease assumes the form of a hyperacute pandemic—for example, in 1961 one such outbreak caused an estimated loss of 20 000 pigs in Petauke and Chipata Districts. Morbidity and mortality are almost 100 per cent in exotic breeds of domestic pigs. Indigenous domestic pigs in Eastern Province seem to have some resistance to the disease.

At present disease outbreaks can only be controlled by strict quarantine and other veterinary sanitary measures. A total embargo is enforced on movements of pigs and pig products from Eastern Province to other parts of Zambia.

East coast fever is an acute disease of cattle caused by the protozoan parasite *Theileria parva* and characterized by high fever, swelling of the lymph-nodes, emaciation and high mortality rate. It is the most serious tick-borne disease in East African cattle and in Zambia is limited to areas adjacent to the Tanzanian and Malawian borders. Transmission is through ticks of the genus *Rhipicephalus*, especially *R. appendiculatus*. Mortality may reach 90–100 per cent, death occurring within two weeks. Recovered animals, usually calves, have a sterile immunity. As yet, the most effective control is by three-day dipping of cattle in insecticidal solutions. Infected ticks may, however, remain alive on pastures for up to fourteen months.

Foot and mouth disease is a highly infectious viral disease chiefly confined to cloven-hoofed animals, particularly cattle and pigs. It has been recorded in buffalo and antelope in Zambia. The Namwala District has been regarded as Zambia's sole enzootic area, although no outbreaks have occurred there for five years. During the preceding twenty-five years, however, there were eight outbreaks in or near this district. During the same period four other outbreaks occurred in neighbouring territories to the south and west, from which infection spread into Zambia.

Zambia has so far experienced only two of the so-called South African types of the causal virus—SAT2 and SAT1. The O and A (so-called European) types are enzootic in areas bordering north-eastern Zambia, and it is amazing that these have not yet spread into this country. Incubation periods average three to six days. An initial high fever is followed by vesicles in the mouth and the interdigital areas and coronary bands of the feet. They may also occur in other thin-skinned areas. They normally burst within twenty-four hours leaving large raw areas which, if uncomplicated by secondary infections, heal within seven to ten days. The acute fever stage is accompanied by anorexia, profuse salivation, acute pain of the feet, almost total drop in milk yield and rapid and marked loss in body condition. The spread of infection to all in-contact animals at this stage is remarkably rapid. Morbidity is 100 per cent in a susceptible cattle population but mortality is low—under 5 per cent except in young calves. However, deterioration of animals in the acute stage causes such serious economic losses that government control is imposed everywhere, and the spread of the diseases is internationally prevented by strict application of the International Zoo-Sanitary Code regulations governing trade in animals and animal products. In most African countries, including Zambia, application of the slaughter policy is deemed impracticable and undesirable, but modern homologous vaccines are applied to all susceptible animals within *cordons-sanitaires* and have proved highly efficient in 'smothering-out' disease outbreaks.

N D McGLASHAN

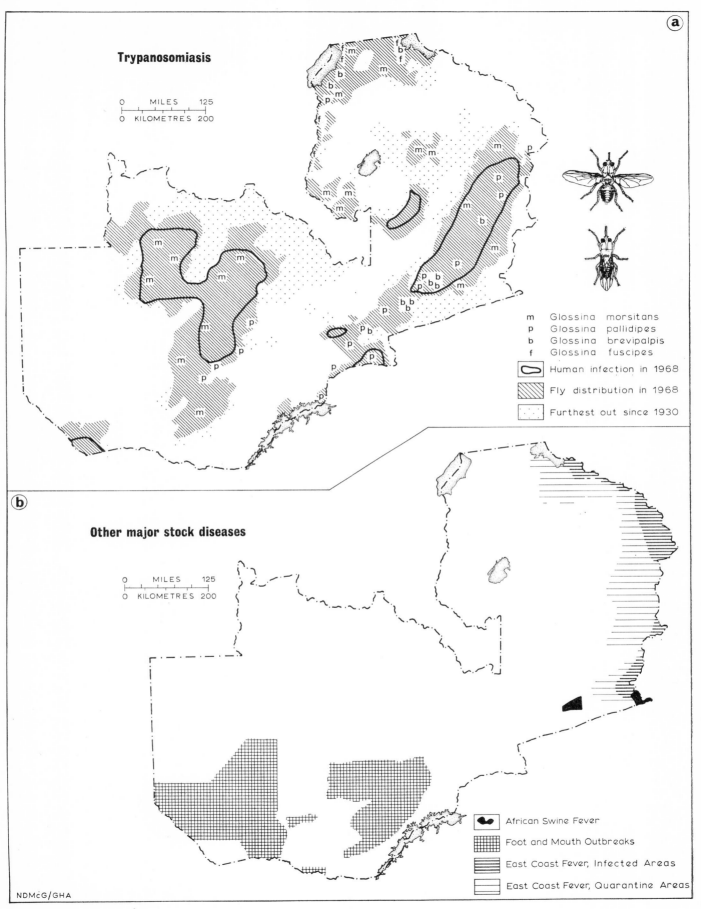

Trypanosomiasis

O— MILES —125
O— KILOMETRES —200

m   Glossina   morsitans
p   Glossina   pallidipes
b   Glossina   brevipalpis
f   Glossina   fuscipes

Human infection in 1968

Fly distribution in 1968

Furthest out since 1930

Other major stock diseases

O— MILES —125
O— KILOMETRES —200

African Swine Fever

Foot and Mouth Outbreaks

East Coast Fever, Infected Areas

East Coast Fever, Quarantine Areas

NDMcG/GHA

25 TRADITIONAL AGRICULTURAL SYSTEMS

Complex interpenetrations of different tribal traditions, a wide range of cultural and physical micro-environments, and the spatially varying impact of economic development combine in differing degrees throughout the country to make for a variety of agricultural systems and sub-systems. In making the considerable simplifications necessary to produce a map at this scale it has been necessary to adopt broad principles rather than to concentrate on more specific areal variations. The poor sandveld and ferrallitic soils and low rural population densities that predominate throughout much of Zambia have given rise to cultures based on pastoralism or on shifting cultivation with long fallow rotations, using various combinations of the country's five main staple cereal crops—maize, finger millet, bulrush millet, sorghum and cassava. Traditional systems have here been defined in relation to two factors; the staple crops, and the degree of sophistication of farming practice. In the interests of simplicity no specific attention has been paid to the local importance of cattle and fishing, and this map must be read in conjunction with others dealing with those aspects (pp. 74 and 78). Three broad categories of agricultural system have been distinguished in this way (i) *Bush-fallow ash-cultures*, which are generally, but not exclusively, associated with the plateaux; (ii) *transitional ash-cultures*; (iii) *hoe-and-plough cultures*, which are generally but not exclusively associated with the valleys and lowlands.

Bush-fallow ash-cultures

These involve 'topping' or felling trees over an area many times greater than that to be cultivated. The branches are usually heaped and burnt and the seeds sown in the ash, either broadcast or by using a planting stick. The simplest form of ash-culture is that practised in the north-eastern parts of the Central Province (1b: small-circle chitemene). Here trees are felled to two feet (60 cm.) above the ground. Numerous small circles of heaped branches, about five to six feet (1·5 to 1·8 m.) in diameter, are then made and burnt, in which, traditionally, a single finger millet crop is sown with a few catch crops. Irregular areas of ten to twenty acres (4·3 to 8·3 ha.) are cleared and these may contain up to 150 small ash circles. 'Catch' crops are planted around the margin of the circle (e.g. pumpkins, Livingstone potatoes, cowpeas) and millet is sown broadcast as soon as these have sprouted. Some circles may be sown for groundnuts and beans in the following season, but most are abandoned for (ideally) up to twenty years of regeneration, though in practice much shorter periods are common. The ash gardens in the Northern Province (1a: large-circle chitemene), in which only top branches of trees are lopped over an area of two or three acres (about 1·5 ha.) and piled into much larger heaps before firing, are less wasteful of land. Other variant forms of chitemene culture are practised throughout the wooded plateaux, e.g. the 'block and strip' system of the northern plateaux in which branches are not heaped so systematically.

Throughout the plateaux the arrangement of village lands depends on the position of the site in relation to the farming resources. Commonly the settlement is close to water, either a permanent stream or a well site, and is surrounded by a few village gardens containing relish crops or cassava. Food staple gardens may be more distant from the settlement, perhaps as far as 8 miles (13 km.) away, though more usually within 3 miles 5 km.). Suitable valley or *dambo* soils are often reserved for relish crops and may be cultivated on a permanent or semi-permanent basis. For all these systems forage resources (berries, fruits, roots, caterpillars, grasshoppers, small mammals) form a valuable protein supplement in economies in which animal husbandry is usually restricted to the keeping of a few chickens or goats.

Transitional ash-cultures

Contact cultures with lowland systems (2 a, b, c, d) are all adaptations to this general upland system of primitive shifting cultivation, in which new crops (like cassava) and improved agricultural techniques are practised. Some of these transitional cultures may soon become 'hoe-and-plough' systems.

Hoe-and-plough systems

Although subsidiary ash plant gardens often play some part in hoe-and-plough economies, these systems are generally characterized by careful soil selection and mounding. Grass-manuring is also practised, rather than the fertilizing of the soil by burning as in the ash-cultures. Rotations are often followed in sequences of five or six years before allowing a similar period of fallowing and a higher proportion of land may be under permanent cultivation. Typical staples are cassava, bulrush millet and maize and there is often a wide range of subsidiary gardens for the cultivation of special crops (vegetables, tubers, rice, tobacco). It is from these systems where animal husbandry plays a more significant role that transitions to ox and tractor ploughing for commercial crops are more easily made.

These more advanced forms of agriculture are practised in alluviums and upper valley soils in the Southern, Central and Eastern Provinces (3h, 3d, 3e), while cash cropping for maize, groundnuts and cotton is also most common in these areas. Land units of 60 to 200 (24 to 81 ha.) acres may be cultivated and there is an increasing trend towards permanent land occupancy, encouraged by government farming schemes and relative proximity (except in Western Province) to marketing facilities. The task of producing the stimuli that lead to improved commercial agriculture and stock rearing is easier in these areas where traditional economies are more varied and sophisticated, and where settlement tends towards permanency. The 'upper-valley' systems of the Eastern and Southern Provinces have already seen considerable improvement through peasant and co-operative farming schemes as well as individual enterprise (pp. 64 and 70) and will no doubt be areas where further developments will take place most rapidly. Other areas of natural improvement may be where more permanent settlements have developed in association with the mixed agriculture and fishing economies of rivers and swamps (p. 78).

Elsewhere, in the predominantly ash-culture regions, the beginnings of permanent occupancy and improved farming may be related to the pervasive spread of the soil-tolerant cassava as a food staple instead of shifting cultivation crops like millets. In many ash-culture areas, however, successful improvement in crop production will be restricted to a few areas of good soil (not always in the most favoured locations). Over large tracts of upland Zambia traditional shifting cultivation should probably give way to extensive ranching and forestry rather than attempt costly and uneconomic transformation to cash agriculture.

D J SIDDLE

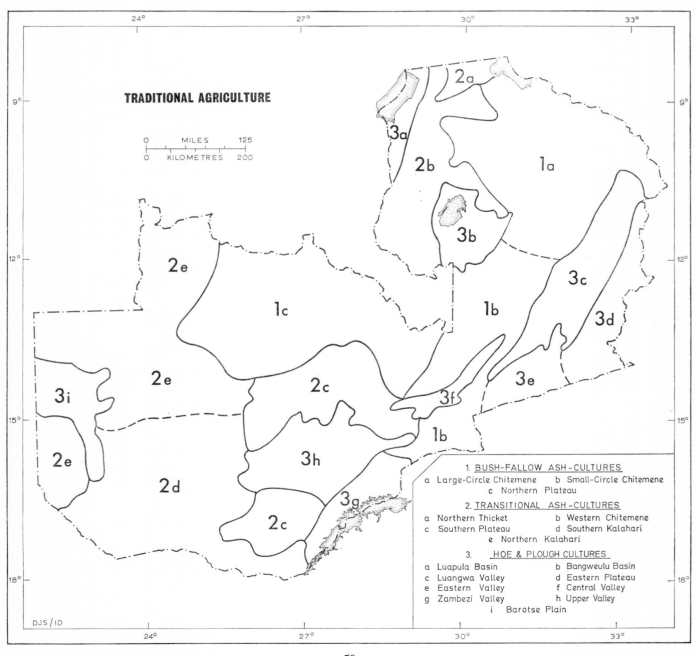

TRADITIONAL AGRICULTURE

MILES 0 — 125
KILOMETRES 0 — 200

1. BUSH-FALLOW ASH-CULTURES
a Large-Circle Chitemene   b Small-Circle Chitemene
c Northern Plateau

2. TRANSITIONAL ASH-CULTURES
a Northern Thicket   b Western Chitemene
c Southern Plateau   d Southern Kalahari
e Northern Kalahari

3. HOE & PLOUGH CULTURES
a Luapula Basin   b Bangweulu Basin
c Luangwa Valley   d Eastern Plateau
e Eastern Valley   f Central Valley
g Zambezi Valley   h Upper Valley
i Barotse Plain

DJS/ID

26 SOME RURAL SETTLEMENT FORMS

Subsistence economies in Zambia are widely based on shifting cultivation and pastoralism (pp. 58 and 75): consequently, many people traditionally tend to live in small kin groups, frequently moving their settlements. In such circumstances most buildings are regarded as temporary rather than permanent homes and little is done to preserve them from the ravages of tropical nature. Settlements sub-divide and change their sites following various disturbances, the most common being diminishing fertility in village gardens, failure of wells, outbreaks of disease and intra-group social conflicts. The characteristic settlement in such circumstances is a small, rather formless group of from five to twenty single room, thatch and wattle ('pole-and-dagga') dwelling huts, around which are a number of food storage bins, pigeon lofts, hen coops and (in the case of cattle keepers) one or two 'kraals' (p. 63 [a]). *Katuwa* (a) typifies this most common settlement form. It has thirty-four inhabitants, has changed site three times in the last thirty years and has a very low investment in material possessions.

Such hamlets (erroneously called villages) are found throughout Zambia, but there is a trend towards larger and more stable rural settlements, resulting from two main causes. Firstly, the tide of cash remission from major urban areas has found expression in increasing numbers of more permanent brick-built dwellings, very often with galvanized iron roofs (p. 63 [f], Map 26). Secondly, increasing population pressures and diminishing soil fertility under traditional practices have locally added weight to government exhortations to change to crop-rotation agriculture, implying more stable settlement forms. Instead of being constantly divided, such settlements being to grow and develop village traits, including some basic social services. *Milambo* (b) represents the first stage in this process. The settlement is still small and has occupied its present site for only eight years, following three moves in the past twenty-five. Buildings and outbuildings are much as in Katuwa, but there are important structural differences. The appearance of brick buildings reflects increasing stability in an area with an emergent cash economy, and hence more capital to invest in building improvements, and more permanent occupation of the land to encourage villagers to do so. The hamlet's economy is based entirely on rotation cropping and plough agriculture, principally for cash crops of maize and groundnuts. Capital wealth in the form of bicycles, radios and farm equipment is increasing, and one building has been established as a small 'village shop'. There seems no reason why Milambo should not now become a viable and permanent village community.

Coalescent settlement forms are already quite well advanced in a few other areas which have long been developing more stable rural economies. Fringing the swamps and lakes of Bangweulu and Mweru, where fishing and rotation agriculture are practised, permanent linear settlements form almost continuous ribbons along motor roads and tracks. Some of these have occu-

pied their present sites for fifty years with little change of character, but the more important are now developing nodal forms. *Chief Bwalya Mponde* (c) is such a settlement. It was established in 1949, only 300 yards (275 m.) from its previous site, following the death of the former chief. The village has a stable oval shape and houses are usually replaced within the established settlement form. However, modern growth structures do not readily fit into such a village form: new buildings, such as a shop, a community hall and a school, are appearing on the periphery away from the traditional focus provided by the chief's compound. Similarly disorganized growth may also be noted in *Kathumba* (d), where services (two community areas, shop, grinding mill, garage) are inconveniently situated on the outskirts of a settlement which is essentially no more than a formless coalescence of smaller family groups.

Natural growth is not always so haphazard. *Chinyanta* (e), a fishing village on Lake Mweru, has developed an almost regular grid-plan, due partly to its roadside alignment and partly to its adoption of square houses, reflecting wealth from fishing.

More regular linear forms can also develop along motor roads in association with government-sponsored improvement schemes. *Chikunga* (f) is a good example of a settlement with a gradually stabilizing linear form. Having moved several times since originally 'hiving-off' from a larger settlement in 1926, the village was finally established at its present site in 1959. Since then it has abandoned shifting cultivation and formed itself into a co-operative, farming 20-acre (8 ha.) blocks for maize, groundnuts and beans. With capital accumulating, Chikunga now supports a shop and many of its houses are brick-built, some with galvanized iron roofs. Future growth will probably take the form of linear infilling, eventually producing the kind of settlement represented by *Chikumbe* (g), a resettlement village co-operative established since 1950, which now has 131 residents and a permanent land tenure system.

Finally, there is the artificial development of planned 'scheme resettlements' on a far larger scale. Some of these are now operating (p. 70) and *Mufubushi* (h) is selected as illustrating two different types of induced growth in one scheme—individual farms and co-operatives. The site was selected in 1966. Forty individual farm blocks of 40 acres (16 ha.) were laid out and 4000 acres (1619 ha.) allocated to four co-operatives. The remaining lands in the scheme were given over to communal grazing, irrigation channels, forestry and access roads. Housing is dispersed in widely separated 'hamlets', while a central area has shops, mechanical services and community halls. Other schemes are similarly laid out: all of them attempt to reconcile traditional social values with economic progress.

Even from this brief survey it emerges that rural settlement forms provide a clear index of increasing rural stability. At present there are considerable opportunities for directing development from central planning units, but this can be effective only if based on a clear understanding of the natural processes of rural change. To this end more research is urgently needed.

D J SIDDLE

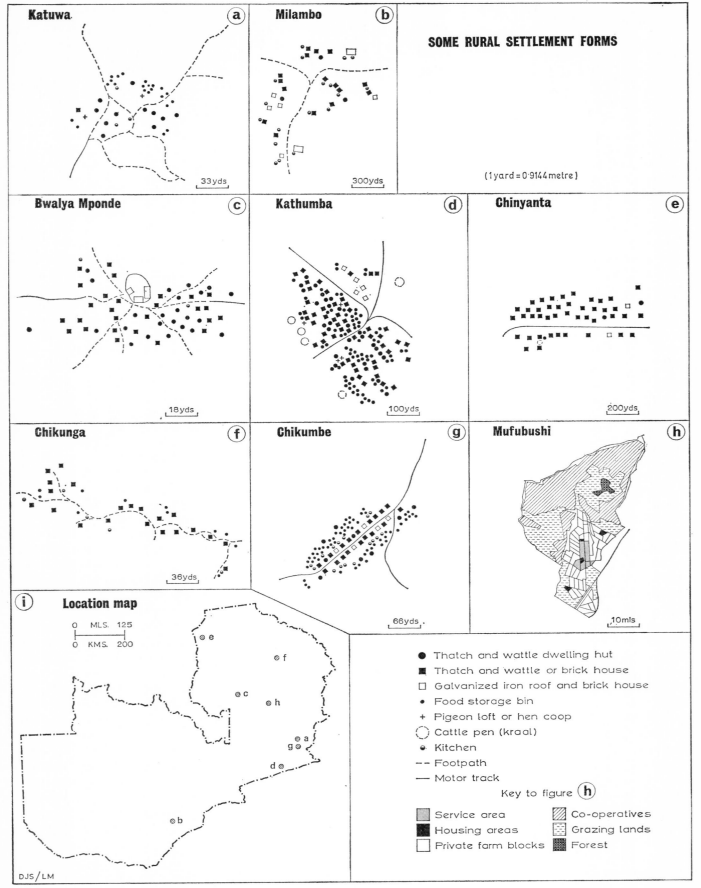

Katuwa (a)

33yds

Milambo (b)

300yds

SOME RURAL SETTLEMENT FORMS

(1 yard = 0·9144 metre)

Bwalya Mponde (c)

18yds

Kathumba (d)

100yds

Chinyanta (e)

200yds

Chikunga (f)

36yds

Chikumbe (g)

66yds

Mufubushi (h)

10mls

(i) **Location map**

0 MLS. 125
0 KMS. 200

⊘e
⊘f
⊘c
⊘h
⊘a
g⊘
d⊘
⊘b

DJS/LM

● Thatch and wattle dwelling hut
■ Thatch and wattle or brick house
□ Galvanized iron roof and brick house
• Food storage bin
+ Pigeon loft or hen coop
◌ Cattle pen (kraal)
◓ Kitchen
-- Footpath
— Motor track

Key to figure (h)

▨ Service area   ▧ Co-operatives
■ Housing areas   ▦ Grazing lands
□ Private farm blocks ▩ Forest

61

27 SOME RURAL HOUSE TYPES

Rural dwellings reflect the availability of particular building materials and the technical abilities, cultural attributes, social and economic circumstances and personal preferences of their builders, who are usually their occupants. These determinants are dynamic and have been changing rapidly during recent decades. Given the variety of peoples, environments and even of rates of change in Zambia, a great variety of house types is inevitable. Within any locality numerous quite distinct styles and sub-styles may be recognized, and it is not possible nowadays to identify a particular type of house with a group of tribes or with a region.

Most recent changes stem from the impact of colonial rule and western technology: however, house types were subject to quite dramatic changes before the colonial era. For example, Sheane (1911), writing of the northern Zambian plateaux, reported that 'square or rectangular houses are found near (mission and government) stations and where East Coast influence has made itself felt'. Cunnison's (1959) description of Lunda housing in the Luapula valley is also illuminating:

'Until about sixty years ago (i.e., c. 1890) there were no mud huts ... Houses were small, high structures built of grass and pliant wood ... It was later immigrants from the plateau who brought with them the knowledge of building mud houses. From that time until after the turn of the century, when missionaries at Mbereshi taught the art of making sun-dried (Kimberley) bricks, mud houses were the rule. Nowadays there is a gradual replacement of mud houses by sun-dried brick houses'.

Turner (1957) reported similarly of the Ndembu of Mwinilunga District. Their 'ancient hut type was the round or square grass hut ... replaced in the present century by the pole and mud hut which was introduced, say informants, from Angola by Lwena immigrants ... (by 1954) the pole-and-mud hut was everywhere giving way before the house of sun-dried Kimberley brick'. As in the lower Luapula valley, the latest development appears to be a product, in the first place, of mission teaching. In both Kawambwa and Mwinilunga Districts there seem to have been two total changes of house type in seventy years or so.

It should be noted at this point that in African rural society the 'house' is often little more than the sleeping quarters and private retreat of a man and wife and their very young children. It is but one of a collection of buildings together comprising the family's living quarters—their homestead. Such a building complex is composed according to dynamic factors such as the constitution of the family group, nature of domestic work (necessarily closely related to the products of their subsistence economy), and the degree of abandonment of traditional items (spirit huts, enclosed verandas, open-air shelters for meetings, etc.) and the adoption of innovations such as detached kitchens, latrines and bathing shelters. Fig. a indicates the possible variety of buildings: it deliberately includes an unusually wide range of traditional and novel features.

Further discussion is limited to recent and current change from pole-and-dagga to 'Kimberley brick' houses. The character and construction of a pole-and-dagga dwelling are shown in figs. b and c. Such buildings are generally characteristic of non-brick dwellings, although temporary settlements for hunters and fishermen, etc.) are often of much flimsier structures (d). Substantial 'modern style' houses can also be built in traditional materials (e). Most buildings not of pole-and-dagga, however, are of Kimberley brick, and the 1963 census recorded the relative use of such materials for dwelling houses.[1] These data are plotted in fig. f. This shows extraordinary spatial variations, from those prevailing in Kawamba District (91·5 per cent of all dwellings of brick) to Kalabo District (1·7 per cent brick). Figs. g and i illustrate different styles of substantial brick-built houses and h shows the transitional phase in which a modest brick house supplants a pole-and-dagga structure, relegating it to a kitchen and supplementary quarters. It also shows traditional food storage huts or bins, which may disappear if pantries within brick houses become popular, and the newly adopted pit-latrine, which is likely to remain separate until water-borne sanitation permits indoor facilities.

Fig. f invites consideration of factors influencing the adoption of brick houses. First and foremost, this change requires a certain technology—the skills to make bricks and build scientifically with them, and the carpenter's ability to make suitable frames for roofs, doors, windows, and so on. Such skills have been taught on mission stations and by government agencies, but clearly in 1963 they were not available everywhere, or were not fully used. Secondly, building in brick demands suitable local clays. In most of Zambia adequate materials can be found, the chief exceptions being the western areas, heavily mantled with Kalahari sand. On the other hand, particularly in densely populated areas, severe shortage of suitable timbers for pole-and-dagga houses may promote the use of Kimberley brick.

Thirdly, some cash is needed to construct even a small brick house. Owners may provide their own labour, but most must pay for the skills of the bricklayer and carpenter and must purchase cement, glass, paint, nails, hinges, etc., which are not freely available in the countryside. The need for cash for building leads to the final group of factors; namely personal inclinations and social (and perhaps administrative) pressures that may or may not persuade rural peoples to spend money on brick houses. Thus in Luapula Province the brick-built house has become the standard; to live in less indicates poverty, sloth, lack of pride, or some similar factor. On the other hand, in Eastern Province in 1964, people seemed satisfied with housing that would have embarrassed Luapula peoples. Eastern Province people saw no reason to spend money on housing and there was need to stimulate changes of attitudes by teaching the real benefits of improved housing.

Since 1963 change has continued apace. Construction of improved housing proceeds under the development plan, while Zambia's National Council for Scientific Research is experimenting with new, inexpensive indigenous building materials.

G KAY

[1] Equivalent data from the 1969 census were not available at the time of writing.

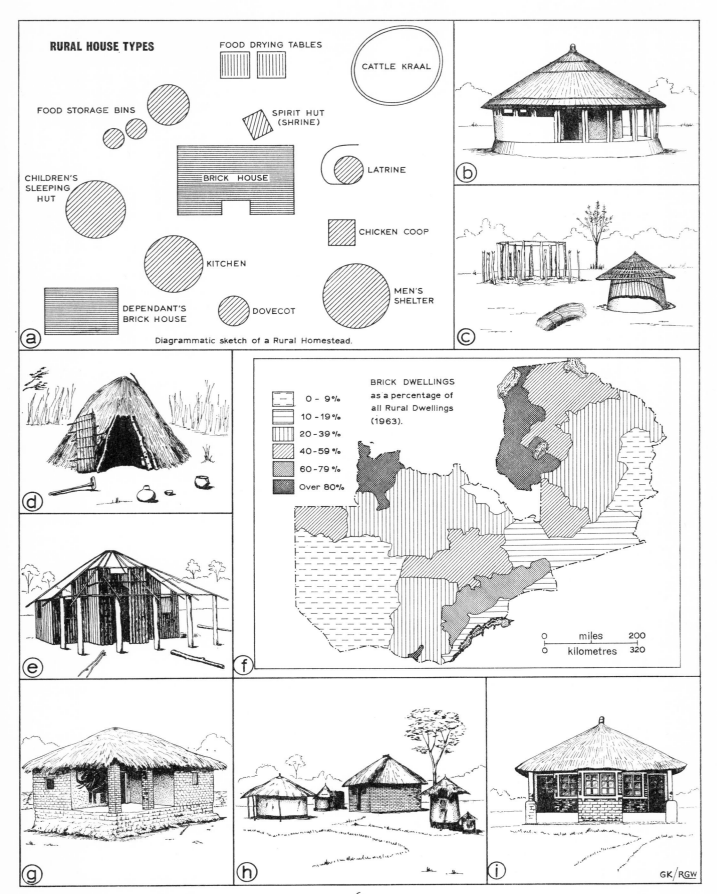

RURAL HOUSE TYPES

FOOD DRYING TABLES

CATTLE KRAAL

FOOD STORAGE BINS

SPIRIT HUT (SHRINE)

BRICK HOUSE

LATRINE

CHILDREN'S SLEEPING HUT

CHICKEN COOP

KITCHEN

MEN'S SHELTER

DEPENDANT'S BRICK HOUSE

DOVECOT

(a) Diagrammatic sketch of a Rural Homestead.

(b)

(c)

(d)

(e)

BRICK DWELLINGS as a percentage of all Rural Dwellings (1963).

0 - 9 %
10 - 19 %
20 - 39 %
40 - 59 %
60 - 79 %
Over 80 %

0   miles   200
0   kilometres   320

(f)

(g)

(h)

(i)

GK/RGW

63

28 CO-OPERATIVES

The co-operative movement in Zambia has passed through several phases of development since the first group was formed in 1914. It is useful to examine the present character and distribution of co-operatives in the light of these changes.

Almost all the early co-operatives were established to allow individual European farmers the advantages of buying and selling in bulk. These 'consumer and marketing unions' were, therefore, chiefly concentrated in the European farming areas along the line of rail and in Eastern Province. Most of the first African societies, which were formed after the Second World War, were similar in character. These too were marketing unions catering for the more advanced 'emergent' farmers who had made progress in areas alongside European farming areas, and who were particularly well developed in Eastern Province. In the same period a number of consumer groups, thrift and loan societies and artisans' co-operatives were also established in most parts of the country. During the six years before independence there was a constant number of about 200 co-operatives of all types, with about 30 000 members. The movement would therefore seem to have reached its limit of expansion under colonial terms of reference by 1958.

The most dramatic changes have taken place since independence and particularly since 1966. In that year the government announced a policy of massive expansion in a new type of association—the 'farming co-operative'. These co-operatives were designed not only to boost agricultural production and build entrepreneurship but also to foster the spirit of communal enterprise, a keynote of the new régime as well as of the co-operative concept. To encourage growth of the new co-operatives the government announced a subsidy of K30 for each acre (0·405 ha.) of land officially certified as completely cleared of woodland (i.e. 'stumped') for cash crops by a registered co-operative with at least ten members, imposing a 10 acre (4·05 ha.) lower limit on the area to be cleared to qualify for the subsidy. It also affirmed that any group which cleared 50 acres (20·25 ha.) would qualify for a grant to purchase a tractor.

The response was immediate. By the end of 1967 there were 466 registered farming co-operatives, who had cleared a total of 45 000 acres (18 225 ha.). This rate of expansion took place among people who had not been encouraged during the colonial era to regard democratic governmental processes as including responsible public participation; who were over-stimulated by frequently extravagant pre-independence promises; who rarely understood fully the meaning of the term 'co-operative' and who were not used to the responsibilities of loan management or the techniques of cash agriculture. The results were almost catastrophic. Family groups in isolated areas registered themselves as co-operatives, crudely cleared considerable acreages of land, some of it unsuitable, and claimed both subsidies and the prestigious tractors. Much of the new land was turned over to maize, a staple crop which most of the members already knew how to grow, a trend further stimulated by the high price of maize in 1967. In that year the Northern Province, for example,

produced 68 609 bags, a 20 000 bag surplus above local requirements. Transport facilities, already strained to breaking point by the commitment to essential services along the north road to Dar es Salaam following the Rhodesian political crisis, could not hope to market this surplus and the crop was left to rot in many small depots established on ill-maintained feeder roads. A total of 177 tractors were distributed to co-operatives in 1967. In many areas some of these now stand idle for want of spare parts or effective servicing and management. In the same year over K3 000 000 was made available by the government in long term loans and K907 000 in seasonal loans for fertilizer and insecticides. Only a small proportion (perhaps 30 per cent) of these loans has been repaid and there is a limited prospect of early improvement in this situation.

In the latter half of 1967 and early 1968 five main measures were introduced which aimed to close this Pandora's box. Small isolated and uneconomic co-operatives were disbanded or persuaded to move to more accessible areas. Most farming co-operatives were induced to group themselves into 35 supply and marketing unions to allow them the facilities of bulk purchase and to supply proper management. The number of new societies permitted to register was severely limited. Acreage requirements for subsidy qualification were reduced to five acres (2·03 ha.). Some additional farm managers and mechanics were employed and foreign voluntary organizations provided technical staff to advise the farmers and to assist local extension staffs already overburdened well beyond rational limits. This period of consolidation continues, although the whole future of the movement, while more promising at present, remains rather in doubt.

Despite the problems generated by over-rapid development there have been some real achievements. Co-operative producers marketed K4 720 302 of agricultural produce in 1967, 90 per cent of which was in maize, tobacco and groundnuts. There has been an encouraging expansion in artisans' co-operatives (building, brickmakers, carpenters and sawyers) of which there are now 140 in the country. There have also been some notable advances in poultry production, especially in Southern Province, largely due to the successful expansion of women's poultry co-operatives.

It is difficult to account for some regional variations in the number of co-operatives shown on this map. The surprisingly large numbers of co-operatives in Luapula Province (156) contrasts rather strangely with the smaller number (71) in the agriculturally more advanced and more populous Southern Province. It would be generous to assume that this is due mainly to the individualism of emergent farmers in the South. The physical isolation of much of Western Province, virtually detached from the rest of the country by the Zambezi floods for half the year, has simulated a seemingly anomolous expansion in artisans' co-operatives, particularly of brickmakers and builders: Western Province being the only one in which this type of co-operative predominates. This is because sands and clays are the only local materials in plentiful supply. The wider variety of societies in the line of rail 'urban' provinces reflects a range of opportunity for expansion. In Eastern Province the long history of co-operative enterprise and the growth of an 'emergent' farmer class since the end of the Second World War has stimulated development of over 100 farming co-operatives.

Ministerial responsibility for co-operative has been a little uncertain and there is urgent need of co-ordination with other rural extension services (agriculture, social services, community development). At the same time government and credit organizations are somewhat reluctant to grant further seasonal loans, without which most farming co-operatives will collapse. Clearly, the future of co-operatives depends upon the emergence of a firm policy for rural development covering all aspects of the social and economic environment. This is the present policy.

D J SIDDLE

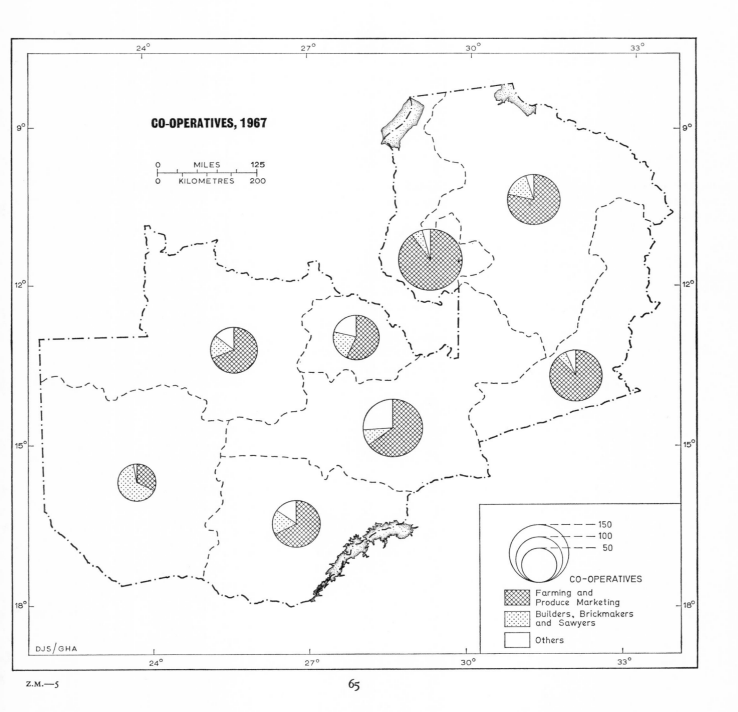

CO-OPERATIVES, 1967

0 MILES 125
0 KILOMETRES 200

150
100
50

CO-OPERATIVES

Farming and Produce Marketing

Builders, Brickmakers and Sawyers

Others

DJS/GHA

29 COMMUNITY DEVELOPMENT

During the colonial period the rural population of Zambia was only marginally involved in the process of government, and naturally came to assume that those who control should also provide. This dependent attitude has carried over into the first years of independence. It has been the task of the Department of Community Development, therefore, to encourage people to take the initiative in improving their circumstances instead of waiting for the government to provide services from central funds.

In the decade before independence, community development was interpreted as 'the encouragement of rural crafts', and the relevant department (of Rural Development), operating with meagre funds, could only establish a few training centres offering courses in homecraft, basketmaking, weaving and improved farming methods. There was little or no extension work in the villages. In 1962 the department was reconstituted as the Department of Community Development and began to encourage the growth of self-help projects and community endeavour. Despite serious staff shortages, limited financial assistance and transport and communication difficulties, the department has pursued a vigorous policy of extension service. By the end of 1965, over 500 self-help groups had been established in the rural areas and 200 ward committees were helping in the organizing of such projects. Three years later there were over 5000 such groups throughout the country covering more than a dozen different types of enterprise. Although the department is concerned with a wide range of educational extension activities (youth clubs, literacy classes, men's and women's groups) the map concentrates attention on 'self-help' projects in the rural areas which have been completed during the first four years of independence.

The distribution of these projects closely reflects four factors: the distribution of population (p. 42), previous contact with development programmes, the varying abilities and enthusiasms of extension officers stationed in each district and ease of communications. Heavy concentrations occur in areas of the Southern Province where peasant farming schemes had produced a development awareness during the colonial period in areas close to the line of rail and in areas near to urban centres. Development in more isolated districts has been restricted by the social difficulties of extension work, further aggravated by poor communications and by petrol restrictions during the three years following Rhodesia's Unilateral Declaration of Independence.

By far the most popular project has been the housing scheme, in which groups of not less than five people have been able to claim a small 'floating grant' of K20 per person for the purchase of essential materials to build a new brick house for each member of the group in turn. At the end of 1968 over 5000 houses had been built in this way throughout Zambia, with particularly heavy concentrations of this activity in the Southern, Northern, Northwestern and Luapula Provinces.

Other projects have been of more local significance. Irrigation projects are most common in regions peripheral to the main commercial farming areas in association with co-operative farming schemes and where the advantages have been tangibly demonstrated by advanced farmers. Road and bridge improvements seem to be more common in the centre and north-west rather than the south and east, though no firm conclusions can be drawn on the evidence of such a scanty distribution.

The question must be asked why self-help projects have been such a conspicuously successful aspect of rural development work while the farming co-operative movement has failed to generate the same enthusiasm and has met many more problems. The difference may partly be attributed to the firm commitment in community development to self-improvement rather than government sponsorship. During the last five years the department has distributed an annual average of only K50 000 in grants. It is worth comparing this record with the enormous sums expended on co-operatives during the same period.

Perhaps a more important reason may be found in the different nature of co-operation expected in the two types of project. Self-help projects demand only limited and temporary co-operation from people who are clearly not going to spend all their time in group activity. The social system of rural Zambia has developed in an economy that generates small, constantly dividing family groups (p. 60). This is very different from the stable village of a crop rotation economy where co-operative activities are already an essential part of the system. Education for total corporate activity in a rural society where there is only limited economic co-operation for specific ends is obviously going to be a much slower process than in a less mobile society. The limited co-operation over a short period of time that is a characteristic of the 'self-help' project does not disturb the social order, and it could be argued that participation of this sort should form a prerequisite training for membership of a farming co-operative.

It would seem, therefore, that the entire rationale of rural development might bear closer examination in the light of experience in community development (see also the chapter on Radio Farm Forum Groups and Young Farmers' Clubs) compared with that with the co-operatives and major resettlement schemes (p. 64 and 70). The main obstacle to co-ordination has been the diffusion of control of various development extension services through different ministries and departments, all operating different policies and even working in the same village or on the same scheme. Re-organization in central administration can usefully bring all these services under the control of one ministry with the prospect of a more carefully considered and integrated approach to these complex problems. Such re-organization was, in fact, achieved recently with the creation of the Ministry of Rural Development, but unfortunately departments of this ministry have since begun to hive off again.

D J SIDDLE

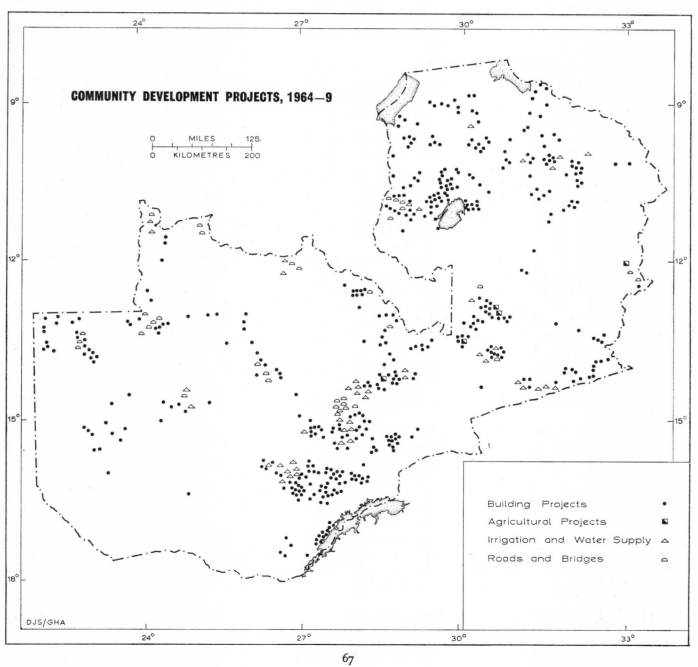

COMMUNITY DEVELOPMENT PROJECTS, 1964—9

O	MILES	125.	
O	KILOMETRES	200	

Building Projects •
Agricultural Projects ◨
Irrigation and Water Supply △
Roads and Bridges ⌂

DJS/GHA

30 YOUNG FARMERS' CLUBS; RADIO FARM FORUM GROUPS

The two distributions represented here draw attention to two of Zambia's more successful agricultural extension services. While it is obviously impossible to measure the impact made by enterprises of this kind in terms of directly improved farming methods and increased yields, there can be little doubt of the long term benefits of these popular services. One might reasonably claim, therefore, that the areas showing the highest densities of participants in these two schemes will be those where marked agricultural progress can be expected over the next two decades.

Young Farmers' Clubs

The Young Farmers' Club movement was initiated in 1958 and in the six years preceding independence approximately 100 clubs were established, largely in the line of rail provinces. Since 1964, however, the expansion has been at the rate of almost 180 new clubs per annum, so that by the end of 1968 there were 910 clubs with 26 000 members, forty per cent of whom were women and girls.

There are two types of young farmers' association: the *school club* and the *open club*. School clubs embrace almost the entire range of educational institutions in the country from the primary school to the teachers' training college, covering an age range of approximately ten to thirty years. Open clubs are usually established at village level, although some have been started by youth clubs and community centres in the towns. Most of the members, whose ages vary from about sixteeen to thirty years, are actively engaged in farming. Both types of association function fairly informally and concentrate on small scale intensive agricultural projects (fruit, vegetables and small livestock). Those with female members also seek to promote skills in home economics and rural crafts. Technical, and some financial, assistance is provided by the Department of Agriculture, and the efforts of each club are guided by an adult leader. Participation is entirely voluntary, and the essence of the success of the movement has been the involvement of individual club members in the planning and implementation of suitable and profitable enterprises.

The distribution of Young Farmers' Clubs is not entirely a reflection of farming enterprise in a particular area. Some high densities may be partly attributed to the proselytizing skill and enthusiasm of local extension officers. The school clubs in particular may be largely indicative of the distribution of educational facilities (p. 104) and the enthusiasm of individual teachers. Nonetheless it is probably significant that a high density of both open and school clubs are to be found in those areas where some progress towards commercial farming has already been made, as in Southern and Eastern Provinces. The distribution also emphasizes the importance of main roads, especially in the north and east (p. 111 [b]).

There are clearly opportunities for using the Young Farmers'

Clubs as a vehicle for introducing an even wider range of rural improvement and community development, and the government will certainly try to capitalize on the success of the movement and on the enthusiasm which it has generated among young people.

Radio Farm Forum groups

While the Young Farmers' Club movement had already begun to gain momentum at independence, the development of the Radio Farm Forum scheme was a specific project under Zambia's First National Development Plan (1966–70). This UNESCO-sponsored scheme was initiated in June 1966, and the pilot project began in May 1967. In this first stage, radio programmes were designed to serve the needs of farmers in the Bemba-speaking areas of Northern, Luapula, Copperbelt and Central Provinces, but the initial success of this development encouraged the organizers to offer the service to the seven other main language areas in the country. This was carried out in three stages in May 1967, and January and July of 1968. In 1967 there were 65 Farm Forum groups with roughly equal numbers in Copperbelt, Northern, Central and Luapula Provinces. At the end of 1968 this number had increased to 407 groups, with over 70 groups established in one year in both Eastern and Southern Provinces, and 40 in both Western and Northwestern Provinces. By mid-1969, due to consolidation of the programme, the expansion had slowed slightly and only 53 new clubs had been established.

As with the 'Flying Doctor' service, agricultural extension work by radio is particularly suited to the needs of a country where distances between limited and necessarily centralized technical expertise and a sparse, scattered and shifting rural population pose special problems. Radio programmes are especially designed to serve the needs of farmers in each of the language areas. Forum centres are usually established at the homes of local extension officers of the Department of Agriculture, who are issued with batteries and receivers. These officers then invite progressive farmers in their areas to participate in the series; to attend the broadcasts, to hold discussions on the topics afterwards, to send in their queries to the Department in Lusaka and to spread new ideas in the areas from which they come. Groups of some ten to fifteen farmers assemble in this way for the weekly sessions, usually from a radius of up to 30 miles (48 km.).

To date, the service has been mainly directed towards those engaged in crop production, but the increasing importance of pig and poultry rearing, as well as the need to encourage increases in beef production, mean that it may soon be extended.

The distribution of forum groups now begins to provide a clear index of differential rates of agricultural progress. One expects to find higher densities in developing farming areas of the Central, Southern and Eastern Provinces where interest in improvement is well established, but interesting concentrations also occur in Western and Luapula Provinces, the reasons for which must remain a matter for speculation pending further investigation.

D J SIDDLE

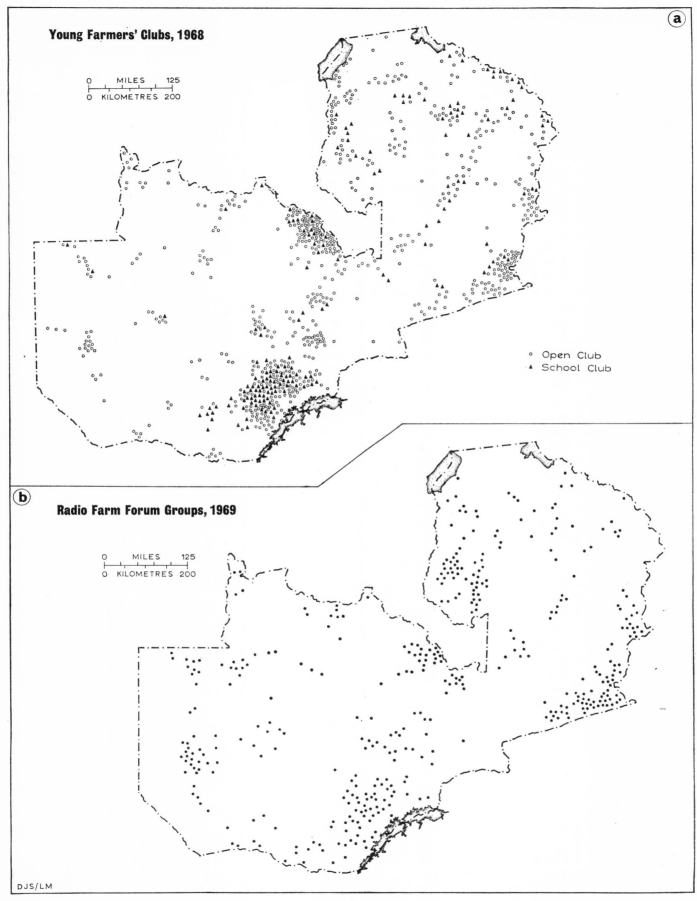

Young Farmers' Clubs, 1968

0 MILES 125
0 KILOMETRES 200

○ Open Club
▲ School Club

Radio Farm Forum Groups, 1969

0 MILES 125
0 KILOMETRES 200

DJS/LM

31 RURAL DEVELOPMENT SCHEMES

There are two basic approaches to rural development in Zambia. The first involves the extension of services (shops, clinics, schools, roads, agricultural advisory services, co-operatives and community projects) throughout the country according to the policies of various government departments and individual entrepreneurs. Such developments may obey socio-economic laws or may serve political ends, but inevitably they take place in a rather piecemeal fashion. The second type of growth aims to concentrate funds and the energies of limited staff in specific 'nodal' development schemes for which sites are chosen in relation to broader national aims. The accompanying maps are concerned with this second type of development.

During the last few years Zambia has been faced with the problem of increasing her food supplies to meet a rapidly expanding market. At the same time, more than 50 per cent of her European producers along the line of rail have left Zambia and the country has been forced to rely increasingly on imports of basic foodstuffs (dairy produce, meat, and, at times, maize) which pass mainly through politically alien countries to the south. Most of the schemes depicted here are principally designed to meet the shortfall in these commodities and to reduce this tide of imports as quickly as possible.

Broadly speaking, three types of nodal scheme operate in Zambia: state farms and ranches; settlement and production units; and a centrally controlled tractor mechanization scheme. *State farms and ranches* aim at a rapid increase of national herds of beef and dairy cattle. Between 1964 and 1968 imports of meat rose from 5·3 million to 19·0 million pounds weight (2·4 to 8.64 million kg.). Consumption of milk products in the same period also increased from 2 400 000 to 4 400 000 gallons (10·9 to 20·0 million litres). During this time, Zambian production of both commodities fell substantially. To close this last gap, the government has taken over an area of more than 300 000 acres (125,000 ha.) for eleven state ranches and six dairy farms. The aim is to stock the ranches with 50 000 head of breeding stock over ten years. The state dairy farms hope to build up a herd of approximately 3000 milk cows by the early nineteen-seventies. These will provide not only milk but also breeding stock for distribution to farmers under supervised schemes.

The aims of the *settlement schemes* are more complex. While a major objective is to increase production, others are to re-settle people from overcrowded reserves, to encourage emergent farmers under expert guidance, and to develop a spirit of communal enterprise. Over twenty settlement schemes now operate throughout the country and several more are planned. Some concentrate on the production of one main cash crop, e.g. Chombwa, cotton; Serenje, tobacco; Ngoli, coffee. Others, like Mufubushi (p. 60), Mungwi and Ngwesi, are mixed farming projects. On most schemes designed to encourage individual farmers, blocks of land in 10 to 40 acre (4·1 to 16·5 ha.) units are laid out and on some schemes crop management is practised under a farm manager. Technical services are provided and costs deducted from the return on each unit. Other variants of this approach use wage labour or co-operative sharing.

The *tractor mechanization project* has developed out of an FAO recommendation for rapid mechanization of agriculture. Under this scheme 200 tractors with hastily trained drivers were established (in 1966) in 40 chosen locations throughout the country. Each unit was provided with mechanical services and supervision. It was quickly recognized that this over-diffusion had increased the already considerable problems of staffing and servicing these units and they were reorganized in twenty-four locations. The tractor units arrange to plough lands on a contract basis for individual farmers and co-operatives, usually within a 30 mile (about 50 km.) range of the unit headquarters. The problems of finding enough work and of maintaining the scheme have not so far been solved. In the first years of operation only two of the units have proved economically viable.

Fig. *b* aims to demonstrate that scheme development of this sort does not provide the permanent answer to rural development problems. Assuming that the aim of rural development is to bring the greatest good to the greatest number of people in the rural population, it will be readily appreciated that the limited service provided by this approach goes only a short way towards achieving this aim. The map was devised in the following way. Around each scheme site (shown on fig. *a*) a circle of 35 miles (56 km.) radius was drawn. This represents, admittedly rather crudely, the typical area of influence of a scheme measured in terms of three complementary distance indices: a normal day's bicycle journey, the area of operation of the tractor units, and the usual catchment area for a settlement scheme that draws on a local population. A 'set' valuation of these overlapping circles allowed demarcation of zones served by from one to (the maximum) of five schemes. The concentration of scheme developments in the line of rail provinces is immediately apparent, but there are more invidious spatial disparities. Interpolation of these circles against dot distribution maps of rural population revealed that of 3.5 million rural inhabitants in Zambia only approximately 52 500 live within 35 miles (56 km.) of five major scheme developments. A further 250 000 live within the range of three or four schemes. Of the remaining 3.25 million only about 800 000 are within range of any scheme at all. This leaves over two million rural dwellers outside the range of any major rural development project. These chances of direct participation are further reduced since there can only be, on the most generous assumption, 1000 beneficiaries of any scheme. It will therefore be readily appreciated that only through a massive input of effort (well beyond the means of a developing country) could these spatial disparities in opportunity be altered through further investment in a policy of expensive uni-nodal development schemes. Such investment would eventually be to the detriment of other more localized forms of 'growth-encouragement' such as the provision of more adequate advisory services and improvements in the rural economic infrastructure. Despite the superficial and partly political appeal of 'major scheme' developments, therefore, their main function is to improve production in certain basic commodities: they do not, in themselves, constitute rural development.

D J SIDDLE

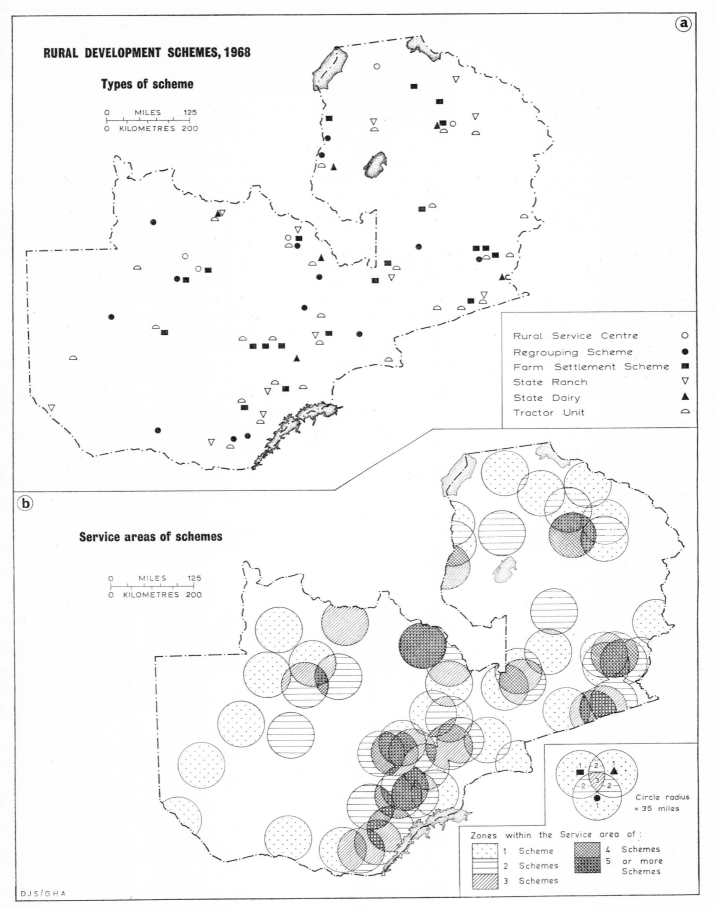

RURAL DEVELOPMENT SCHEMES, 1968

Types of scheme

0 MILES 125
0 KILOMETRES 200

Rural Service Centre	O
Regrouping Scheme	●
Farm Settlement Scheme	▣
State Ranch	▽
State Dairy	▲
Tractor Unit	⌂

ⓐ

ⓑ

Service areas of schemes

0 MILES 125
0 KILOMETRES 200

Circle radius
= 35 miles

Zones within the Service area of:

	1 Scheme		4 Schemes
	2 Schemes		5 or more Schemes
	3 Schemes		

DJS/GHA

71

32 COMMERCIAL CROP PRODUCTION

Until shortly before independence in 1964, commercial farming in Zambia, geographically restricted to a few areas and almost entirely in European hands, was comparatively simple to describe. It is now increasingly difficult to define and locate with precision, due to dualism regarding sources of production. There remain perhaps 450 large-scale, predominantly European commercial farmers (cf. about 1000 in 1962), who still produce most marketed crops. There are also the developing African farmers who, especially in Southern, Central and Eastern Provinces, are in the process of evolving from a near-subsistence economy, via cash sales of surpluses, into outright commercial farming.

It is particularly difficult to distinguish between marketed subsistence crop surpluses and small-scale truly commercial production, because records are inadequate. Official production figures refer only to amounts sold to marketing organizations at their collecting points, while census figures are based on incomplete returns from small operators and co-operatives. The maps are mostly based on 1967 figures—in some respects a more typical year than 1968—but variability in annual production under tropical conditions is emphasized.

Despite data limitations, a broad geographical pattern of present commercial crop production is apparent in Zambia (although the future pattern is a matter for speculation). The railway zone southward from Kabwe, with the Mkushi block forming an outlier, is the main commercial farming area. Offering comparatively developed infrastructure and markets, it also occupies high, healthy ground with moderate rainfall (p. 20) and areas of fertile red clays, red brown loams and sandveld tobacco soils. Here are found virtually all the remaining large-scale producers. Here, too, African farmers, especially in Southern and Central Provinces, soon followed their European neighbours' example in adopting a cash economy. Vacated European farms are now used for expanding African co-operative farms, state ranches and peasant farming settlements. This replacement process will intensify following the 1969 Referendum empowering government, through the National Assembly, to expropriate the land of absentee landowners.

Despite large Copperbelt urban markets, there are fewer farmers north of Kabwe, due to poor soils and the past lack of official encouragement of local farming (p. 84). Away from the railway only the Mkushi block along the Great North Road remains significant in large-scale crop production.

Long-established European commercial farms around Mbala (formerly Abercorn) and Chipata (Fort Jameson) have dwindled to extinction, largely through isolation. The area between Chipata and Petauke in Eastern Province has climate and soil conditions similar to those favouring commercial farming in Southern Province, but is far from markets. However, fertile soils and particularly effective extension work since the nineteen-forties have resulted in thriving peasant farming schemes, which recent tarring of the Great East Road from Lusaka should benefit. Elsewhere commercial crops are produced in scattered localities near main roads and provincial centres, where transport and small markets are available, especially on better soil.

Figs. *a* to *f* refer to selected major commercial crops. Lesser crops include sugar-cane at Nakambala, pineapples at Mwinilunga, coffee in Northern Province, bananas and tea in Luapula Province and a little rice on wetter soils in the north and west.

Maize (fig. *a*) is widely grown for subsistence, but most commercial production comes from the line of rail, where transport and markets are backed by 28 to 36 inches (71·1 to 91·4 cm.) of rainfall annually and summer monthly mean temperatures exceeding 72°F. (22·5°C.). While grown widely on sandy soils, maize does best on heavier red brown loams and red clays. In 1967–68 some 4 132 000 bags were sold to the Grain Marketing Board (GMB), the majority being hybrid maize. Maize is usually grown in rotation with green manures and leguminous crops such as sunhemp, velvet beans and cowpeas. Guaranteed prices have caused overproduction in the past and farmers have been encouraged to diversify because of current low world prices. In 1968–69, however, there was a shortfall in production, the GMB purchasing only 2 700 000 bags.

Tobacco (fig. *d*). Virginia flue-cured tobacco, for long Zambia's principal agricultural export, prefers sandy soils with up to 36 inches (91 cm.) annual rainfall. Demanding both capital and skill, it is confined to larger farms, mostly in the main commercial farming belt. Previously, growers sold on the Salisbury (Rhodesia) auction floors, but today the entire crop is auctioned in Lusaka. Production fell over 50 per cent from 1964 to 1967, but the remaining growers received higher prices.

Burley tobacco, better suited to small-scale farming, is mostly grown in Eastern Province. Production has been declining, but improvement may follow rising prices since 1966. Oriental (Turkish) tobacco is widely grown in small quantities in northern areas. This is a useful cash crop in areas emerging from the subsistence stage, but prices and acreages are declining.

Traditionally, tobacco was exported from Beira, but since the Rhodesian impasse some has been air-freighted to Britain.

Groundnuts (fig. *c*) are widely grown for subsistence, but commercial production, especially of the exported confectionery nut, occurs mainly between Lundazi and Petauke in Eastern Province. Groundnuts are sold for human consumption, or for their oil, and groundnut cake is sold as concentrated protein stockfeed. Some 200,000 bags were marketed in 1967.

Cotton (fig. *f*) grows well in medium to heavy soils below 4000 feet (1219 m.) altitude in areas with 24 to 36 inches (61 to 91 cm.) annual rainfall, and also in the hot, dry Gwembe and Luangwa valleys, where irrigation may be needed. It is produced by a few large-scale farmers who are experimenting with machinery, by co-operatives, and by peasant farmers on customary land. Labour for hand-picking presents a problem. The Lusaka ginnery and the new Kafue textile mill can handle all local production. Production increased from 9 374 400 lb. in 1967–68 to 15 225 000 lb. (3 383 000 kg.) in 1968–69.

The concentration of production of *Vegetables* and *Fruits* (figs. *e*, *f*) along the railway line shows clear response to urban markets and availability of rapid transportation; but there is a serious shortfall in domestic production. Commercial *sorghums* (fig. *b*) are for brewing.

E WILSON

72

COMMERCIAL CROP PRODUCTION

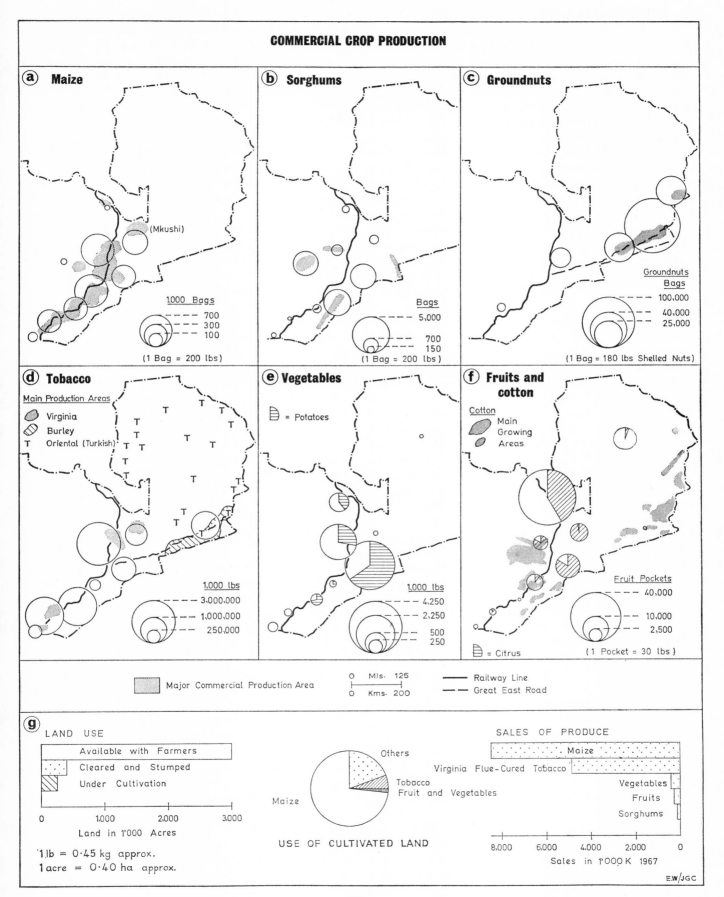

ⓐ Maize

(Mkushi)

1,000 Bags
—— 700
—— 300
—— 100

(1 Bag = 200 lbs)

ⓑ Sorghums

Bags
—— 5,000

—— 700
—— 150

(1 Bag = 200 lbs)

ⓒ Groundnuts

Groundnuts
Bags
—— 100,000

—— 40,000
—— 25,000

(1 Bag = 180 lbs Shelled Nuts)

ⓓ Tobacco

Main Production Areas
◆ Virginia
◇ Burley
T Oriental (Turkish)

1,000 lbs
—— 3,000,000

—— 1,000,000

—— 250,000

ⓔ Vegetables

▤ = Potatoes

1,000 lbs
—— 4,250

—— 2,250

—— 500
—— 250

ⓕ Fruits and cotton

Cotton
◆ Main
◆ Growing
◆ Areas

Fruit Pockets
—— 40,000

—— 10,000

—— 2,500

▤ = Citrus

(1 Pocket = 30 lbs)

Major Commercial Production Area

O Mls. 125
O Kms. 200

—— Railway Line
—·— Great East Road

ⓖ LAND USE

Available with Farmers
Cleared and Stumped
Under Cultivation

0   1,000   2,000   3,000
Land in 1'000 Acres

1 lb = 0·45 kg approx.
1 acre = 0·40 ha approx.

Others
Tobacco
Fruit and Vegetables
Maize

USE OF CULTIVATED LAND

SALES OF PRODUCE

Maize
Virginia Flue-Cured Tobacco
Vegetables
Fruits
Sorghums

8,000   6,000   4,000   2,000   0
Sales in 1'000 K 1967

E.W/JGC

73

33 COMMERCIAL LIVESTOCK PRODUCTION

Because many Zambians have a protein-short diet, livestock farming (with fisheries) is a vital area for development. Beef and dairy cattle, pigs, sheep, goats and poultry are all kept in substantial but still inadequate numbers.

Beef cattle. Where *cattle* are kept in the traditional economy, it had been customary for Africans to measure wealth by numbers of animals, regardless of age, condition or slaughter value: traditionally, few such cattle have been marketed. By December 1966, of 1 359 043 head of cattle in Zambia, only 156 000 were on commercial farms, nearly all owned by Europeans. Nevertheless, surplus cattle were beginning to enter the market from traditional herds, while some 20 000 head were owned by emergent African commercial farmers on customary land. By 1969 there were also 29 166 head on state ranches around the country: some ranches will produce beef, although their main purpose is to supply commercial farmers with good quality weaners.

With present rapid change it is difficult to distinguish clearly between these sources of marketed beef cattle. Fig. *c* therefore merely shows the total numbers of beef cattle by districts, with the three potential sources indicated. Beef supply still comes mostly from commercial farms, with increasing contributions from traditional herds.

Nearly all commercial cattle ranches are in Central and Southern Provinces, near the railway and close enough to markets for beasts to arrive for slaughter in good condition. The main environmental factor limiting cattle rearing is the distribution of tsetse-fly. The line of rail is a tsetse-free belt: other such areas are between Chipata and Petauke, a belt running west and south-west from the Tanzanian border, and the upper Zambezi valley (p. 57 [a]). However, these outlying areas are far from the railway and only in the first has there been appreciable European settlement, with commercial beef production.

Grazing varies seasonally. Lush new grass during early rains grows tall and coarse by March; as the rains retreat the grass dries out and becomes tough and short of protein. Smaller or later rains may force farmers to supplement natural grazing to keep beasts in condition. Frost, fortunately rare, desiccates the grass, which becomes not only poor eating but dangerously inflammable and easily destroyed by bush fires. Where possible, farmers use grazing on dambos and on flood plains such as the Kafue Flats: these areas are flooded in the late rains and early winter, but as the floods recede they provide succulent pasture when plateau grassland is at its driest. A fortunate farmer has perhaps 75 per cent dry land and 25 per cent dambo on his farm. Others may move stock temporarily to nearby floodplains. Plain edges can become overstocked when floods are especially high.

Without planted legume-rich pastures or supplementary feeding a beast may lose 100 lb. (about 45 kg.) in weight during winter and may never grow to full size and quality. Even more extra rations are needed for fattening. Legumes (cowpeas, velvet beans, sunhemp), grains (maize, sorghum, rapoko) and vegetables are grown or bought for direct consumption and for making hay and silage (protein feeds may be needed for milk production). Rotational grazing or the sowing of legume-rich pastures are a means of saving on purchased concentrates.

In 1966–67, over 52 000 officially graded cattle were sold to the Cold Storage Board and to private butchers. About 18 000 ungraded beasts were slaughtered in the rural areas, including some from subsistence farms. With rising living standards, Zambia's beef production falls far below present needs by at least 40 000 carcasses annually.

To increase local supply, the National Beef Scheme encourages subsistence farmers to sell more cattle and to decrease calf mortality by improved management. Subsidies are recommended for building night kraals, calf pens and cattle crushes, for spray pumps and for internal parasite control, and local training centres with demonstration herds are planned. However, on customary land (with its complete absence of secure land-tenure laws) enclosure, fencing and, consequently, commercially viable ranching are minimal.

Dairy Cattle. Despite exhortations from the Dairy Produce Board to drink more milk, by mid-1969 entirely fresh milk was no longer commercially available anywhere in Zambia, varying proportions of reconstituted milk being included across the country. Entirely fresh milk reappeared, however, in some centres late in 1969. In June 1968, ninety-eight registered producers sold to the Board. Most of them farmed in the Mazabuka, Lusaka and Chisamba areas, less than twenty on the Copperbelt (to serve about 750 000 people) and the remainder in Livingstone and Choma. There were two state dairy farms.

Milk production varies seasonally with the condition of grazing, being highest early in the year. Supplementary feeding is required nearly all the year round. Milk and butterfat usually travel to creameries by road and fresh milk travels by road tanker from the Mazabuka area to the Copperbelt. Almost four million gallons are produced annually, mostly sold as liquid milk, although a little butter and cheese are made. Friesland and Channel Island breeds are the principal milk producers.

Pigs. Of 87 000 pigs recorded in 1966–67, only a tenth were on commercial farms. Some 16 000 were slaughtered, half for bacon and over a quarter for pork. Great efforts are made to increase production and improve quality through co-operatives and pig-farming courses.

Sheep. Woolled sheep are ill-suited to Zambian conditions, partly because they have difficulty grazing the long, coarse grass, even more because of the sharp seeds of *Hyparrenia* grass that penetrate their thin skins, matting fleeces into useless tangles. Nevertheless, it should be possible to keep wool sheep successfully where *Hyparrenia* does not grow, and on planted pastures. Black-headed Persian sheep with short, curly coats do better and are kept in small numbers for mutton, although farmers have problems controlling intestinal parasites. Only 651 sheep slaughterings were recorded in 1966–67 and nearly all mutton sold is imported. Sheep on commercial farms totalled 13 000.

Poultry farming is expanding vigorously. Eggs and table birds come mostly from the Copperbelt and Lusaka, but egg production by peasant farmers and co-operatives is increasing rapidly throughout Zambia.

E WILSON

74

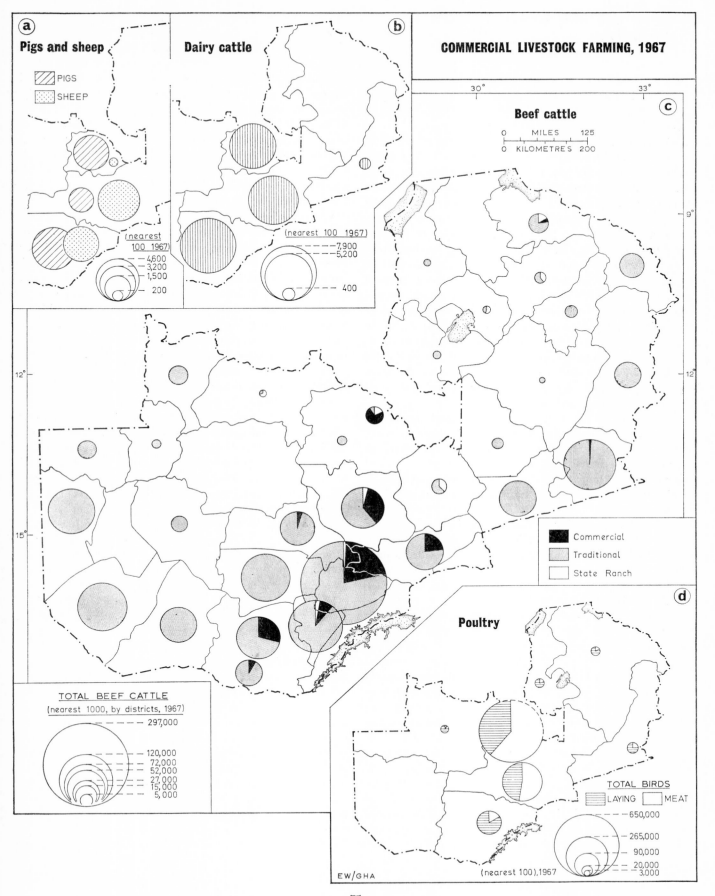

COMMERCIAL LIVESTOCK FARMING, 1967

(a) **Pigs and sheep**

PIGS
SHEEP

(nearest 100 1967)
—— 4,600
—— 3,200
—— 1,500
—— 200

(b) **Dairy cattle**

(nearest 100 1967)
—— 7,900
—— 5,200

—— 400

(c) **Beef cattle**

30°   33°

0   MILES   125
0   KILOMETRES   200

9°
12°

Commercial
Traditional
State Ranch

TOTAL BEEF CATTLE
(nearest 1000, by districts, 1967)
—— 297,000

—— 120,000
—— 72,000
—— 52,000
—— 27,000
—— 15,000
—— 5,000

(d) **Poultry**

TOTAL BIRDS
LAYING   MEAT

—— 650,000

—— 265,000

—— 90,000

—— 20,000
—— 3,000

(nearest 100), 1967

EW/GHA

75

34 LAND USE AND AGRICULTURAL POTENTIAL

Use of land in Zambia (depicted in generalized fashion in fig. *a*) has so far tended to be lavishly extensive. Of the country's 4 057 000 inhabitants (1969 census) some 70 per cent live in 'rural' areas (i.e. outside towns of 4000 people or more) where most rely on subsistence agriculture using systems of long fallow shifting cultivation (p. 58). Generously assuming that under such systems the average cultivated land requirement is about one acre per head per annum, there are only about 5000 sq. miles (12 950 sq. km. or 1 295 000 ha.) under subsistence crops in any one year. This represents about one sixtieth part of the total area of the country. Official statistics concerning the commercial farming sector are no more than estimates, but they do indicate the similarly tiny proportion of the land surface under improved cultivation. In 1967 only 570 square miles (1476 sq. km.), representing about 0·2 per cent of the national area, had been cleared of woodlands for plough cultivation: of this meagre fraction only some 320 sq. miles (615 sq. km.) were actually cultivated.

Thus at present some 98 per cent of the total area of Zambia is occupied by fallow land, unimproved pasture, and by woodland, swamps, marshes, mining land and other non-agricultural uses. Forest reserves and protected forests (p. 24) occupy 13 000 000 acres (5 200 000 ha.), over sixty times the annual arable acreage under the plough and over four times the maximum extent of subsistence cropping in any one year. Nevertheless, only just over one million cubic feet (35 335 cu. m.) of timber are used commercially per annum. Zambia's commercial fisheries, too, are still at an early stage of development, contributing only 30 000 tons (30 m. kilos) of fish in 1968 (p. 78). It is therefore hardly surprising to find that agriculture's share of Zambia's national fixed capital investment in 1967 was only two per cent (K4 000 000) and that this sector provided a mere 8·7 per cent of the gross domestic product. Even allowing for considerable error in official estimates, the severely limited nature of positive land use is amply demonstrated.

It has been suggested that the low level of utilization is in response to two main factors: the very low average population density of 14 per sq. mile (roughly 5 per sq. km.), and adverse physical conditions (see early chapters). The first factor is incontestable. Except in most unusual economic circumstances intensive land use, with its high labour inputs, is scarcely possible where there are few people. Only in limited local areas where agricultural economies are linked with fishing (especially around Lakes Bangweulu and Mweru and along the Luapula River or where 'reserves' alongside commercial farming areas have become overcrowded), do rural densities greatly exceed 10 per sq. mile (2·59 per sq. km.). Long fallow shifting cultivation and extensive pastoralism in the non-commercial sector, and fairly extensive mechanized agriculture and extensive livestock production in the commercial farming areas are natural responses to sparse populations (and vice versa).

The second factor is less easily justified. Undoubtedly much of Zambia has poor, leached sandveld and lateritic soils and the rainfall régime is unfavourable (pp. 20 and 26), yet there remains much scope for increased agricultural production by concentrating activities in physically favoured localities. Even in the comparatively developed and productive areas along the line of rail, the country's agricultural resources are grossly underutilized. At the same time, urban migration and widely increased buying power since independence have created an excess of market demand for local agricultural products over supply, so that Zambia is forced to rely increasingly upon expensively imported foodstuffs, in which there has been a 33 per cent increase in volume since 1964.

This situation where there is inadequate production from under-utilized resources can only be improved by a vigorous long-term programme of rural development. Successful planning to this end in any country depends, however, on the gathering of a sufficient amount of data relating to all aspects of the rural society including the purely physical conditions of the country. Sufficient data is not yet available in Zambia (although much is being collected), and it must be emphasized that the agricultural potential map (fig. *b*), drawn from information kindly supplied by the Department of Agriculture, is intended as a very tentative and highly generalized attempt to indicate wider areas of possibility; it should be regarded as a provisional sketchmap. Areas shaded as potentially productive are merely those within which productive activities might be extended, given favourable socio-economic conditions; they do not imply a uniform degree of suitability throughout a given area. Zones of special production, for example, are those within which market gardening or plantation production of special crops might profitably be introduced. The weakness of the map lies not only in its grossly generalized character but also in the limited number of factors (largely physical) taken into account. Indeed, it serves primarily to emphasize the need for more accurate information analysis. A dearth of such information in most developing states accounts for the rather conjectural character of much rural development planning.

Fortunately, Zambian planners need not build on such insecure foundations: wealth from the country's copper resources has provided capital to invest in obtaining information. Indeed, much material has already been assembled by the various planning branches of government and by teams of consultants who have completed (1967–69) a detailed socio-economic survey of each province in the country, which should be analysed during 1970. Some reconnaissance land use and land potential mapping is also being undertaken during 1970–71 by a team of university geographers working with the Department of Agriculture. A full-scale assessment of land potential must await the results of these exercises. Because the work will take some time, the postponement of the Second National Development Plan until 1972 (which is expected strongly to emphasize rural development in general), is likely to prove beneficial in this respect.

D J SIDDLE

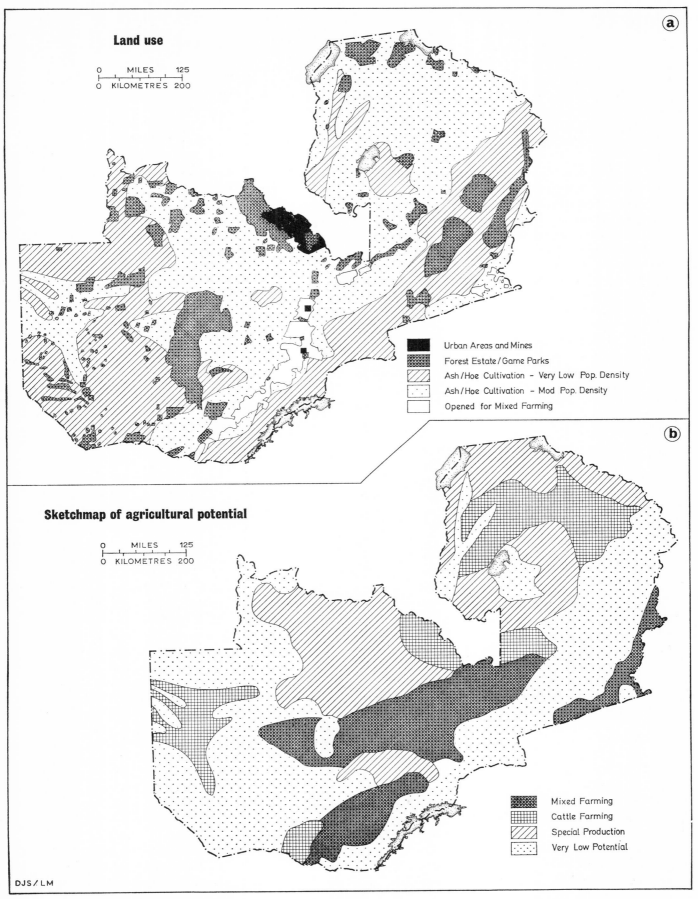

Land use

0 MILES 125
0 KILOMETRES 200

- ■ Urban Areas and Mines
- Forest Estate / Game Parks
- Ash / Hoe Cultivation – Very Low Pop. Density
- Ash / Hoe Cultivation – Mod Pop. Density
- Opened for Mixed Farming

(a)

Sketchmap of agricultural potential

0 MILES 125
0 KILOMETRES 200

- Mixed Farming
- Cattle Farming
- Special Production
- Very Low Potential

(b)

DJS / LM

77

35 FISHERIES

Zambia is a land-locked country, but it is generously endowed with large lakes, swamps and rivers. These provide a wide variety of fish environments and over 300 different species of fish have been identified. Zambians as a people eat considerable quantities of fish; indeed, it is thought that more fish is eaten than meat.

Some 15 000 people are concerned with commercial fishing in Zambia and their trade has a market value estimated to exceed K6 000 000 per annum. At least 35 000 others undertake some temporary or subsistence fishing in the smaller streams and swamps of the country, and their catch, which does not enter the cash economy, has also been estimated and indicated very tentatively on the map opposite.

The total fish production from the major commercial fisheries rose from 12 000 short tons in 1952 to a peak of 34 000 short tons in 1964 and stood at 29 430 short tons in 1968 (26 754 metric tons), a short fall requiring annual importation of roughly 20 000 tons by 1969. (Production figures for dried fish are calculated by the fresh weight equivalent.)

The three major river systems (p. 16) and their associated lakes have differing types of fish. The first, Lake Tanganyika, has the unique ndagaa fishery. Here the fish have evolved in a habitat of internal drainage separated from other sources of fish species and in great depth of water in the rift valley lake. The two species of ndagaa (family *Clupeidae*), commonly known as kapenta or fresh-water sardine, are up to four inches (10 cm.) long. They are either sundried or packed and frozen commercially for sale. Three species of perch (*Lates*) are also caught. These much larger fish, 20 to 30 inches (about 15 to 75 cm.) long, feed on the kapenta. The commonest method of catching the deep-swimming fish is at night with paraffin pressure lamps which attract shoals of kapenta and their predator perch.

The fisheries of the Congo headwaters—Lakes Bangweulu, Mweru and Mweru-Wantipa and the River Luapula—produce over 100 fish species of which some thirty are commercially important and one, *Tilapia* (bream) is outstanding, being highly prized for its flavour. Plank canoes are tending to replace dug-out canoes and the growing use of outboard motors also helps to increase the safe range of fishing out to the less fished middle waters. Here the danger of sudden squalls has always been a deterrent to fishermen in the unstable dugout canoes. Some of the catch in this region is sold to fish traders from the Copperbelt towns, who transport fresh fish in special boxes on lorries and either bring their own ice or buy it on arrival at Lake Mweru. Much of the rest of the catch is partly sun-dried and then smoked for local consumption or sale.

The main commercial fisheries of the Zambezi system are the Kafue Flats and the Lukanga Swamps. A feature of these fisheries is the annual flooding of the plains from December to April, which causes the waters to be especially rich in alkaline salts and in phyto- and zoo-plankton species. The main fish caught are the commercially popular cichlids (*Tilapia* species), the commonest method of fishing utilizing gill nets. Seine nets were made illegal in 1961 because in the low or receding waters from July to September few fish can escape, breeding fish with young being especially vulnerable. However, the nets were again legalized in 1967. The possible effects on the fishing economy of the Kafue Gorge hydro-electric scheme (in changing the flooding régime of the Kafue Flats) is a matter of some concern to local scientists.

As with other man-made lakes, the Lake Kariba fishery (shared with Rhodesia) started with a few boom years (3000 short tons in 1962), after which the harvest declined as the lake stabilized. Tilapia fingerlings introduced into the lake completely disappeared, probably eaten by tiger fish, as did other species, but experimental stocking continues, the best prospects lying with the Lake Tanganyika kapenta.

ZAMBIA'S MAJOR COMMERCIAL FISHERIES

	Area in Sq. miles	Total production 1960	In short tons 1968
Mweru-Luapula	1000[1]	7 306	6 332
Mweru-Wantipa	600	1 282	3 156
Bangweulu	3000	6 580	8 165
Tanganyika	817[1]	2 943	7 720
Kafue	3000[2]	2 705	3 189[3]
Kariba	700[1]	500	868
TOTALS	9 117	21 316	29 430

[1] Within borders of Zambia.
[2] At flood.
[3] 1968 was a very poor year. The normal average is approximately 6 000–7 000 tons.

Every river and stream in Zambia contributes its quota of fish to the subsistence of local people. They use a variety of fishing methods not used by commercial fishermen, including elaborately constructed traps, weirs and scoop baskets and even multi-pronged spears. The use of modern nets and lines is also beginning to spread among them from contact with commercial fishermen.

Zambia has good prospects of increasing her harvest of fish. Some main lines of development at present are the increasing use of larger, more 'sea'-worthy boats, of engine power to increase effective fishing range, and of correctly meshed nets for particular fisheries. Apart from such technical improvements, the market also greatly needs improved organization, particularly because at present the fishermen too often fail to get a fair price by direct negotiation with the traders. Good access roads to central stations in each fishery would facilitate price negotiation and, at the same time, make the setting up of ice plants an economic measure, as at Kashikishi on Lake Mweru. Developments of this kind will also improve the general standard of living of the fisherfolk. Instead of living scattered in small groups in islands among the waters, they could in many cases live in settled communities with shops, education and other services available. Such population re-grouping would accord with national policy for the rural areas.

The First National Development Plan provides for the extension and development of infrastructure at all major fisheries. The principal aim is to reduce the present high wastage of fish caused by inadequate facilities for landing, handling and processing the catch. Credit is made available to fishermen for improved nets and other gear and to boat-builders to encourage local craftsmen. Fish culture schemes, research, training and marketing are also being improved under the plan.

N D McGLASHAN

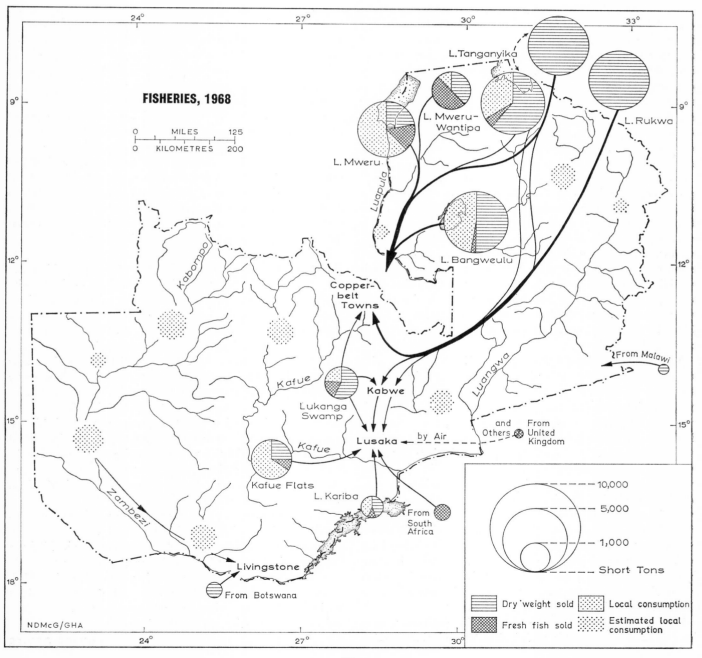

FISHERIES, 1968

36 THE TOWNS

Despite rapid urbanization, today over 70 per cent of Zambians still live in the rural areas. The traditional settlement form is the smallest impermanent village: although there are some larger 'capital villages' such as Lealui (the Lozi royal court) there have never been true indigenous towns. Zambian towns are essentially colonial creations, exotic in concept, form and function. Geographically they fall into two divisions: a dominant group along the line of rail and a scatter of tiny settlements in the outlying 'bush'. Line of rail towns are mainly discussed on pp. 82, 86 and 88. The bush towns are mostly provincial or district administrative headquarters ('bomas'), such as Kasama, Mansa (formerly Fort Roseberry) and Mongu, which have since developed some commercial functions. Chipata (Fort Jameson) and Mbala (Abercorn) are also old route centres expanded as service outlets for surrounding European commercial farmers, who have now nearly all departed. Such centres have always been very small. However, all non-mining towns, large and small, began as European and Asian enclaves in which Africans—government clerks and messengers, labourers and domestic servants —worked rather intermittently for cash wages and were grudgingly accepted as third-class citizens. Today, however, Africans vastly outnumber non-Africans in all towns.

A ranking of towns by size and status classes (Appendix 2) suggests comparatively balanced national urban development. Imbalance lies not in the hierachy of towns but in their geographical distribution, as discussed below. The principal functions of each centre (a subjective listing) indicate that town sizes relate significantly to their variety of functions. Thus Kitwe, a broad-based regional centre, outranks Mufulira, a mining town with subsidiary functions, which in turn outranks Chililabombwe, virtually a mining camp. However, town growth also reflects size of urban economic base, regarded as jobs generated, so that Chililabombwe outranks an outlying administrative and service centre such as Kasama.

The overall geographical distribution of Zambian towns, with sizeable centres wholly confined to the line of rail, is less favourable than their hierarchy. Most tiny bush centres are hardly growing vigorously (bureaucratic growth excepted), a fact with regional planning implications. Government wishes to curb the drift to larger towns of rural people with poor prospects of finding jobs or housing. Recognizing the powerful lure of towns, however, its aim is to regroup rural population in new or replanned settlements, to be provided with some urban-style services and amenities. Existing small outlying towns must form nodes in any such network. Where these have failed to develop the bright lights and above all the jobs to retain and attract people, can new planned centres do so, particularly when built under conditions of financial stringency? The contrast between bush towns and larger line of rail centres in economic growth potential does not auger well for success with some aspects of the rural regrouping programme.

Zambian towns, lying mostly on undulating plateaux, tend to have uninteresting, if fairly varied, sites. These include mining towns near ore outcrops (p. 82); route towns (e.g. Livingstone, Chipata, Kafue); harbours (Samfya); towns at or near precolonial centres (Mongu); sites at rail sidings (Lusaka) and administrative centres sited on grounds of centrality.

Despite variety in size, function and site, the towns have common characteristics. As early twentieth century creations they usually display some rather stereotyped town-planning, which, with usually uninspiring architecture and a general lack of distinctive local building materials, produces rather dull townscapes. All of them, designed with the notion that land was plentiful and in disregard of the economics of public utilities, tend to sprawl luxuriously, a process aided by usually gentle slopes. Sprawl is aggravated by a history of de facto racial segregation, which everywhere caused residential separation into expansive European suburbs, modest Asian quarters, African compounds and, especially since independence, shanty towns. Sprawl is further increased in larger towns by farm subdivisions and by satellite settlements (some incorporated in 1970). Much urban land is held in public ownership and there is general acceptance of responsibility to house employees in both public and private sectors. The relatively few privately-owned urban homes are largely located in ex-European suburbs and areas of peri-urban smallholdings. Commercial and service development is everywhere rather limited, largely because until independence towns were dominated by non-Africans who, although a small minority, possessed most of the purchasing power and all the urban tradition. Past dependence on Rhodesia also restricted commercial development. Finally, despite changing English to Zambian street names, these colonial towns still retain vestigial British characteristics in their 'garden suburbs', an occasional pseudo-Tudor public house, and their faded clubs.

Zambian towns fall into two administrative categories, as explained in the table. Both municipalities (including cities) and townships are still administered in the British local authority tradition and on occasion be-wigged mayors swathed in medieval European finery perspire in African heat.

Nevertheless the Zambian Government is radically changing the colonial physical structure of its country's urban centres. Africans in government, civil service and the professions now reside in low density areas once the preserve of their white neighbours. In an attempt to check emergence of a new élite class, government is promoting 'integrated housing development', with high and low cost properties intermixed. To encourage participation by nationals, foreign-owned businesses are now confined by legislation to more complex activities and to the town centres, a restriction bearing most heavily upon the comparatively few Asian traders, who must either seek Zambian citizenship or move to the 'prescribed areas'.

The larger towns now face grave squatter problems. Squatters are massing in squalor on their fringes, exerting pressures on government to alleviate their plight. Their presence highlights a fundamental dichotomy in Zambian society between the backward rural poor and some increasingly prosperous and sophisticated urban dwellers. While the present socio-economic gradient persists and steepens, urban drift will continue to pose a serious and worsening problem for the fledgling nation.

D HYWEL DAVIES

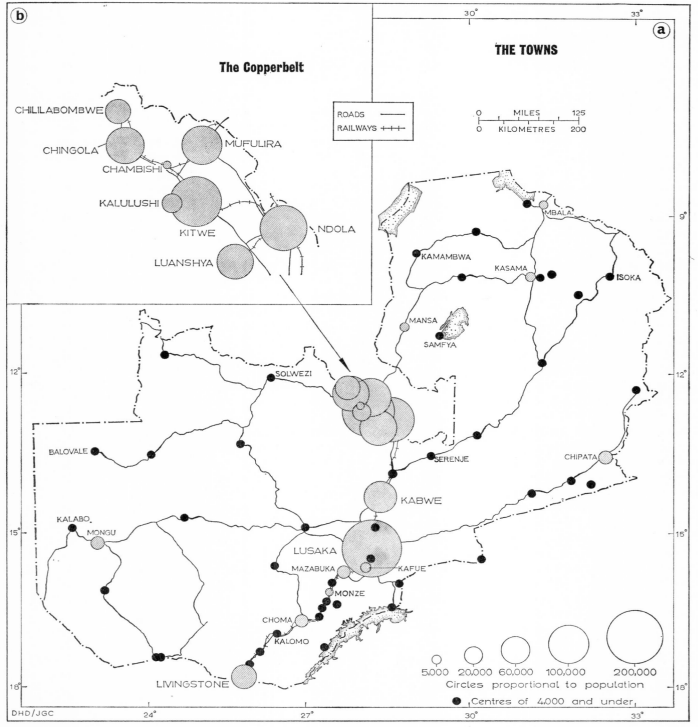

THE TOWNS

b

The Copperbelt

CHILILABOMBWE

CHINGOLA

CHAMBISHI

MUFULIRA

KALULUSHI

KITWE

NDOLA

LUANSHYA

a

ROADS ————
RAILWAYS +++

0   MILES   125
0   KILOMETRES   200

MBALA

KAMAMBWA   KASAMA   ISOKA

MANSA

SAMFYA

SOLWEZI

BALOVALE   SERENJE   CHIPATA

KABWE

KALABO   MONGU

LUSAKA   KAFUE

MAZABUKA   MONZE

CHOMA

KALOMO

LIVINGSTONE

5,000 20,000 60,000 100,000 200,000
Circles proportional to population

● Centres of 4,000 and under

DHD/JGC

The Copperbelt comprises state lands adjacent to the railway in the province of the same name. Alone in Zambia, it has towns sufficiently large, numerous and closely located to form a modest urbanized region. Of its three-quarters of a million inhabitants in 1969, 684 000 or 91 per cent lived in its eight urban centres, which include five of the six largest in the country plus the small new town of Chambishi, and account for over 60 per cent of all Zambian urban dwellers. The region has the best-developed infrastructure and services and some of the most highly paid workers. Eighteen per cent of all Zambians live on the Copperbelt, constituting the largest and most accessible market in the country.

Nevertheless the region is strongly urbanized only by central African standards. Its towns are scattered over an area of 90 by 30 miles separated one from another by miles of thick, mostly uncleared bush which is lightly populated and underdeveloped.

Urban centres

Except for Ndola, the principal urban centres are located at or near each of the seven copper mines. Consequently they lie at irregular intervals around the contact of the 'peninsula' of unproductive basement rocks and the lower Roan orebodies (p. 93, figs *e* and *g*). Hanging wall areas (land overlying possible orebodies) are held as mining special grants and reserved for future mining uses. They may be used for temporary non-mining purposes, such as agriculture and forestry, but no urban development is permitted. Consequently the towns can expand only on to the basement or along the contact zone.

After 1902 a pioneering mining phase saw tin and mud shacks erected around several small-scale diggings. Except for Ndola, however, real towns emerged only in the nineteen-thirties, following consolidation of mining operations into the hands of a few strong companies and consequent growth of a sense of security and continuity. These companies could not wait for a dilatory (because impoverished) colonial government to establish settlements but took the initiative themselves. They quickly built, serviced and administered townships for both European and African employees and continue to run most of them to this day.

In the four pre-war mining centres—Luanshya, Nkana-Kitwe, Mufulira and Nchanga-Chingola—(henceforth all 'twin' towns are referred to only by their local authority names, but the *joint* settlements are referred to) smaller townships were gradually developed by local authorities alongside the mine townships in order to provide administrative and commercial services. In these, central business districts gradually developed on the boundaries of the adjacent mine townships to serve both communities, while small planned industrial areas also grew up after the war. Some of these local authority townships obtain certain basic services—water, electricity or even hospital services — from the mines. However, administratively the 'twin' townships remain quite separate; some even have separate names. The maps (p. 85) show the boundaries between them passing through the centres of what appear on the ground as urban entities with unified street plans.

In the post-war townships a more integrated approach developed. Bancroft mine and local authority township (the latter now renamed Chililabombwe) retain the twin structure, but Kalulushi, built entirely by the mining company, was handed over completely to local authority administration in 1958. The newest settlement, Chambishi (1965), was planned from the outset as a local authority township. Today the mining companies are keen to shed all township responsibilities, but incorporation under local authorities is delayed by remarkable administrative complexities, largely caused by higher standards of amenities and wages levels in the mine townships. Thus the latter remain privately administered for the time being.

The Copperbelt region has still to reach the point of economic 'take-off', in that its manufacturing industry has only recently developed real momentum. Mining dominates and, should it decline, some smaller centres would become 'ghost' settlements. However, mining dominance decreases with the increasing size of towns. *Chambishi, Kalulushi*, and to a lesser extent, *Chililabombwe*, are purely mining centres. A group of towns in the 90 000 to 100 000 population range—*Mufulira, Chingola* and *Luanshya*—are principally mining towns but also have significant manufacturing and service functions and, in some cases, local administrative activities.

Kitwe, largest city on the Copperbelt, is a mining centre with regional functions. In addition to Rhokana Mine, its mining sector at Nkana includes regional administration, technical services and copper refining for the entire Nchanga Consolidated Copper Mines' Group (formerly the mines of the Anglo American Corporation). Its size is mainly due to its central location, which has stimulated relatively strong development of retail and service functions and of manufacturing industry (p. 95), the latter increasingly broadly based but retaining strong connections with the mine. Only Ndola rivals it as a regional 'capital'. Kitwe has a neatly planned, compact central business district around Kaunda Square. It is inadequately served by two hotels (an amenity entirely lacking in most Copperbelt towns) and has one or two cinemas, a theatre, a mine airfield accepting commercial flights and relatively good educational facilities.

Ndola, Kitwe's great rival, is the oldest large centre, originating as an African trading and Arab slaving centre. Already a boma in 1902, it is now capital of Copperbelt Province. With the arrival of the railway in 1907 it became a regional distribution point and, with its railway yards and international airport, retains this function today, although with competition from Kitwe. Ndola became a mining centre for the first time when the nearby historic Bwana Mkubwa mine, within its present municipal boundary, reopened in late 1970. However, the city is already linked with the mining industry through the presence of Roan Consolidated Mines' regional headquarters and one of its two refineries. But Ndola's economic base rests firmly upon commerce and manufacturing industry. Its sprawling business district compares well with Kitwe's in range of goods and services. It is comparable with Lusaka in its industrial structure, numbering 123 establishments in 1969. Industrial growth prospects are bright, with an oil storage depot opened in 1968 at the Zambia–Tanzania pipeline terminal (to which will be added a refinery in 1971–72), a large new cement factory and other new enterprises. Good educational facilities include the Northern Technical College and the city has four hotels, a theatre and cinemas. Ndola claims to be the fastest-growing urban centre on the Copperbelt.

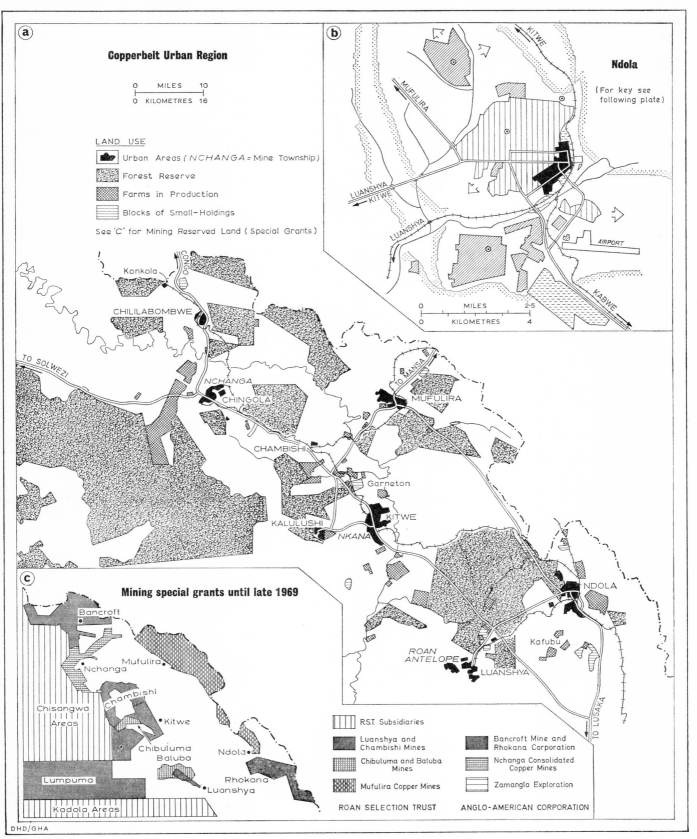

Satellite settlements are characteristic of Copperbelt towns. Some, like Konkola, are residential outliers of parent centres (Chililabombwe); others are separately administered African townships. The latter originated because housing was tied to employment, no provision being made for the self-employed, for retired workers not wishing to return to their villages, or for those simply disliking 'compound' life. To curb the growth of unauthorized settlements the colonial government had selected five sites for satellite townships by 1943. Here basic services were provided, most occupiers building their own homes. Although far superior to later squatter settlements, they have not proved very successful, largely because of the lack of employment there.

Other satellites are 'rural suburbs', originally exclusively European, with large plots of 3 to 5 acres (1·2 to 2 ha.) or more. The main example is Garneton (Itimpi) near Kitwe, planned as a subdivision of 20-acre (about 8 ha.) plots, where retired mine-workers would farm for the local urban market. As this scheme failed, plots were progressively subdivided and sold off for almost any purpose, usually as 'exurbia' residences. Such developments are unpopular with local authorities because of their high cost of servicing. A rather similar scheme for Africans at Kafubu, near Ndola, also languished, until recently revived as a co-operative venture. Such schemes have developed piecemeal, resulting in uneconomic and sometimes unsightly extensions of towns into their rural fringes. (The Government has recently announced its intention to incorporate the satellite developments into parent settlements—mine townships excepted.)

The town maps illustrate major morphological characteristics of all the towns except Chambishi and satellites. Points to notice are the adjustment of settlement form to the edges of mining land and the limited directions for expansion; the distribution of high and low density residential areas (the former somewhat nearer workplaces); central business districts located within local authority townships yet central to both 'twins'; planned small industrial areas; and the meandering boundaries dividing twin settlements. Most striking of all on the ground are the tailings dams, pithead gear and open pits on mining land. Squatter areas, which cannot accurately be displayed, are omitted.

The rural area

Containing only 9 per cent of the population, the Copperbelt rural area, divided among seven rural districts, is sparsely populated and surprisingly undeveloped considering market potential and existing infrastructure.

Agriculture is poorly developed, most of the region's food supplies coming from commercial farms to the south and from outside the country. In part this is due to generally poor, leached soils with a low base exchange capacity (the limited good soils also tend to be badly located with respect to water supply) and to the expense of irrigation from the slightly incised Kafue drainage system. Given the market, however, heavy capital input to horticulture, dairying and the like would be justified and

it is clear that human constraints have operated. Under colonial rule state land was effectively reserved for Europeans who, as urban workers, lacked both farming skills and motivation, preferring to sub-divide and use smallholdings for basically residential purposes. African smallholders have also lacked the skills needed for intensive commercial farming, and training programmes to remedy this are only beginning to achieve results. In future, however, the region must provide far more of its food needs from local African smallholders in the Copperbelt rural areas and elsewhere within the province. The colonial government also failed to encourage local farming, preferring to protect large-scale commercial farmers on the line of rail farther south. Thus by 1959 only 93 out of 274 listed farms on the Copperbelt were productive. Since independence, production of perishable foodstuffs has suffered from a partial exodus of European farmers but some government-sponsored developments, including a ranch near Kitwe, may lead to improvements.

Mining Reserve Land (special grants) occupies much of the Copperbelt and is virtually unproductive apart from mining. Almost a third of the surface area is held under *Forest Reserves* (p. 24). These provide some indigenous hardwood timber for the mines, while portions are now under plantations of tropical pines and eucalypts, some just beginning to produce. Forest reserves enable the rural poor to supplement their diet with collected produce and the lands are also used to some extent for illegal cultivation. A few thousand charcoal burners also use the reserves. The area actually available for farming is thus much smaller than might be thought, although sufficient for a far greater volume of food production than is now achieved.

Additional to these major uses of land is an untidy scatter of *minor rural land uses*. These include rural smallholdings (productive and unproductive); government, basically residential use, such as army and police barracks; and ribbon development of roadside cafés, bars, stores, road camps and petrol stations. Near to towns thousands of squatters occupy mine reserve land, old brickfield camps and other sites. Many rural people are unemployed and most live at lower standards than the townsfolk. The rural area is thus somewhat depressed economically as well as being administratively and aesthetically untidy.

In regional planning terms the Copperbelt is rather chaotic. A serious weakness is that precise data are lacking, but it is nevertheless apparent that the naturally-evolved hierarchy of central places is not capitalized upon in planning policy (if such can be identified). Some towns tend to compete with one another and regional services are limited and unco-ordinated. The rural hinterland is largely neglected and is not linked to the towns in any plans—for example, rural areas are not effectively used for recreation purposes. Intra-regional public transportation is inadequate and main roads are too narrow for today's traffic.

These problems were realized in the early sixties, when a Copperbelt Planning Authority was created to prepare a regional plan. Unfortunately, its restrictive terms of reference specifically excluded planning for the large areas of state and mining lands: furthermore, it was not provided with any executive 'teeth' to implement its own programme. Inevitably the plan proved disappointingly negative and it has had virtually no visible effect upon the landscape. As with Lusaka (p. 86), there is still physical space for some bold comprehensive planning, but, with the present influx of industries and squatters, very little time. A new regional plan, preceded by thorough research and followed by effective execution, is urgently needed for Zambia's economic and urban heartland.

D HYWEL DAVIES

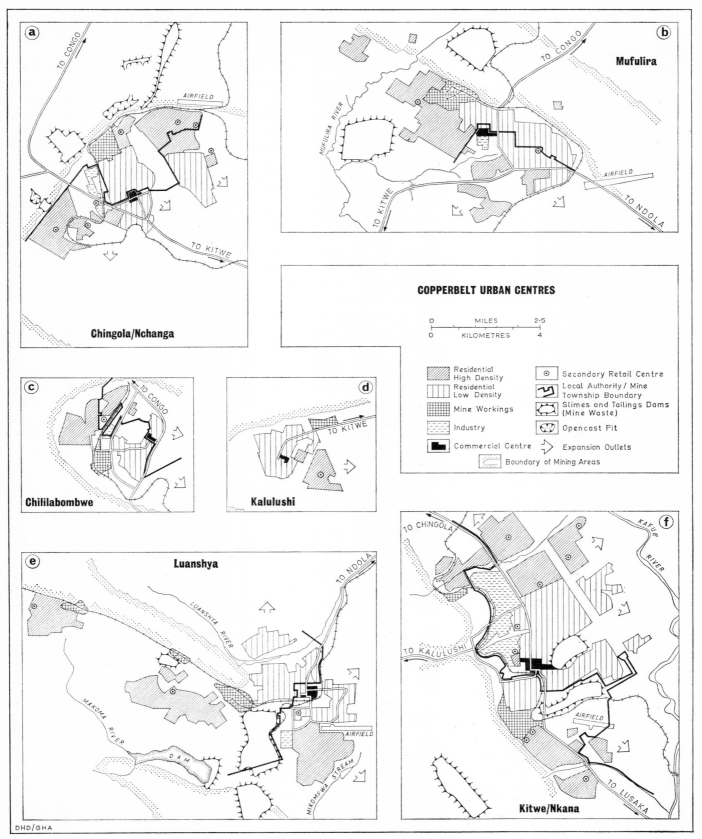

COPPERBELT URBAN CENTRES

	MILES	2·5
0		
0	KILOMETRES	4

Residential High Density — Secondary Retail Centre
Residential Low Density — Local Authority / Mine Township Boundary
Mine Workings — Slimes and Tailings Dams (Mine Waste)
Industry — Opencast Pit
Commercial Centre — Expansion Outlets
Boundary of Mining Areas

Chingola/Nchanga

Mufulira

Chililabombwe

Kalulushi

Luanshya

Kitwe/Nkana

DHD/GHA

85

Lusaka is the capital and largest city of Zambia. Its population in 1969, including adjacent but administratively separate townships (some since incorporated) was 238 000, of whom perhaps 15 000 were non-Africans. Situated around 4150 feet (1265 m.) above sea level on the mid-Tertiary plateau surface, it is fairly centrally placed on the line of rail, with road links to Western and Eastern Provinces (p. 110). Its plateau climate is generally pleasant and healthy, with ample sunshine, day breezes and cool nights. Primarily the seat of government, Lusaka is also the leading single financial, commercial and industrial centre in Zambia. The main branches of manufacturing are foodstuffs and beverages, clothing, building materials and light engineering and repairs (p. 95). The city has leading educational establishments and, with its new international airport, has become the principal centre for transport and communications (p. 113).

Lusaka originated in 1905 as a siding on the single-track railway built to serve the new Broken Hill mine (Kabwe), taking its name from Lusaakas, the headman of a nearby village. The site lies on the flat Lusaka Dolomite surface near its eastern contact with more varied country, developed mainly on schists, to the north and east (fig. d). European farms were gradually taken up nearby, producing maize, beef and hides for railing to Kabwe and Katanga. A small agricultural service centre consequently developed around the siding, officially recognized in 1913 by the creation of a village management board and dignified with a gridiron streetplan, which today encloses the main business district.

Site disadvantages soon become apparent. The dolomite forms a karstic terrain devoid of surface drainage. During the dry winters water proved hard to obtain as the water table fell. During summer rains the water table rose to the surface, streets flooded and solution hollows filled with stagnant water, causing disease. With such physical handicaps and a limited economic base the little settlement grew only slowly until 1931, when it was chosen to be the new capital of Northern Rhodesia, a turning point in its short history.

The colonial government had considered moving the capital from Livingstone to a more central location since amalgamation of Northwestern and Northeastern Rhodesia. A British planner, Professor Adshead, was commissioned to recommend a site. This was to be accessible to the entire territory and from Southern Rhodesia, reasonably close to the emergent Copperbelt yet distant enough to discourage dominance by mining interests. Good water resources were essential and high ground desirable for health reasons. Lusaka was duly chosen from various claimants. Although its surface water supply was inadequate, large proven underground supplies along the dolomite contact could be tapped with the resources of a government town.

Adshead also presented an outline plan and his basic recommendations laid the planning foundations for the city. He proposed building the capital away from the unattractive existing settlement and on the Ridgeway, a low, breezy schist ridge a mile or so to the east (figs. c, d). Here he designed a 'garden city on an imaginative and spacious groundplan, in contrast to the original gridiron. Ample space and greenery were planned, with large building plots for European officials centred around the Ridgeway axial road (now Independence Avenue), with its government offices, legislature, High Court and Government House. Plot sizes decreased somewhat away from this 'Snobs Hill', but densities were everywhere low. Adshead also accepted the colonial de facto residential segregation of races. A limited African population was envisaged, mostly humble government employees and domestics. Some servants' families would be housed on European plots, but most Africans would occupy separate locations, mainly south and west of the capital area. These had somewhat higher densities and much lower standards of amenity than European areas. An Asian residential quarter, with a secondary business district, later emerged near the old town, and police and army camps and other institutional areas developed. Segregation was virtually complete until the eve of independence. The development of both industry and services was somewhat inhibited by reliance on Southern Rhodesia, especially during Federation, and by growing dominance of the Copperbelt regional market. Lusaka grew steadily without again changing its character until independence in 1964.

Today the fast-growing capital faces serious planning problems. Water, obtained solely from boreholes, was in limited supply from 1965 to 1969, when piped Kafue water became available. Low density sprawl, stemming from 'garden city' thinking and uncontrolled subdivision of farms, provides some pleasant suburbs and avenues, but makes servicing costly and causes lengthy journeys to work, shop and school. Low density central areas largely restrict essential new low-income housing to the periphery, where the poorer people face the worst commuting problem. The eccentric western location of the 'central' business district is away from the general growth direction and generally inefficient, the more so because of inadequate connections across the railway barrier. The best-equipped schools, clubs and other facilities are in the low density areas, readily accessible only to upper-income Zambians.

The worst problem today, however, is chronic shortage of housing and jobs for the large influx of unskilled villagers since independence. Unauthorized shanty towns have mushroomed around the city, where perhaps half of Lusaka's residents live in conditions approaching social breakdown and disease. Repeated in other major Zambian urban centres, the squatter problem is a national one.

Lusaka's growth problems demand bold, flexible and comprehensive planning. It is encouraging that the city planning authority area now extends well beyond the municipal boundary: it is to be expanded to encompass Kafue, 27 miles south a new town which will serve as Lusaka's heavy industrial area (p. 88 and 119[c]). Consultants have reported to government the findings of comprehensive surveys and their new master plans have been approved. Their implementation is anxiously awaited, for while the city's low density provides enviable elbow room for constructive planning, the present growth rate affords precious little time.

D HYWEL DAVIES

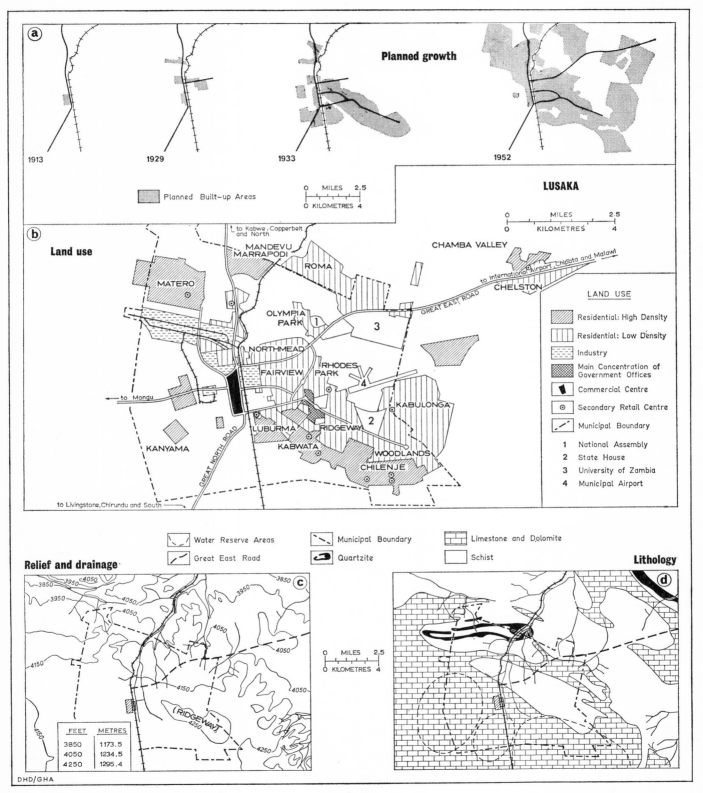

a
Planned growth

1913   1929   1933   1952

Planned Built-up Areas

| 0 | MILES | 2.5 |
| 0 | KILOMETRES | 4 |

LUSAKA

| 0 | MILES | 2.5 |
| 0 | KILOMETRES | 4 |

b
Land use

to Kabwe, Copperbelt and North

MANDEVU MARRAPODI
ROMA
MATERO
OLYMPIA PARK
NORTHMEAD
FAIRVIEW
RHODES PARK
to Mongu
KANYAMA
LUBURMA
RIDGEWAY
KABWATA
CHILENJE
WOODLANDS
KABULONGA
CHAMBA VALLEY
CHELSTON
GREAT EAST ROAD
to International Airport, Chipata and Malawi
GREAT NORTH ROAD
to Livingstone, Chirundu and South

LAND USE

Residential: High Density
Residential: Low Density
Industry
Main Concentration of Government Offices
Commercial Centre
Secondary Retail Centre
Municipal Boundary

1 National Assembly
2 State House
3 University of Zambia
4 Municipal Airport

Water Reserve Areas   Municipal Boundary   Limestone and Dolomite
Great East Road   Quartzite   Schist

c
Relief and drainage

3850 3950 4050 3850
3950 4050
4050
4150
4150
4050
(RIDGEWAY)
4250
4250
4150

FEET	METRES
3850	1173.5
4050	1234.5
4250	1295.4

| 0 | MILES | 2.5 |
| 0 | KILOMETRES | 4 |

d
Lithology

DHD/GHA

The pattern of urban settlement along the railway is closely related to the need for sidings at frequent intervals along the single track system, and to the superior agricultural value of much of the country through which the line runs. Most towns grew from small administrative or commercial posts established near railway sidings. Although Ndola and Lusaka, because of their present size and functions, are dealt with elsewhere, generically they too belong to this group.

Along the northern section of the line towns are far fewer than between Livingstone and Lusaka. This is partly due to the dominance of Kabwe and Lusaka—only eighty miles apart —both of them comparatively large centres with extensive hinterlands. North of Kabwe commercial farming is relatively unimportant and Kapiri Mposhi, strategically situated at the junction of the Great North Road and the main road to the Copperbelt, is the only significant centre.

From Livingstone to Lusaka the road and railway, running alongside each other for long stretches, traverse the oldest and most prosperous commercial farming region in Zambia. Here small towns are strung out at fairly regular intervals. Only Chilanga, with its cement plant, and more recently Kafue, have industry of any consequence. Choma (11 000) and Maza-buka (9000) are the largest centres between Livingstone and Kafue, but they and their smaller neighbours are essentially commercial and market centres serving an agricultural hinterland to which their fortunes are closely tied.

Three towns, Livingstone (43 000), Kabwe (67 000) and Kafue merit separate consideration.

Livingstone

The original settlement at Livingstone was at the 'Old Drift', a ferrying point on the Zambezi eight miles above the Victoria Falls. On completion of the railway bridge in 1905, ferry traffic disappeared and the settlement, which occupied a notoriously unhealthy site, was moved to higher ground and renamed Livingstone. The town's importance stemmed from its position on the principal routeway from the south and, in the years prior to 1935, from its role as territorial capital.

After the Second World War the tourist trade, based on the Victoria Falls, became the mainstay of the local economy. However, increasing political separation of Zambia and Rhodesia following the break-up of the Central African Federation, Zambian independence and deterioration of relations between the two countries since Rhodesia's Unilateral Declaration of Independence in 1965, have drastically reduced the numbers of tourists visiting Livingstone (p. 108).

The need to expand the employment base of the town has become considerably more urgent since the decline (perhaps temporary) of tourism, but efforts to attract new industry have not met with much success. A factory producing radios and record players opened in 1965 and the long-established textile and clothing industry has seen some expansion. The much-hoped-for fertilizer plant (600 jobs), was finally re-located at Kafue.

Despite government's decision in November 1969 to establish the Fiat vehicle assembly plant in Livingstone, the economic outlook is not bright, for the town's prosperity rests upon political and economic ties with the south that no longer exist.

Kabwe (Broken Hill)

Unlike most other towns under discussion, Kabwe existed before the arrival of the railway, which was deliberately routed through it. Its lead and zinc mine opened in 1902 and is the only one of the pre-1914 generation to survive in production, if somewhat precariously, to the present day.

The urban structure of Kabwe is haphazard and poorly planned due to its development by three separate agencies. As in most Copperbelt mining towns, the mine still maintains its own township. The railways, whose headquarters have been in Kabwe for many years, also developed a separate township, although this now falls within municipal control. Of special interest is the presence of mine farms. Dating from the late nineteen-twenties, these plots were intended to make mine employees more self-supporting. Unfortunately, over the last few years, they have been over-run by hordes of squatters, over 21 000 at the last count.

Kabwe, like Livingstone, has seen better days. Broken Hill mine is troubled by technical problems of extraction, by low metal prices and the need to replace the South African market, which once took 75 per cent of its production. Alternative sources of employment are very limited. In 1970 Zambia Railways opened large new workshops (1000 jobs) and the state-owned Industrial Development Corporation (INDECO) brought into production a plant producing grain sacks and hessian, employing nearly 600 people. In open competition with Lusaka and the Copperbelt, however, Kabwe is unlikely to attract many new concerns.

Kafue

Whereas Livingstone and Kabwe are colonial towns inheriting past economic problems, Kafue is the product of the post-independence era, embodying the ambitions of a young nation. In 1967 planning consultants produced a master plan incorporating the old settlement of Kafue (population under 3000) in an extensive development that will transform the little township into a major industrial centre with a projected population of 100 000 by the end of the century.

The riverside site has much to commend it. The Great North Road and the railway pass through it and ample supplies of water and electric power are at hand. Construction of the new town and its first industries is well advanced, involving contractors and specialists from many countries. At present the industrial area houses an ammonium nitrate fertilizer plant, a fully integrated textile mill and a small firm producing fibre-glass fishing boats. The first two projects between them employ about 1200 people. Should a national iron and steel industry be developed, it is almost certain to be located in Kafue.

Separated from the industrial zone by a 'green belt' lies the residential area, planned in communities of 10 000 people, each with its own shops and service facilities (p. 119 [c]). Already one community is substantially developed and two more are partially developed to house a population that will reach 20 000 in the early nineteen-seventies. Much use is being made of higher density housing types—flats, terraced housing, two and three storey units—all features comparatively rare in Zambian urban settlements.

J E GARDINER

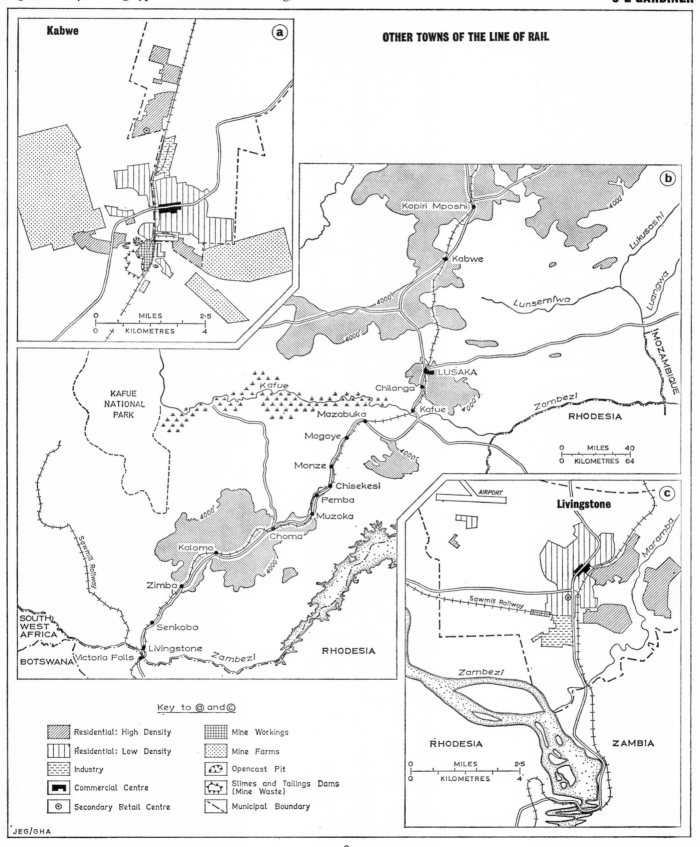

OTHER TOWNS OF THE LINE OF RAIL

Key to ⓐ and ⓒ

Residential: High Density		Mine Workings	
Residential: Low Density		Mine Farms	
Industry		Opencast Pit	
Commercial Centre		Slimes and Tailings Dams (Mine Waste)	
Secondary Retail Centre		Municipal Boundary	

JEG/GHA

41 MINERAL CONCESSIONS AND PRODUCTION (EXCLUDING COPPER) TO 1969

As from the close of 1969 all existing prospecting concessions in Zambia were cancelled and all mineral rights came under state control. Companies active since independence in 1964 were granted prior claim on some of their previous concessions, but inactive companies were required to re-apply in open competition. In January 1970 the then Ministry of Trade, Industry and Mines (whose Mines Department regulates all mining operations) was preparing a completely new Register of Mineral Titles to record all valid prospecting rights in Zambia and international companies entirely new on the scene were expressing interest in acquiring prospecting rights. At the time of writing, therefore, it is not possible to describe adequately the new concessions following this wholesale reorganization. However, since mineral concessions prior to 1969 provided the basis for present mining—Zambia's key industry—it is relevant to outline their development and distribution very briefly.

Mineral concessions

When the British South Africa (BSA) Company obtained its Charter to administer territories north of the Zambezi in 1889, it naturally wished to establish their economic value: the company accordingly organized mineral prospecting from 1896 onwards. Prospecting companies and individuals usually searched for traces of the old malachite and azurite workings from which local Africans had obtained copper, probably for several centuries. These indigenous coppersmiths exploited only shallow oxide ores and, even with simple smelting methods, obtained metal of a high degree of purity. Much of their production was cast into bars and crosses for trade and currency, and some was drawn into fine wire for body ornaments.

The high hopes of early European prospectors were rarely justified, and considerable financial losses on gold and copper ventures led to a decrease in prospecting by about 1910, although several copper mines had achieved brief periods of production. Indeed, the BSA Company itself suffered continuous losses administering the territory and paid no dividends until after 1924, when government was taken over by the British Crown.

In 1922 the post-war dollar shortage emphasized that if mining were to be made profitable so far from sea ports, only large-scale, well-capitalized prospecting companies could be expected to overcome the difficulties. Exclusive prospecting rights were accordingly offered for stated periods of time to responsible mining interests with the resources to carry out thorough investigations. This policy led to a second wave of prospecting; in fourteen years, from 1926 to 1940, 203 000 square miles (525 770 sq. km., roughly 70 per cent of the surface of Zambia) were examined at some time for mineral occurrences. Barotseland (now Western Province) was excluded from prospecting under the terms of separate treaties dating from 1900.

During the period from 1926 to 1940, the two major groups, Anglo American Corporation and Roan Selection Trust, became dominant and carried out prospecting through several subsidiary companies (fig. b). The actual mining areas of the Copperbelt and their immediate surrounds were covered by Special Grants of mining rights (p. 83 [c]).

Building minerals, clay, limestone, phyllite and magnesite are also separately controlled on long term licences under Special Grants. Several major companies in these fields were taken under state control in 1968.

Mineral production

Copper from the Copperbelt, dominating all mining in Zambia (fig. d), is described on p. 92.

Zambia Broken Hill Development Company (Anglo American Corporation) started lead and zinc production in 1906. In recent years more easily accessible ores have become exhausted, labour and transport costs have increased, and capital equipment has needed replacement. Consequently, mining costs have risen, share values have fallen and no dividends are being paid: only tax concessions have allowed the company to continue to finance operations. In 1968 the production of zinc was 58 659 short tons and of lead 24 126 short tons, worth respectively over K8 million and K3 million. Some silver is produced as a by-product of zinc and lead mining and some from copper mining. Cobalt is also produced at four of the copper mines.

Many small-scale mining operations have lived and died in Zambia. For example, two small companies, Mwewa and Kalaba Manganese, used to mine manganese by special grant in one large and one small area near Mansa in Luapula Province. The companies experienced difficulties in exporting their ore, which had to travel by road across the Chembe pontoon over the River Luapula and via the Congo Pedicle road to the railhead at Mufulira. In 1968 another small property, Kampumba (east of Kabwe), still produced 27 962 short tons of manganese, partly of ore graded to 54 per cent metal content and partly undifferentiated ore: the total value was K382 826.

Zambia's independence in 1964 and Rhodesia's Unilateral Declaration of Independence in 1965 stimulated exploitation of coal from previously known low-grade deposits in the Gwembe valley, thereby decreasing reliance on imported Rhodesian coal from Wankie. Open cast methods were used at the short-life mine at Nkandabwe (now closed), while shaft mining is being developed to reach deeper coal of high calorific value at nearby Maamba. The coal travels 50 miles (80 km.) by a new road up the Gwembe escarpment to Batoka railway siding, 13 miles north-east of Choma. The 1968 production stood at 632 019 short tons, valued at K1 128 604.

There are an estimated five million tons of high grade iron ore at Sanje, near Mumbwa. Together with coal from Maamba, this may soon form the basis of a local iron and steel industry (p. 94); local manganese resources would be complementary.

Small quantities of precious and semi-precious stones (except diamonds) are obtainable in Southern Province, including amethysts valued at K210 960 in 1968. Small-scale exploitation of mica has occurred sporadically in Eastern Province. Production of some other minerals is indicated in fig. a, c and d.

N D McGLASHAN

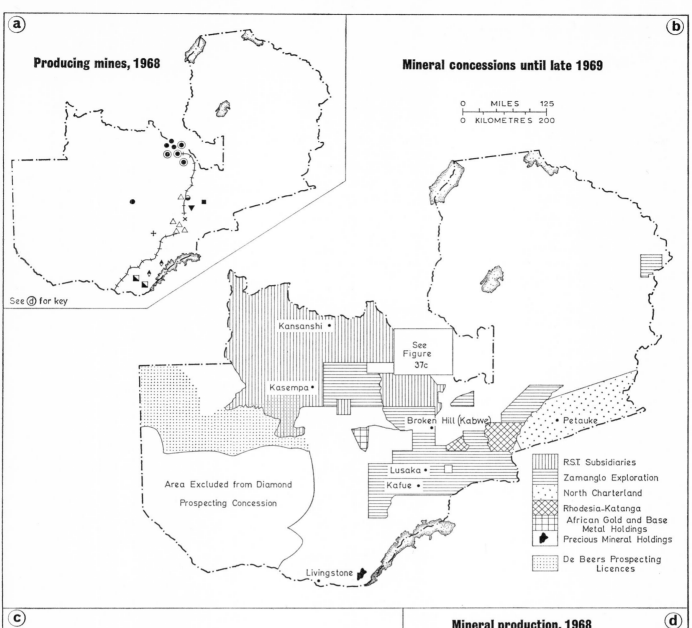

a) Producing mines, 1968

See (d) for key

b) Mineral concessions until late 1969

```
0      MILES      125
0   KILOMETRES   200
```

Kansanshi •

Kasempa •

See Figure 37c

Broken Hill (Kabwe) •

• Petauke

Lusaka •

Kafue •

Area Excluded from Diamond Prospecting Concession

Livingstone •

	R.S.T. Subsidiaries
	Zamanglo Exploration
	North Charterland
	Rhodesia-Katanga
	African Gold and Base Metal Holdings
	Precious Mineral Holdings
	De Beers Prospecting Licences

c) Production in short tons

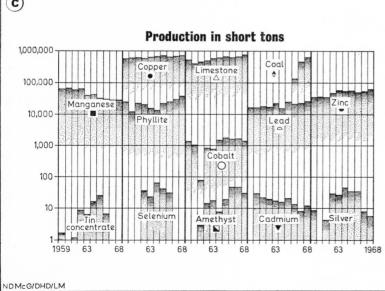

Copper
Limestone
Coal
Manganese
Phyllite
Zinc
Lead
Cobalt
Tin concentrate
Selenium
Amethyst
Cadmium
Silver

1,000,000
100,000
10,000
1,000
100
10
1

1959 63 68 63 68 63 68 63 68 63 1968

d) Mineral production, 1968

Mineral	Value in Kwacha
● Copper	514,817,008
▾ Zinc	8,365,729
⌐ Lead	3,193,542
○ Cobalt	2,638,623
△ Limestone	2,033,749
Silver*	1,954,540
♦ Coal	1,128,604
■ Manganese	382,826
◨ Amethyst	210,960
Gold*	153,339
Selenium*	108,647
▼ Cadmium	49,704
+ Gypsum	10,580
Phyllite	9,709
× Talc	2,769
* By-product from Copper (Silver not entirely)	

NDMcG/DHD/LM

Anglo American Corporation (AAC)	*Roan Selection Trust (RST)*
(now Nchanga Consolidated	*(now Roan Consolidated Mines Ltd.)*
Copper Mines Ltd.)	
Bancroft Mines Ltd.	Mufulira Copper Mines Ltd.
Nchanga Consolidated Copper	Mufulira Division
Mines Ltd.	Chibuluma Division
Rhokana Corporation Ltd.	Chambishi Division
	Luanshya Mines Ltd.

The Copperbelt is here considered solely as a *mining* region (see p. 82). This gently undulating bush country, roughly 90 miles (144 km.) long by 30 miles (48 km.) wide, is Zambia's economic heartland. Graphs *c* and *a* show, respectively, how the region's copper industry dominates the national economy and makes Zambia the world's third largest producer of copper. In 1968 total production was 733 000 short tons (733 000 short tons or 755 000 metric tons in 1969) and sales totalled K515 millions, excluding a little cobalt, and were higher for 1969. Ore reserves, 'indicated and possible', total 765 000 000 sorts tons, sufficient for 22 years at the 1968 rate of 34 000 000 tons hoisted.

The copper ores, mostly sulphides (pyrites, chalcopyrites, bornite, etc.) with important secondary oxide ores, are found in the Katanga system, which overlies schists and old granite of the Basement Complex. Regional folding of Katanga sediments between massifs formed the Kafue Anticline, the north-west-southeast axis of the region, which controls the Kafue drainage pattern. Subsequent peneplanation removed Katanga sediments, exposing the basement. The Katanga is preserved in the Mufulira Syncline to the north-east and in a set of *en echelon* synclines, bordering a major synclinorium, to the south-west (fig. *g*). The orebodies are located in the lower Roan group in the Katanga Mines series. The ore formations are mainly argillites and micaceous dolomites, only locally mineralized to ore grade. They are mostly 15 to 50 feet (4·6 to 15·2 m.) thick with an ore content around three or four per cent. Their origins remain controversial, with geologists supporting both syngenetic and epigenetic hypotheses.

Roan Antelope (Luanshya) and Bwana Mkubwa were discovered in 1902 but prospecting became really effective only from 1923, when sole rights were granted to financially strong companies. The oldest fully working mine began production only in 1931. This time lag reflects awareness that in neighbouring Katanga the industry had developed on rich surface oxide ores, below which were much leaner primary ores. Heavy leaching had impoverished the Copperbelt oxide ores, which were unpromising. Only after deep drilling in the nineteen-twenties was it realized that, unlike Katanga, the sulphide ores were the richer resource. Since then the present mines have gradually come into operation—Luanshya 1931, Rhokana 1932, Mufulira 1933, Nchanga 1939, Chibuluma 1956, Bancroft 1957 and Chambishi 1965. Because the giant Nchanga mine now exploits oxide ores, the proportion of copper won from sulphide ores has fallen recently to perhaps two-thirds of total Copperbelt production.

Consolidation gradually placed the industry entirely under control of the Anglo American Corporation and Roan Selection Trust, both registered in 1928, mining operations being conducted by subsidiary companies (see table). On 1 January 1970 the state took 51 per cent share control of mining, subsequently setting up the Mining and Industrial Development Corporation of Zambia (MINDECO) to hold the shares and options attached to new prospecting licences.

Only Mufulira mine lay on the eastern syncline, although re-opening of Bwana Mkubwa in 1970 adds a second: the other six mines lie on the western synclines. Fig. *e* distinguishes underground from open cast mines and shows the distribution of smelters and refineries serving groups of mines. The inset chart reveals complex intra-regional movements of copper products based on technology as much as on group ownership. Copper was exported southward by rail until the Rhodesian impasse, since when northern routes are being developed, particularly to Lobito and Dar es Salaam (p. 111). In 1968 large tonnages were still tied up in transit stock owing to continuing difficulties with these routes. Principal customers are shown in fig. *b*. Fuel and power requirements of the mines are discussed on pp. 90 and 98.

From 1965 to 1968 a Zambianization policy displaced 1077 skilled expatriate mineworkers, while 1358 others left voluntarily and have been replaced by Zambians. On 31 December 1968 there remained 4862 expatriates out of a total labour force of 47 851. Fig *f* shows that most mine labour is Zambian, drawn particularly from rural, populous areas in Northern and Luapula Provinces. The middle Zambezi plain and Eastern Province, also populous, have provided fewer workers because traditionally these were recruiting areas, respectively, for Witwatersrand mines and Rhodesian farms and mines. Although such labour migration is now forbidden this recruitment pattern is only slowly fading.

In the twenties and thirties African employees usually worked short periods to earn money for taxes, bride price and consumer goods. This turnover proving inefficient, the companies offered career opportunities in permanent employment, with tied housing and services. Average length of service subsequently rose to 8·9 years in 1969.

The industry planned to spend over K150 million on capital expansion—including three new open pits plus expansion of the existing huge pit at Nchanga; an oxygen plant and smelter extensions at Rhokana; two ball mills at Bancroft; re-opening of Bwana Mkubwa mine in 1970; increased smelter capacity at Mufulira and Luanshya; a pilot project at Baluba mine (Luanshya); investigation of possible underground mining at Chambishi; and continued exploration. The government regarded this programme as inadequate and the 1970 partial take-over may result in more rapid growth, as well as the spread of copper mining to new areas, especially westwards.

Development of the industry (and of Zambia itself) depends on copper price maintenance. In 1968 the price rose to a record K1076·66 (£628·06) a ton following an American copper industry strike. After settlement it fell sharply to K758·42, rising again to K859 at year's end. This fluctuation illustrates the vulnerability of Zambia's key industry to external influences (which include stockpiling and substitution policies) and explains the government's efforts to diversify the economy. For the forseeable future, however, copper will dominate the Zambian economy.

D HYWEL DAVIES

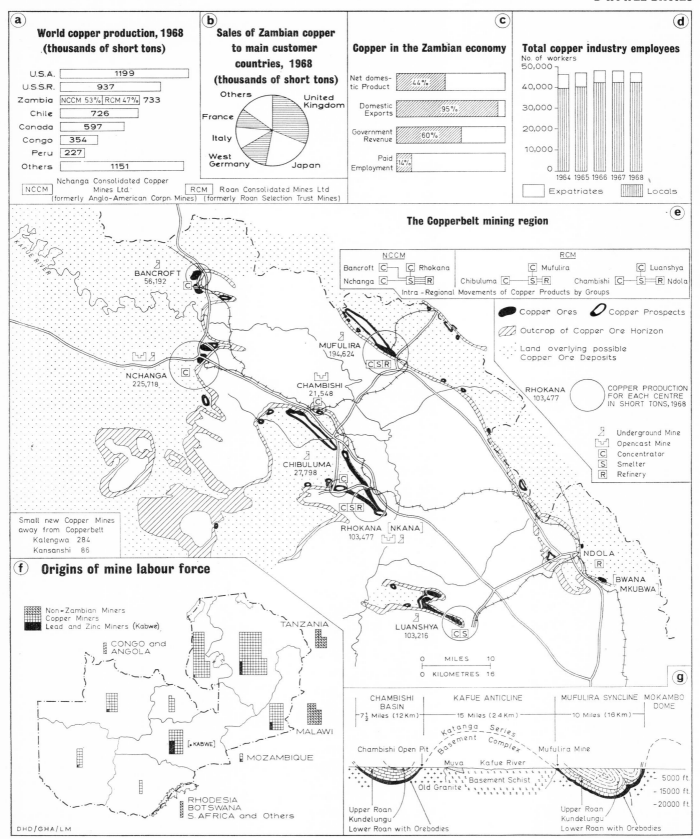

(a) World copper production, 1968 (thousands of short tons)

U.S.A.	1199
U.S.S.R.	937
Zambia	NCCM 53% RCM 47% 733
Chile	726
Canada	597
Congo	354
Peru	227
Others	1151

NCCM — Nchanga Consolidated Copper Mines Ltd. (formerly Anglo-American Corpn Mines)
RCM — Roan Consolidated Mines Ltd (formerly Roan Selection Trust Mines)

(b) Sales of Zambian copper to main customer countries, 1968 (thousands of short tons)

Others, United Kingdom, France, Italy, West Germany, Japan

(c) Copper in the Zambian economy

Net domestic Product	44%
Domestic Exports	95%
Government Revenue	60%
Paid Employment	14%

(d) Total copper industry employees

No. of workers — 50,000, 40,000, 30,000, 20,000, 10,000, 0 — 1964 1965 1966 1967 1968

Expatriates   Locals

(e) The Copperbelt mining region

NCCM
Bancroft C — C Rhokana
Nchanga C — S — R

RCM
C Mufulira   C Luanshya
Chibuluma C — S — R   Chambishi C — S — R Ndola

Intra-Regional Movements of Copper Products by Groups

Copper Ores   Copper Prospects
Outcrop of Copper Ore Horizon
Land overlying possible Copper Ore Deposits

COPPER PRODUCTION FOR EACH CENTRE IN SHORT TONS, 1968

Underground Mine
Opencast Mine
C Concentrator
S Smelter
R Refinery

BANCROFT 56,192
NCHANGA 225,718
MUFULIRA 194,624
CHAMBISHI 21,548
CHIBULUMA 27,798
RHOKANA 103,477
RHOKANA NKANA 103,477
LUANSHYA 103,216
NDOLA
BWANA MKUBWA

KAFUE RIVER

Small new Copper Mines away from Copperbelt
Kalengwa 284
Kansanshi 86

0 MILES 10
0 KILOMETRES 16

(f) Origins of mine labour force

Non-Zambian Miners
Copper Miners
Lead and Zinc Miners (Kabwe)

CONGO and ANGOLA
TANZANIA
MALAWI
KABWE
MOZAMBIQUE
RHODESIA BOTSWANA S. AFRICA and Others

DHD/GHA/LM

(g)

CHAMBISHI BASIN — 7½ Miles (12 Km)
KAFUE ANTICLINE — 15 Miles (24 Km)
MUFULIRA SYNCLINE — 10 Miles (16 Km)
MOKAMBO DOME

Katanga Series
Basement Complex
Chambishi Open Pit
Muva   Kafue River
Mufulira Mine
Old Granite
Basement Schist
Upper Roan Kundelungu Lower Roan with Orebodies
Upper Roan Kundelungu Lower Roan with Orebodies
5000 ft.
15000 ft.
20000 ft.

43 MANUFACTURING INDUSTRIES

Until independence the development of manufacturing in Zambia was seriously inhibited. Throughout the life of the Central African Federation (1953–63) Zambia and Malawi provided the principal markets for secondary industries which were being fostered in Southern Rhodesia, largely on the proceeds of the Zambian copper mines. A high wage level, created by the mining industry, was another obstacle to development in the north.

In 1964 Zambia stood in need of a large expansion in manufacturing on several counts, but principally to help redress the imbalance in an economy dominated by mining, to reduce imports and so plug the drain of foreign exchange, and to stimulate new centres of development away from the line of rail. In addition Zambia's position was exacerbated by pressing political considerations. As trade with her traditional suppliers in Southern Africa became less acceptable, especially after Rhodesia's Unilateral Declaration of Independence in 1965, the drive towards autarchy gathered added momentum. The expansion of the economy that took place in the early years of independence is the more remarkable when considered against the background of supply shortages and bottlenecks that resulted from hurried attempts to open new external routes and to adjust the pattern of trade. The index of industrial production rose from 124.2 in 1964 to 221.2 in 1967 (1961 = 100), and the value of gross domestic production from manufacturing trebled over the same period. These figures must be treated with caution, but they do indicate the strength of the upsurge experienced in the manufacturing sector of the economy.

Notwithstanding progress during recent years, all manufacturing sectors, with the exception of metals, are backward to some degree. The importance of metals is not obvious from fig. a because in the Zambian census of production copper smelting and refining are classified with mining. Food, beverages, tobacco, wood, rubber and non-metallic minerals have a longer history than most other sectors, and are consequently rather better developed. Chemicals, clothing, footwear, paper products, printing and publishing are very backward, and leather and textiles even more so. Industries in these sectors suffered most from the importing of highly competitive goods from the south.

It is difficult to obtain a detailed and accurate picture of manufacturing at the time of writing (late 1969) because of the dearth of statistics for the last three years. The new census of production will help to fill this gap, but is not expected to be completed until 1970. What is fairly certain is that growth has approximated fairly closely to the targets set for manufacturing in the First National Development Plan, 1966–1970. For much of this expansion government, through the medium of the Industrial Development Corporation of Zambia (INDECO), has been directly responsible.

INDECO (now subsidiary to MINDECO, p. 92) formed by the then Northern Rhodesia Government in 1960 to operate as a development bank, has vastly extended its activities since 1965. It works in conjunction with the private sector and also on its own account. Although its interests are not restricted to manufacturing this sector accounted for well over half its total investment in 1969.

The construction boom has been an important factor in the expansion of the metals sector. Here private concerns still dominate, although government participation is sure to increase. Metal Fabricators of Zambia, an INDECO Company (51 per cent rating shareholding) will shortly produce wire and cable from local copper in a new K2·5 million plant at Luanshya. Technical and financial aspects of proposals for an iron and steel industry are being studied. This project is likely to cost at least K30 million and is not expected to be justifiable solely on economic grounds. A vehicle assembly plant is being established at Livingstone by the Fiat Company.

Rising demand from the construction industry has also led to greater output from the non-metallic minerals sector. Production of cement at the Chilanga factory increased by over 80 per cent between 1966 and 1968, and with the opening of the new plant near Ndola in 1969, Zambia will shortly be independent of external suppliers. Unfortunately the production of sewer pipes and face bricks has been hindered by technical problems. The establishment of a glass industry was announced by President Kaunda in August 1969.

Zambezi Sawmills, acquired by INDECO (51 per cent) in 1968, is currently enlarging the sphere of its operations in Western Province.

The K16 million nitrogen chemicals plant at Kafue will make Zambia self-sufficient in fertilizer and produce ammonium nitrate for the explosives factory at Kafironda on the Copperbelt. Plans for an oil refinery have been approved, to be located near the oil pipeline terminal on the outskirts of Ndola.

A substantial boost will be given to the textile sector by the new mill at Kafue, and the grain bag factory at Kabwe.

Before 1964 most industrial and financial supporting services were located in Southern Rhodesia. Many of these facilities, including a Standards Bureau, a Patents and Trade Marks Registry and an additional Assize Office are now operating in Zambia. A Stock Exchange is presently being organized.

By partially relieving Zambia's heavy reliance on external suppliers, the progress made in manufacturing over the past five years has significantly strengthened national confidence. It has also established the basis for the development of a rounded industrial structure hopefully capable in certain sectors of producing for export.

Despite INDECO's laudable efforts in establishing rural industry—for example, grain milling, food processing—by far the largest portion of private and public investment has added to the concentration of activity on the Copperbelt and line of rail. Fig. b and c show this concentration by firms and by employees. The largest towns—Lusaka, Kitwe and Ndola—have experienced the most rapid industrial growth and even middle order centres such as Mufulira, Kabwe and Livingstone have experienced difficulty in attracting new concerns.

Such concentration of activity is economically justifiable, even inevitable, but it can only increase the disparities in wealth between the urban and rural areas giving added impetus to the urban drift, further complicating the lack of rural development.

J E GARDINER

MANUFACTURING INDUSTRIES

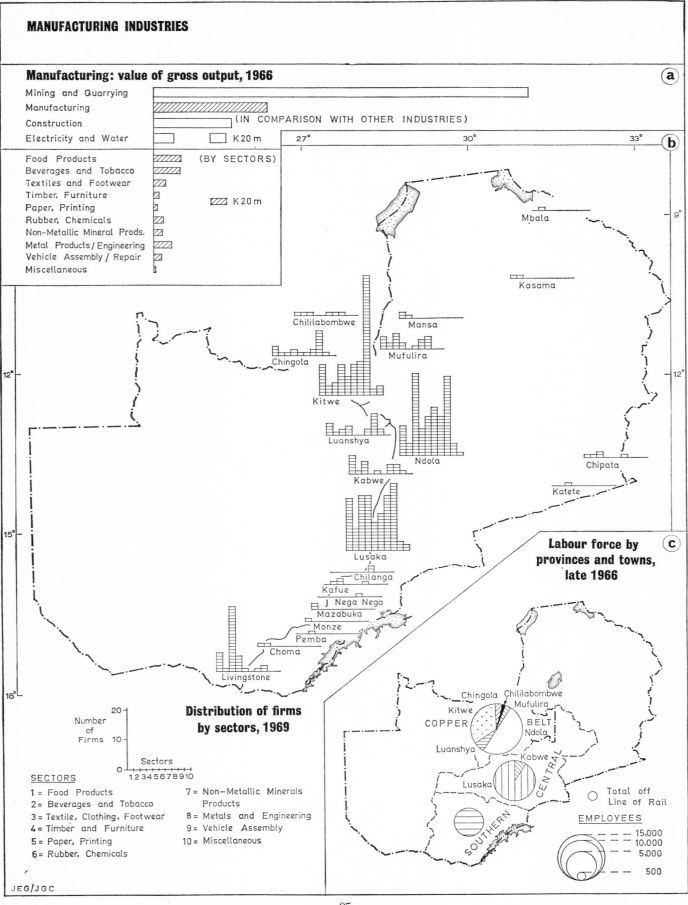

Manufacturing: value of gross output, 1966

Mining and Quarrying
Manufacturing
Construction (IN COMPARISON WITH OTHER INDUSTRIES)
Electricity and Water ☐ K 20 m

Food Products (BY SECTORS)
Beverages and Tobacco
Textiles and Footwear
Timber, Furniture
Paper, Printing ▨ K 20 m
Rubber, Chemicals
Non-Metallic Mineral Prods.
Metal Products / Engineering
Vehicle Assembly / Repair
Miscellaneous

a

b

27° 30° 33°

9°

Mbala

Kasama

Chililabombwe Mansa

Chingola Mufulira

Kitwe

12° 12°

Luanshya

Ndola Chipata

Kabwe Katete

15°

Labour force by provinces and towns, late 1966

c

Lusaka

Chilanga
Kafue
J Nega Nega
Mazabuka
Monze
Pemba
Choma

Livingstone

18°

Chingola Chililabombwe
Kitwe Mufulira
COPPER BELT
Ndola
Luanshya
Kabwe CENTRAL
Lusaka
SOUTHERN

Total off
Line of Rail

EMPLOYEES
15,000
10,000
5,000
500

Distribution of firms by sectors, 1969

Number
of 20
Firms 10
0
Sectors
1 2 3 4 5 6 7 8 9 10

SECTORS

1 = Food Products
2 = Beverages and Tobacco
3 = Textile, Clothing, Footwear
4 = Timber and Furniture
5 = Paper, Printing
6 = Rubber, Chemicals

7 = Non-Metallic Minerals Products
8 = Metals and Engineering
9 = Vehicle Assembly
10 = Miscellaneous

JEG/JGC

95

44 WATER SUPPLY

Water supply may be derived from either surface or underground sources: Zambia depends fairly equally on each source.

The extent and availability of *groundwater* depends on two main factors, the bedrock geology (p. 18) and the depth of weathering, which is related to the age of the plateau surfaces (p. 14). Limestones and dolomites of Katanga age are generally the best aquifers. Solution along joint planes in these rocks has often produced extensive fissures which hold and permit the extraction of water. Sandstones and conglomerates of the Karroo system are also useful sources but the more widespread shales of the same system yield little water. Yield from boreholes in the Kalahari sands has not yet been extensively investigated but a system of water extraction from shallow depths in unconsolidated rocks, known as 'well points', has proved successful. Schists, gneisses and granite are variable in character as aquifers, the more deeply and irregularly weathered providing the best water sources. Quartzites are usually poor aquifers, being massive and little decomposed, although those of low grade metamorphism may yield moderate flows. The basalts of the Livingstone area are poor aquifers except in vesicular zones at the top and base of the lava flows, and Luapula porphyry similarly has very low groundwater potential.

The greatest groundwater potential in the country is fortuitously located along the line of rail and has been exploited by several urban centres. Until early 1970 the entire water supply of Lusaka was derived from a number of large diameter boreholes in a brecciated zone in dolomite south-west of the city, with a maximum extraction rate of 12 million gallons (54·5 million litres) per day. Kabwe's domestic supply is also derived from boreholes in dolomite, augmented by water pumped from the mines. In Southern Province, Mazabuka also obtains its water from boreholes in dolomite.

On the Copperbelt, several towns, notably Chililabombwe, Mufulira, Chingola and Kalulushi, depend at least partly on groundwater pumped from the mines. Chililabombwe, with the largest pumping installations in the country, extracts up to 65 million gallons (295 million litres) a day from this source. Only a small fraction of this is treated, some raw water being used in mineral processing but most being discharged directly into the Kafue River.

Away from the line of rail, township water requirements are small and can often be met by less extensive groundwater supplies from decomposition basins in schists and gneisses. Petauke and Chipata in Eastern Province each depend on several such sources, but in 1971 surface sources will enlarge Chipata's water supply. In Northern and Luapula Provinces, underground sources are used in Mbala, Mpika and Kawambwa.

In addition to the townships, institutional supplies for rural schools, missions and agricultural stations are most commonly derived from boreholes, while commercial farms frequently use underground sources for household supplies.

Surface water has been the only source for many towns since they were established, but several others, which originally depended on sub-surface sources, have reached the limit of groundwater exploitation and must now either supplement or replace these by surface supplies.

The Kafue River system is the most extensively used, and several Copperbelt and Central Province towns extract water from it. Kitwe's domestic water supply, the largest in the country with a total installed capacity of 23 million gallons (104·5 million litres) of treated water a day, is taken entirely from the Kafue River. Like many Copperbelt towns (p. 82), Kitwe has two separate domestic water supply systems, one operated by the city council and the other by the mine at Nkana. The latter authority treats about three quarters of the total, supplying the mine townships and selling the surplus to the city council. Part of the water supply of Ndola, Luanshya, Chingola, Garneton, Kalulushi and Chililabombwe is derived from the Kafue or its tributaries, so that on some tributaries it has been necessary to build dams to maintain supplies throughout the dry season.

Water for Namwala and for Kafue Town is also taken from the Kafue River, while since 1970 Lusaka's supply is being augmented by Kafue water brought 37 miles (59 km.) by pipeline and raised approximately 1050 feet (323 m.) above the river level. In the first phase this contributed an additional 10 million gallons (45·5 million litres) a day, but as demand increases the full pipe capacity of 20 million gallons (90 million litres) will be pumped daily.

The Zambezi River supplies Livingstone and several smaller townships, while Lake Kariba provides water for adjacent settlements. In Northern and Luapula Provinces, the headwaters of the Chambeshi and Luapula Rivers supply several towns, while Lakes Tanganyika, Mweru and Bangweulu are all used by lakeside settlements.

Throughout Zambia, chlorination is standard treatment of domestic water supplies for cities and townships and most are also treated with filtration and sedimentation or both, exceptions being some borehole supplies which may have few impurities.

Since water supply for towns may be brought considerable distances or from deep boreholes, it is not a limiting factor in urban growth. However, with the rapid urban development over the past five years (Appendix 2) demand has often exceeded expectation and either water rationing is introduced or the installations are made to exceed their designed capacity, e.g. by pumping for a greater part of the day than intended.

A perennial water supply is a more fundamental factor in the distribution of rural settlement and most of Zambia's rural population depends on surface sources or groundwater sources that can be tapped by wells at shallow depth. Consequently, there is a low density of population in areas where such supplies are severely limited, such as the escarpment zones, the western plateau areas covered by Kalahari sands and on the floor of the rift valleys. Elsewhere, although settlement may not be restricted by water supply, the precise location of villages often depends on this factor, settlements being concentrated along perennial streams and dambos. The provision of deep wells and well points, largely through rural councils, has allowed expansion into areas not previously suitable for settlement.

D R ARCHER

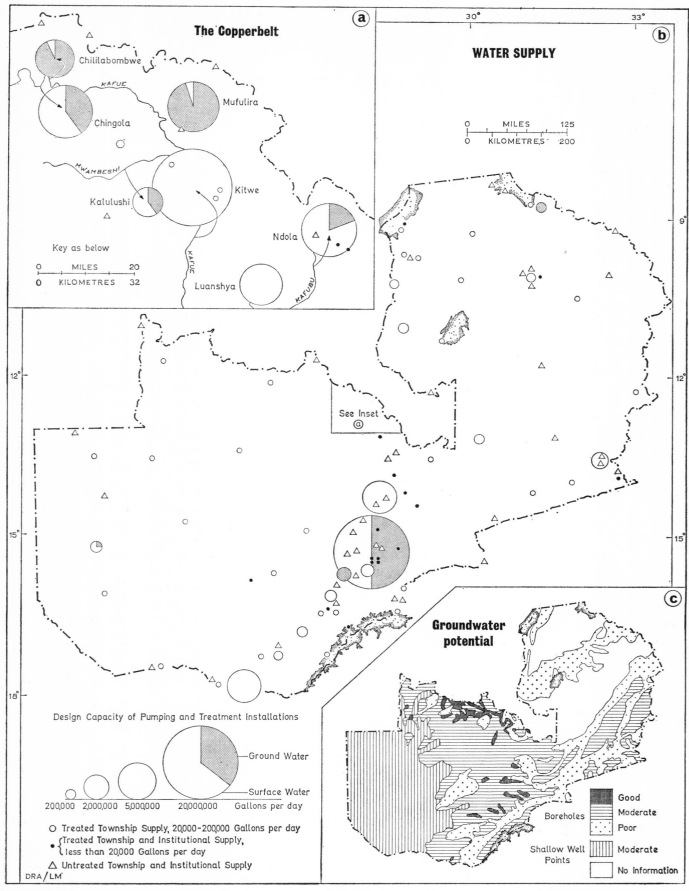

The Copperbelt

Chililabombwe

Mufulira

Chingola

KAFUE

MWAMBESHI

Kalulushi

Kitwe

Ndola

Key as below

| 0 | MILES | 20 |

| 0 | KILOMETRES | 32 |

Luanshya

KAFUE

KAFUBU

WATER SUPPLY

30° 33°

| 0 | MILES | 125 |

| 0 | KILOMETRES | 200 |

9°

12° 12°

See Inset
ⓐ

15° 15°

18°

Design Capacity of Pumping and Treatment Installations

Ground Water

Surface Water

200,000 2,000,000 5,000,000 20,000,000 Gallons per day

○ Treated Township Supply, 20,000-200,000 Gallons per day

● {Treated Township and Institutional Supply,
  {less than 20,000 Gallons per day

△ Untreated Township and Institutional Supply

DRA/LM

Groundwater potential

Boreholes

Good

Moderate

Poor

Shallow Well
Points

Moderate

No Information

ⓒ

45 ELECTRICITY PRODUCTION AND SUPPLY

The opening of large copper mines during the nineteen-thirties gave the first major stimulus to the production of electricity in Zambia by providing a large and guaranteed consumer demand. The requirements were met in the first place by each mine building and running its own thermo-electric plant fired by coal easily imported by rail from Wankie in Rhodesia. In 1938 Luanshya and Mufulira power stations were linked, and in 1948 Rhokana and Nchanga were added to give a power grid covering all the Copperbelt towns. The supply situation was further strengthened in 1956 by the linking of the Congo supply from the huge hydro-electric power station of Le Marinel in Katanga to the Copperbelt grid in Zambia. Amounts as large as 110 MW have been received from Katanga in emergency.

In the pre-Kariba years other Zambian towns had their own local supply undertakings, notably Lusaka's 12 MW thermal station. Livingstone's 8 MW hydro-electric supply, powered by a small channel taken off the Zambezi beside the Victoria Falls, utilized the drop of about 360 feet (111 m.) into the Silent Pool between the third and fourth gorges (p. 109 [c]).

During the Federal years, 1953–63, it became clear that piecemeal erection of minor power stations would be completely insufficient for the rapidly increasing demand for electricity both in Zambia and Rhodesia. Two alternative major schemes for hydro-electric power development were suggested, each estimated to cost some K200 million. These were the now world-famous schemes on the Zambezi River at the Kariba Gorge and the ecologically more complex plan for the Kafue Gorge.

For economic and political reasons the Kariba scheme was selected for immediate development. During the years 1955–9 builders and engineers struggled against river floods in the sultry heat of the low-lying valley. The first stage, consisting of six turbines in the south bank, giving a total installed capacity of 600 MW (later uprated to produce 705 MW), was inaugurated on 17 May 1960. Overhead pylons carrying transmission lines supply electricity at 330 KW northward to Lusaka, to Kabwe and the Copperbelt as well as southward to Salisbury and the towns of the Rhodesian Midlands.

Behind the 420 feet (129 m.) high dam, a lake of some 2 000 square miles (5180 sq. km.), 175 miles (282 kqm.) long and up to 20 miles (32 km.) wide, has built up in the deep Zambesi valley. In Zambia 34 000, and in Rhodesia 23 000 Valley Tonga tribesmen were resettled above the level of the new man-made lake. During the celebrated 'Operation Noah' thousands of wild animals were rescued from the rising lake waters and transferred to habitats above the flood.

Beside its use for power production the lake has great potential as a major fishery and for communications, recreation and tourism, although to date actual developments in all these fields have been disappointing.

The original plan called for a second power station of 600 MW to be installed in the north bank at Kariba, followed eventually by a third stage of 300 MW, to give a total of 1600 MW. Work on the second stage started at the end of 1970.

The Kafue scheme, currently (1969) under construction, will initially have a dam in the Kafue Gorge controlling a six mile long tunnelled head race to the turbine house. The installed capacity will be 600 MW provided by turbines of 150 MW each, but to obtain this full output all the year round it will be necessary to proceed with a second stage involving a storage dam at Iteshi-Teshi near the head of the Kafue Flats. This has now been deferred until Kariba north bank station has been constructed.

The original 8 MW station at Victoria Falls was recently supplemented by a new 60 MW underground power-house in the fourth gorge, while another 40 MW station is being built in the third gorge, to give a total installed capacity of 108 MW. A 330 KW high-tension line runs from the Falls to Kafue so that this power can be fed into the national grid.

The Central African Power Corporation was responsible for the generation and bulk supply of electricity from Kariba. In Lusaka and Central Electricity Corporation (CEC) transformed this power and distributed it to domestic and industrial consumers. The CEC area has now been taken over, together with the Victoria Falls supply, by a new body known as the Zambia Electricity Supply Corporation (ZESCO) which co-ordinates and controls all electricity generation, transmission and distribution throughout Zambia.

On the Copperbelt, where demand is rising at an average of 6 per cent per annum, the Copperbelt Power Company distributes power to the mines through its Copperbelt grid, which distributes over 85 per cent of all power used in Zambia, most of it from Kariba. The coal-fired power stations on the Copperbelt are all old and would, in normal circumstances, have been replaced before now. In addition their plant was built to burn Wankie coal rather than the Zambian coal of lower calorific value currently being consumed. When both Kafue and a new gas-turbine station at Luano (a second is proposed for Chililabombwe) are operating, it is anticipated that the mines' power-stations will be greatly reduced in size and load.

The Northern Electricity Supply Corporation is responsible for some lesser hydro-electric schemes and diesel-electric generators at district centres and other towns. Major users of electricity in minor town areas are often water supply undertakings, hospitals and secondary schools, in addition to domestic and minor industrial users.

The sparsely populated rural areas of Zambia are so far without electric power and there are only limited immediate plans to supply villages. When this time comes the rural areas of the Luapula valley and of the Eastern Province appear to be the most suitable areas. Here are dense rural populations with, in each case, a cash-oriented economy. Suggested new transmission lines into western and eastern Zambia, the former associated with the future expansion of mining activities, are shown on the figure.

N D McGLASHAN

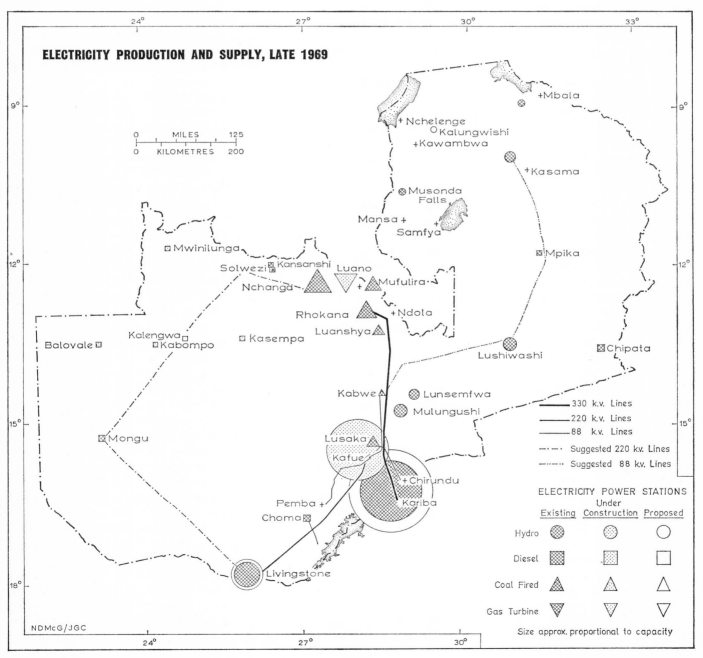

ELECTRICITY PRODUCTION AND SUPPLY, LATE 1969

MILES
0   125
0   200
KILOMETRES

+Mbala

+Nchelenge
○Kalungwishi
+Kawambwa

⊗Kasama

⊗Musonda
Falls

Mansa +
+
Samfya

Mwinilunga

⊠Mpika

Solwezi⊠ ⊠Kansanshi   Luano
Nchanga   Mufulira
+

Rhokana   +Ndola
Luanshya

Balovale ⊠   Kalengwa ⊠
⊠Kabompo   ⊡Kasempa

⊗Lushiwashi   ⊠Chipata

Kabwe △   ⊗ Lunsemfwa
⊗ Mulungushi

330 k.v. Lines
220 k.v. Lines
88 k.v. Lines

Suggested 220 k.v. Lines
Suggested 88 k.v. Lines

Mongu ⊠

Lusaka △
Kafue

+Chirundu
Kariba

Pemba +
Choma ⊠

Livingstone

ELECTRICITY POWER STATIONS
Under
Existing   Construction   Proposed

Hydro   ⊗   ⊙   ○
Diesel   ⊠   ▣   □
Coal Fired   △   △   △
Gas Turbine   ▽   ▽   ▽

Size approx. proportional to capacity

NDMcG/JGC

Medical facilities

Zambia's hospitals, rural health centres, urban clinics, leprosaria and air-strips are widely distributed throughout the country. A third of these have been built since independence in 1964. Previously, health facilities were provided mainly by missions in outlying regions and mines on the Copperbelt, with government hospitals mostly along the line of rail. The First National Development Plan (FNDP) radically changed this pattern, aiming to bring basic facilities within reach of all, even in the vast sparsely-populated areas. Priority was given to preventive and rural health centre services, to siting new projects in rural areas, and to focusing development on two main types of unit—many small, widely-distributed health centres and clinics, and smaller numbers of fully-equipped district hospitals. Mission and mines establishments, now quasi-government, have also been extended, whilst many industries run departmental clinics. All health services are obtainable free of charge.

Medical and preventive services are organized by the Department of Health and the Provincial Medical Officers. The basic unit, the rural health centre, provides all services except full-scale hospitalization, and aims to extend sub-clinics, preventive work and health education throughout its locality. Run by a Medical Assistant, it is supervised by the Provincial Medical Officer, and, in some cases, by a doctor from a nearby hospital; most health centres have some in-patient beds. Many of Zambia's health hazards—malnutrition, tuberculosis, parasitic infestations, leprosy—respond adequately to out-patient treatment. Recently, 'under-five' clinics have been developed for maternal and child health education, vaccinations and immunizations, and nutrition teaching. In 1969, 276 government and 75 mission health centres provided 3660 in-patient beds and 420 babies' cots; over half these centres organized under-five clinics.

Urban and departmental clinics operate, in towns, similarly to rural centres, with perhaps more doctor-supervision and slightly more emphasis on preventive work. There were sixty-three government and twenty-eight mines' urban clinics in 1969, and they are increasing rapidly; many operate sub-clinics and under-five clinics elsewhere in their towns.

The Flying Doctor Service, a government body, administers twelve airstrip clinics in remote areas; each has a medical orderly in radio contact with Ndola headquarters and is visited two or three times weekly by a doctor and a qualified nurse. Somewhat different is Mission Medic-Air, whose volunteer pilots and doctors fly every Sunday to mission health centres to treat in-patients; at present it serves six Copperbelt mission centres.

The district hospital provides fully-qualified doctor services, in-patient wards, maternity beds; operating theatre, X-ray and laboratory facilities and an out-patient department. A centre of referral for health centres and clinics, it is run by one or more Medical Officers and registered nurses, with medical assistants and enrolled nurses (often trained here before going to rural health centres. A few district hospitals have visiting specialists and dentists, but the latter (like radiographers and laboratory technicians) are in very short supply. There are now 56 district hospitals—20 government, 26 mission and 10 mines' hospitals—with 6600 beds and 620 cots; a few have fee-paying wards. The mines hospitals' facilities are comparable with those in central and general hospitals.

Zambia retained 22 leprosaria in 1969, with 2000 long-stay patients living in huts under simple medical care. Leprosaria will continue to close down in the future, due mainly to the new policy of treating non-infectious leprosy in out-patient and rural health centres. In Eastern Province a mobile intensive care unit is bringing excellent results.

At the highest level are central, general and specialist hospitals, with many beds and consultant staffs to whom patients are referred from all Zambia. There are 3 central, 2 general and 3 specialist hospitals in Lusaka, Livingstone, Kabwe, Kitwe and Ndola. Staffed by 45 specialists and 75 doctors, they have 2950 beds and 250 cots. The largest, in Lusaka, is being greatly expanded to accommodate the University Teaching Hospital, where some wards are already open.

Rapid growth in hospitals, treatment centres and in-patient beds is shown in fig. c. Excluding leprosaria, there are now 518 treatment centres with some 14 500 beds and cots. For an estimated population of 4 054 000, this averages 1 treatment-centre per 7830 persons and 1 in-patient bed per 280 persons—1.28 centres per 10 000 population and 3.58 beds per 1000, of which 2.57 are hospital beds. These averages differ somewhat between provinces (fig. a). In Central, Copperbelt and Southern Provinces the bed-ratios are better than average, whereas in the out-lying provinces there are relatively more treatment-centres but (except in Northwestern Province) lower bed-ratios. Northwestern Province, with only 4.7 persons per sq. mile, has more treatment-centres and better bed-ratios than any other province; yet it still has localities (as do most other provinces) where the nearest centre is more than 25 miles' walk distant. So, in many localities, the people's participation in medical services and disease-prevention is very limited, and sickness is dealt with mainly by traditional healers.

Medical facilities for employees and dependants are provided by some private industries, usually at a clinic at the work-place; occasionally a special hospital has been built (e.g. Kafue Gorge dam site). Private doctors and dentists practise in Lusaka, on the Copperbelt and in line of rail towns. Altogether there are some 340 doctors in Zambia, a ratio—comparatively favourable for Africa—of one doctor per 11,900 persons.

Medical training is increasingly provided in Zambia, and grants are also given for overseas training. The University of Zambia Medical School which opened in 1968 (pre-medical courses in 1966), expected its first output of doctors in 1973. Nurses are trained at two levels: a full course at two schools of nursing leads to State Registration, and a two-year course to become a Zambia Enrolled Nurse is offered. Men train for three years to become Medical Assistants, with emphasis on diagnosis, treatment and preventive work rather than ward nursing; specialized training (mental health, tuberculosis, leprosy) can be taken subsequently. Technicians' training is beginning at the

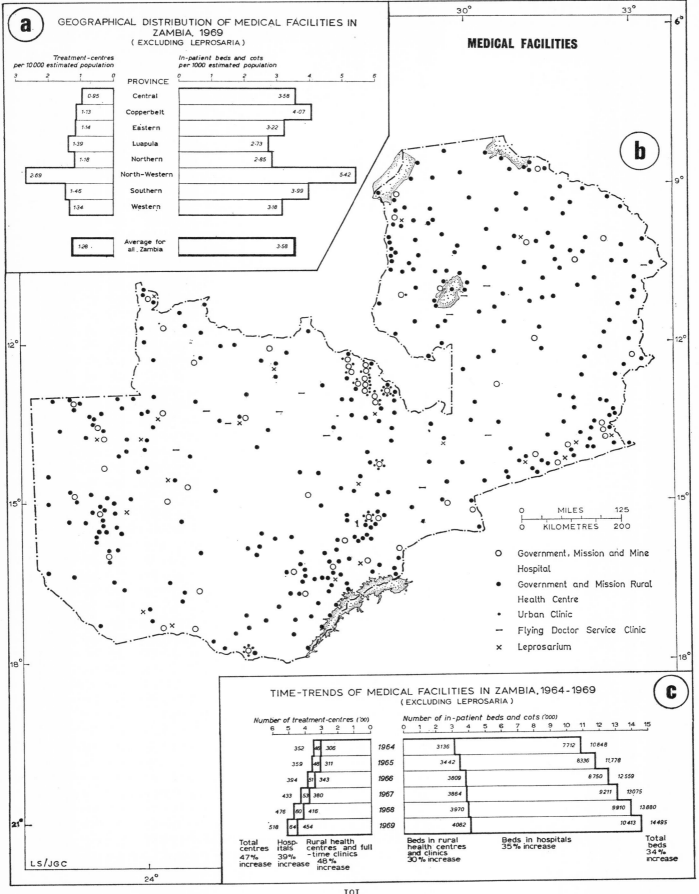

a GEOGRAPHICAL DISTRIBUTION OF MEDICAL FACILITIES IN ZAMBIA, 1969
(EXCLUDING LEPROSARIA)

Treatment-centres per 10 000 estimated population

In-patient beds and cots per 1000 estimated population

	Treatment-centres	PROVINCE	In-patient beds and cots
	0.95	Central	3.58
	1.13	Copperbelt	4.07
	1.14	Eastern	3.22
	1.39	Luapula	2.73
	1.18	Northern	2.85
	2.69	North-Western	5.42
	1.46	Southern	3.99
	1.34	Western	3.18
	1.28	Average for all Zambia	3.58

b MEDICAL FACILITIES

MILES 125
KILOMETRES 200

○ Government, Mission and Mine Hospital

● Government and Mission Rural Health Centre

· Urban Clinic

— Flying Doctor Service Clinic

× Leprosarium

c TIME-TRENDS OF MEDICAL FACILITIES IN ZAMBIA, 1964-1969
(EXCLUDING LEPROSARIA)

Number of treatment-centres ('00)

Number of in-patient beds and cots ('000)

Year	Rural health centres and full-time clinics	Hospitals	Total centres	Beds in rural health centres and clinics	Beds in hospitals	Total beds
1964	306	46	352	3136	7712	10 848
1965	311	48	359	3442	8336	11 778
1966	343	51	394	3809	8750	12 559
1967	380	53	433	3864	9211	13 075
1968	416	60	476	3970	9910	13 880
1969	454	64	518	4082	10 413	14 495

Total centres 47% increase

Hospitals 39% increase

Rural health centres and full-time clinics 48% increase

Beds in rural health centres and clinics 30% increase

Beds in hospitals 35% increase

Total beds 34% increase

LS/JGC

new College of Technology, but the shortage of qualified technical staff will continue for some years.

Zambia's medical facilities compare well with other African countries, although inferior to those in Europe, unevenly distributed geographically, and often lacking in quality. Some health centres are still without a Medical Assistant; some hospitals have insufficient doctors or nurses; dental and other services suffer from severe shortages of technicians; almost all medically qualified staff are expatriates; and training programmes have not yet reached FNDP targets. Demands on services increase steadily, and improvements in standards and skills are needed. However, expansion since 1964 has been phenomenal—47 per cent more treatment centres, 39 per cent more hospitals, and 34 per cent more in-patient beds. Government expenditure on health approaches 7 per cent of the annual budget, and expansion of services continues, with increasing emphasis on improved quality. This will depend largely on training programmes, on extensive hygiene and nutrition education, and on increased participation in disease-prevention.

Health and the prevention of disease

Lying mainly at high altitudes, Zambia has a pleasant sub-tropical climate. Most temperate and some tropical diseases are common, but other major tropical diseases—notably yellow fever and onchocerciasis—do not occur. Smallpox has recently been eradicated.

The tropical diseases most prevalent are malaria, bilharzia, and other parasitic infestations including hookworm, and leprosy. These endemic diseases are fairly evenly distributed throughout the country, with a few exceptions. Preventive measures are increasingly practised, so far without producing a significant decline, except in malaria in Lusaka and Copperbelt towns where regular insecticidal spraying of houses has brought great success.

By far the most important tropical disease is malaria, causing nearly 20 000 in-patient admissions a year (about 4·8 per 1000 population), over 300 deaths (mostly children) in hospitals alone, and great disability, sickness and mortality outside hospitals. Although total prevalence is unknown, it is believed that over 25 per cent of children have malaria parasites present which—though not causing acute malarial illness—with malnutrition cause debility and long-term lowered function. Moreover, when these children contract measles or some gastro-intestinal or respiratory infections, an unnecessarily high proportion die. Wider spraying campaigns are planned for the future, and research into other control measures continues.

Bilharzia admissions to hospital average about 2100 a year (0·5 per 1000) and only about 10 hospital deaths. However, except where local absence of surface water or the snail hosts make it rare, it is widely prevalent, especially among boys, and causes long-term disability if untreated. Bilharzia and other parasitic infestations are now widely treated by modern drugs; eradica-

tion of snail hosts is also being attempted, notably in Lake Kariba, so far with little success.

Long-stay leprosaria inmates numbered nearly 2000 in 1969 and almost 1000 hospital admissions for short-term treatment were made; some 15 000 out-patients were under treatment at health centres and clinics. These known cases represent a prevalence of 4·43 per 1000 population, but there is probably a similar number of unknown cases. Preventive measures are directed mainly to early treatment to convert infectious into non-infectious cases; and in Eastern Province the mobile 'Lepra' clinics concentrate also on early case-finding and contacts of known cases. Leprosaria in-patients have decreased steadily since 1966.

Other tropical diseases no longer represent a serious threat. Trypanosomiasis (sleeping sickness) occurs in some game reserves and other sparsely-populated areas (p. 56); tsetse-fly control is carried out on all vehicles leaving such areas. Few human cases occur nowadays, only seventy-five cases being reported in 1969; but it is economically important in rendering areas unsuitable for cattle-raising, e.g. Luapula Province.

Strict preventive measures have also made rabies rare. Regulations enforce inoculation of all dogs, and whenever rabies is suspected, human contacts are vaccinated; any case must immediately be notified to the authorities by telegram. In 1969 only twelve cases were reported.

The anti-smallpox campaign has been so successful that smallpox has not occurred in Zambia since 1968. Vaccination on a tremendous scale is practised—babies and pre-school children at health centres, children at school, adults in the villages—totalling about 1 400 000 each year; the mobile teams also do BCG (tuberculosis) vaccination. In November 1969 a sample survey in all provinces showed that 75 to 80 per cent of the population now have protection—but preventive measures will continue while smallpox occurs elsewhere in Africa.

The 'temperate' diseases—measles, whooping-cough, chicken-pox, poliomyelitis, tuberculosis, gastro-intestinal infections, respiratory disorders, malnutrition, anaemia, accidents and injuries, etc.—are prevalent in Zambia, though total incidence rates are known only for notifiable diseases. Hospital admissions and deaths indicate the relative importance of the different disease-groups: the largest is the respiratory group (influenza, bronchitis, respiratory tract infections, pneumonia, etc.) causing about 20 000 admissions and over 1300 hospital deaths a year. Accidents and injuries cause over 19 000 admissions annually; motor accident rates in Lusaka and the Copperbelt are among the world's highest. Next in magnitude are gastro-enteric disorders, causing nearly 15 000 admissions and over 900 hospital deaths (many of babies and children) and measles, with 12 000 admissions and nearly 1000 hospital deaths (again, mainly of babies and children). Preventive measures are not easy; measles vaccination is practised in special local and national campaigns and in hospitals and clinics where refrigeration is available for the vaccine. In 1970 paraffin refrigerators were being installed in all rural health centres, and an extension of measles vaccination is planned. Vaccination and immunization against other child-

(*Concluded in Appendix 3, p. 127.*)

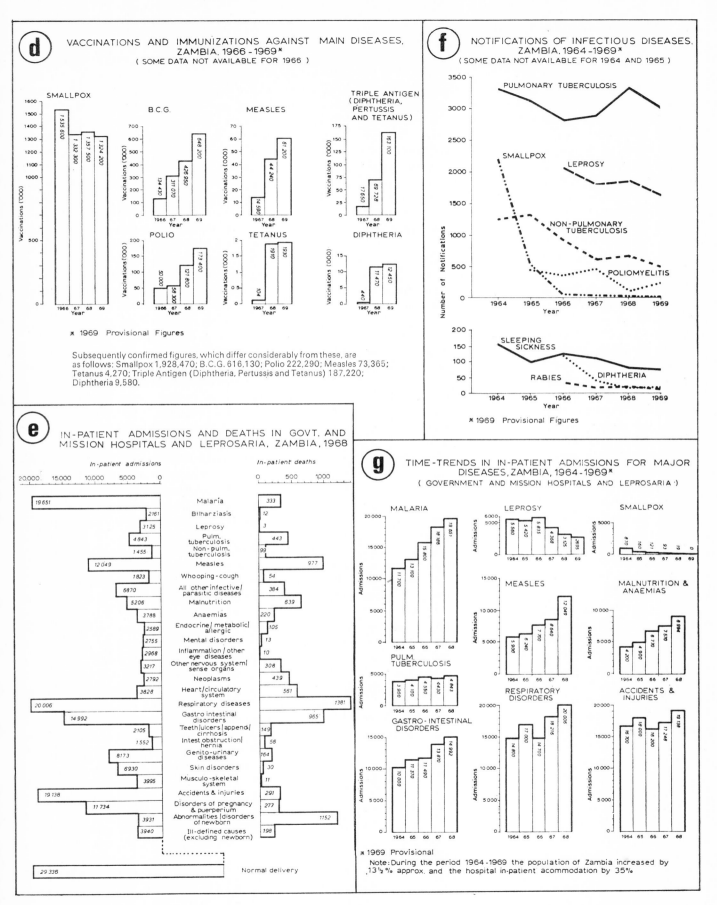

d VACCINATIONS AND IMMUNIZATIONS AGAINST MAIN DISEASES,
ZAMBIA, 1966-1969*
(SOME DATA NOT AVAILABLE FOR 1966)

SMALLPOX

B.C.G.

MEASLES

TRIPLE ANTIGEN
(DIPHTHERIA,
PERTUSSIS
AND TETANUS)

POLIO

TETANUS

DIPHTHERIA

* 1969 Provisional Figures

Subsequently confirmed figures, which differ considerably from these, are
as follows: Smallpox 1,928,470; B.C.G. 616,130; Polio 222,290; Measles 73,365;
Tetanus 4,270; Triple Antigen (Diphtheria, Pertussis and Tetanus) 187,220;
Diphtheria 9,580.

f NOTIFICATIONS OF INFECTIOUS DISEASES,
ZAMBIA, 1964-1969*
(SOME DATA NOT AVAILABLE FOR 1964 AND 1965)

PULMONARY TUBERCULOSIS

SMALLPOX

LEPROSY

NON-PULMONARY
TUBERCULOSIS

POLIOMYELITIS

SLEEPING
SICKNESS

RABIES   DIPHTHERIA

* 1969 Provisional Figures

e IN-PATIENT ADMISSIONS AND DEATHS IN GOVT. AND
MISSION HOSPITALS AND LEPROSARIA, ZAMBIA, 1968

In-patient admissions

In-patient deaths

In-patient admissions	Disease	In-patient deaths
19 651	Malaria	333
2161	Bilharziasis	12
3125	Leprosy	3
4843	Pulm. tuberculosis	443
1455	Non-pulm. tuberculosis	99
12 049	Measles	977
1823	Whooping-cough	54
6870	All other infective/parasitic diseases	384
5206	Malnutrition	639
3788	Anaemias	220
2589	Endocrine/metabolic/allergic	105
2755	Mental disorders	13
2968	Inflammation/other eye diseases	10
3217	Other nervous system/sense organs	308
2792	Neoplasms	439
3828	Heart/circulatory system	561
20 006	Respiratory diseases	1381
14 992	Gastro intestinal disorders	965
2105	Teeth/ulcers/append/cirrhosis	149
1552	Intest.obstruction/hernia	56
8173	Genito-urinary diseases	164
6930	Skin disorders	30
3995	Musculo-skeletal system	11
19 138	Accidents & injuries	291
11 734	Disorders of pregnancy & puerperium	277
3931	Abnormalities/disorders of newborn	1152
3940	Ill-defined causes (excluding newborn)	198
29 336	Normal delivery	

g TIME-TRENDS IN IN-PATIENT ADMISSIONS FOR MAJOR
DISEASES, ZAMBIA, 1964-1969*
(GOVERNMENT AND MISSION HOSPITALS AND LEPROSARIA)

MALARIA

LEPROSY

SMALLPOX

MEASLES

MALNUTRITION &
ANAEMIAS

PULM.
TUBERCULOSIS

RESPIRATORY
DISORDERS

ACCIDENTS &
INJURIES

GASTRO-INTESTINAL
DISORDERS

* 1969 Provisional

Note: During the period 1964-1969 the population of Zambia increased by
13½% approx. and the hospital in-patient accommodation by 35%

103

With the coming of independence, Zambia planned massive and far-reaching educational expansion, with three major objectives in view. Equal opportunities for education were to be provided as far as possible for all citizens irrespective of race, tribe, religion or means, in contrast to racial (and, by implication, class) segregation prevailing until 1964. Secondly, the colonial legacy of grossly inadequate trained manpower was to be overcome. (In 1964 Zambia had only just over 1200 Cambridge School Certificate holders and barely 100 university graduates, the latter all trained abroad.) Thirdly, mass education was to serve as a catalyst of change from tribalism to nationhood.

In outline, the educational aims of the First National Development Plan (1966–70) were: to expand primary schools (especially in rural areas) so that by 1970 every child aged seven years could attend Grade I (this target was reached nationally in 1968, but the practice of accepting children at ages five to seven years has created continuing shortages of places in urban primary schools); to provide seven years of primary education for all urban area children and 75 per cent of rural area children, the remaining rural children to get at least four years education; to expand secondary education to allow one-third of all primary school leavers to enter secondary school; generally to train and retrain more teachers, provide many more technical, vocational and adult educational facilities, and open a national university.

Fig *a* and the following table show the growth in school enrolment since 1964.

	1964	1965	1966	1967	1968	1969
Primary	378 639	410 150	473 432	539 353	608 893	645 679
Secondary	13 871	17 187	24 005	34 139	42 388	48 136

The achievement of greatly increased secondary enrolment between 1966 and 1968 can be attributed mainly to two factors. Firstly, there was a double output from the primary schools in 1965 occasioned by the shortening of the primary stage from eight to seven years. Secondly, from 1965 onward, the government's Transitional Development Plan in education emphasized self-help by local people in the building of classrooms. In consequence greatly increased enrolment proved possible in primary schools, and more secondary schools followed to cope with the resulting increased demand.

The distribution of primary schools (not mapped for lack of sufficiently precise data) broadly reflects population distribution (p. 45). The greatest concentrations of pupils are in urban centres, represented by the three line of rail provinces—Copperbelt, Central and Southern. The 1963 Census had revealed an already marked rural-urban migration, forcing government to build many urban primary schools. Preliminary results of the 1969 Census indicate that urban drift continues unabated and faster than urban classrooms can be built. Consequently, some rural schools are not filling their quotas of Grade I pupils, while many urban schools have to turn children away.

Figs. *b* and *c* indicate the proportions of secondary to primary enrolments by provinces, while fig. *d* shows actual locations of secondary schools in 1969. Their distribution and enrolment patterns are roughly similar to those for primary schools, but reflect a deliberate policy of siting many new secondary schools at district headquarters in rural areas—a facet of a wider attempt to check urban migration. Most secondary schools are residential. By the end of the 1965–69 quinquennium all but two districts in Zambia had a secondary school, although urban areas continued to have the lion's share. Numbers of secondary schools had increased from 46 in 1964 to 113 in 1969, with enrolments similarly rising from 13 871 to 48 157. Placement is on a national, not a provincial basis and there is considerable mobility among secondary school pupils, most of whom are boarders. The distribution plots in figs. *c* and *d* therefore do not accurately reflect distribution of opportunity for secondary education.

An encouraging trend is the improving ratio of girls to boys in all schools. At primary level, where more girls are completing all grades, the ratio is now about two to three (fig. *b*), while at secondary level it is roughly one to two (fig. *c*). Even at the university, one woman student is enrolled for each seven men, a ratio unmatched in much of Africa.

Fig. *e* shows student numbers in centres of higher and further education: these include colleges of further education and technical training institutions (which, with vocational training schools in urban areas are now the responsibility of the Commission for Technical Education), teacher training colleges and the University of Zambia. The figure shows inevitable concentration of such institutions in urban centres along the developed line of rail. The wholly independent University of Zambia in Lusaka opened in 1966; by 1969 it had an enrolment of almost 1000 full-time students, plus hundreds of part-time students, making it perhaps the fastest-growing university in Africa. Lusaka also has the College of Further Education and the Natural Resources Development College. The three line of rail provinces each has both teacher training and technical colleges. Of the outlying provinces, Northwestern and Luapula have no such institutions, while the remaining three have teachers' colleges only. To increase the national output of junior secondary teachers, the Ministry of Education has set up a teachers' college at Kabwe and plans another on the Copperbelt in 1971. Under the second development plan beginning probably in 1972, new teachers' colleges are earmarked for Luapula and Northwestern provinces, while the university is to expand to its planned peak of around 5000 full-time students by 1980.

Thus, in some five years of independence, Zambia has virtually achieved the broad quantitative aims of its first development plan: corresponding major changes in thinking are also taking place in curriculum planning and other qualitative aspects of education that cannot be touched upon here. Expansion is, indeed, impressive, but, in view of the urgent national requirements for trained manpower and an insatiable demand for education from the populace at large, it is apparent that problems of supply will abound for the forseeable future.

M M KAUNDA

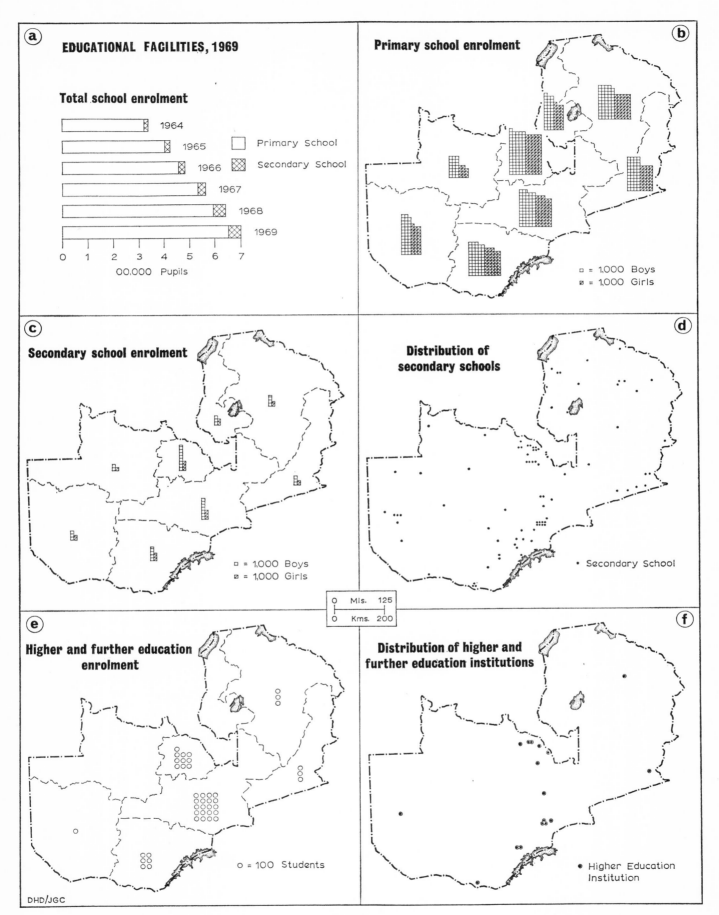

a

EDUCATIONAL FACILITIES, 1969

Total school enrolment

1964
1965
1966
1967
1968
1969

☐ Primary School
▨ Secondary School

0 1 2 3 4 5 6 7
00,000 Pupils

b

Primary school enrolment

□ = 1,000 Boys
▨ = 1,000 Girls

c

Secondary school enrolment

□ = 1,000 Boys
▨ = 1,000 Girls

d

Distribution of secondary schools

· Secondary School

0 Mls. 125
0 Kms. 200

e

Higher and further education enrolment

○ = 100 Students

f

Distribution of higher and further education institutions

● Higher Education Institution

DHD/JGC

105

49 SOME SERVICES

Road passenger transport

Improvement of the road transport system is vital to national economic development, but among a population where private car ownership is still a rare privilege, the rapidly growing demand can only be met by more public transport facilities.

The largest bus operator is the United Bus Company of Zambia (UBZ), formerly Central African Road Services, in which government, through the Industrial Development Corporation (INDECO), has a controlling interest. In 1968 UBZ operated a fleet of 222 buses, of which 153 were on scheduled services at a given time. Of the total fleet, 73 vehicles worked local routes in the principal towns of the Copperbelt and line of rail. At the time of the 1968 Report on Passenger Road Transport in Zambia a further 76 buses were owned by individuals and various companies.

The pattern of bus services described by fig. *a* bears a close relationship to inequalities in regional development and to distribution of population—factors dealt with in other parts of the book. Traffic along the line of rail, particularly between Lusaka and Ndola, is less than might be expected because of the considerably cheaper fares offered by Zambia Railways.

Of 280 taxis licensed in March 1968, 202 operated on the Copperbelt and 72 in Lusaka. Most of them were the station wagon type authorized to carry seven persons.

With one bus to every 13 000 and one taxi to every 14 000 people in Zambia, the road passenger transport system as a whole is as overloaded as individual buses to be seen on the streets of of the major cities. However, UBZ expected delivery of new and bigger buses to bring its fleet up to 330 by the end of 1969.

Postal services

Fig. *b* shows the distribution of post offices in 1968, all of which handle mail for personal collection from post boxes. At many rural offices local chiefs arrange for the collection of incoming mail for distribution in their villages. Road, air and particularly rail routes are used for carrying mail. The General Post Office also operates a widespread network of telephone communications, including land lines with automatic standard trunk dialling (STD) exchanges at all major centres on the Copperbelt and line of rail. These still linked up with Salisbury, Bulawayo and Victoria Falls in Rhodesia in 1969. Outlying areas are linked by radio telephone. Since independence a micro-wave link has been built to channel telephone conversations and television programmes between Lusaka and the Copperbelt.

Petrol stations

Fig. *c* shows the 1968 distribution of 188 petrol stations in the country. Of 132 along the entire line of rail, 55 were on the Copperbelt and 32 in Lusaka. In outlying areas east of the Copperbelt there were 38, mostly along the Greath North and Great East Roads; but the entire western rural areas had only 18 petrol stations. By 1969 the total number of stations had risen to 208.

The largest company in Zambia in 1969 was Shell/BP with 117 stations, followed by Mobil with 46, Caltex with 26 and Total with 17. Esso and Agip were newcomers with one station each. Near the end of 1969 the government announced its intention of acquiring 51 per cent share control of Shell/BP, but the smaller firms remain wholly private. In addition to these company stations, many farms and schools in rural areas have their own tanks, which are filled by the companies.

Petrol stations have so far been located according to demand, with no established policy of locating at planned distances along major arteries. Thus long stretches of major trunk roads, such as the Mumbwa-Mankoya stretch on the Lusaka-Mongu road, still remain without facilities.

Zambia lacks oil resources of her own and all requirements are imported in a refined state, but a refinery is to be built at Ndola. Formerly, petroleum products were imported from Rhodesia. During the emergency following that country's seizure of independence, petrol was rationed in Zambia while alternative routes were being developed. For a time petrol moved (at times hazardously) in drums, later in road tankers, down the then unsurfaced and seasonally difficult Great North Road (the 'Hell Run') and the Great East Road, and at one stage was even flown in from Dar es Salaam. This situation stimulated early completition of the 1000-mile (1609 km.) 8-inch (20·3 cm.) pipeline from the Dar es Salaam refinery: when this opened in 1968 supplies reverted to normal and rationing quickly ceased. The pipeline carries diesel and premium and regular grade petroleum, but for technical reasons aviation spirit and lubricants are still brought in by road. The Zambian terminal, four miles (about 6·5 km.) south of Ndola, has storage tanks for all companies, from which fuel is taken to depots in Ndola, Lusaka, Choma and Livingstone.

There has been a greatly increased consumption of petroleum products since independence, due to more widespread prosperity but also to an increased government vehicle fleet, a process of changeover of Zambia Railways to diesel locomotives and to consumption by major development projects. Most of this increased consumption is still along the line of rail.

Banks

Banking facilities are provided by five commercial banks: in descending order of size of operations in Zambia these are Barclays, Standard, National and Grindleys, Commercial Bank of Zambia, and National Commercial Bank of Zambia, the latter opening only in 1969. The Bank of Zambia, established in August 1964, issues the national currency and controls foreign exchange. In addition to commercial banks, the post office operates an increasingly popular savings bank.

Commercial banks handle most of the credit facilities in urban areas but have limited activity in the rural areas. Loans for smaller businessmen and small farmers come largely from the Credit Organization of Zambia. In addition there are seven co-operative credit unions (with which the churches are associated) and several building societies, while a number of firms offer hire purchase facilities. In general the 'banking habit' is growing steadily in the urban centres of Zambia.

J JENKINSON

SOME SERVICES, 1968

a Bus services (excluding local urban services)

KEY
□ Number of Buses operating entirely within the Province
○ Number of Buses operating on Inter-Provincial routes
--- Provincial Boundaries

b Post offices

Kasama
Mansa
Solwezi
Kitwe • Ndola
Kabwe
Mongu
Lusaka
Livingstone

All maps are 1969 data
0   Mls.   125
0   Kms.   200

c Petrol filling-stations

Kasama
Mansa
Solwezi
Kitwe • Ndola
Chipata
Kabwe
Mongu
Lusaka
Livingstone

↗ Tazama products Pipeline to Dar es salaam

d Banks

Kasama
Mansa
Solwezi
Kitwe • Ndola
Chipata
Kabwe
Mongu
Lusaka
Livingstone

JJ/JGC

50 TOURISM

Like most developing countries Zambia is expanding her small tourist industry as a potentially valuable source of foreign exchange. (Developed facilities will also meet a growing local demand for weekend and vacation recreational outlets.) The unspoiled Zambian scenery, dominated by plateau country, is not generally spectacular, but there are local areas with fine views and one or two world-famous beauty spots. The country is rich in wild life, including superb bird life in the rather inaccessible floodplains and swamps. Zambia offers a delightful dry season climate (October excepted) with warm, sunny days and cool nights, particularly during April, May, August and September. The Zambian National Tourist Board (ZNTB) is the agency for all aspects of tourism.

Keys to tour routes, national monuments and other places of interest (figs. *b, c, d*), are in Appendix 4, p. 128.

The majestic Victoria Falls (fig. *c*), (renamed by David Livingstone but known locally by its charming Lozi name Mosi-oa-Tunya ('The Smoke that Thunders')) are probably the only Zambian scenic attraction of world renown, one which it shares with Rhodesia. A new footbridge built over the Knife Edge in 1969 greatly improves viewing from the Zambian side, but a comprehensive visit requires tourists to cross into Rhodesia, with the inconvenience of customs and immigration checks in each direction.

The Livingstone Museum in the town mounts scholarly displays of central African history and pre-history, while local dancers perform regularly at the Open Air Museum. Other sights near Livingstone include the gorges below the Falls and a small game park (extended in 1969). Some routes of ZNTB tours by bus and motor launch are shown.

Other major attractions are Zambia's game parks, rich in big game, with a total area equal to Switzerland. Kafue National Park alone covers 8650 square miles (22 403 sq. km.) and is the largest in Africa. Lodges accommodate visitors on game viewing or photographic safaris, and the Luangwa Park offers the additional unique attraction of game-watching on foot accompanied by an armed ranger, selected as being a crack shot! Game park visitors increased from 2300 in 1960 to 5615 in 1968, but most were Zambian residents. The best season for game viewing is July to September when grass is usually short, tracks are firm, and animals are congregated around water sources. Parks generally close from about October to March during the main rains.

The Kasaba Bay area on bilharzia-free Lake Tanganyika offers game fishing, and water sports and the Sumbu Game Reserve. Near Mbala are the Kalambo Falls, Africa's second highest, with a sheer drop of 726 feet (223 m.), twice the height of Victoria Falls. Above the Falls is a pre-historic site, not yet open to the public. At the other end of Zambia, the 170-mile (273 km.) long man-made Lake Kariba also has some small fishing and boating centres with chalet accommodation.

The main entry port and capital, Lusaka, has few tourist attractions, but several ZNTB tours start and finish there (fig. *b*). The striking new House of Assembly and the developing University of Zambia campus are attractions. From the Copperbelt cities, tours of the mines can be arranged.

Hunting safaris started in 1950 and now operate in the Luangwa valley and the Sichifula area. Two commercial companies are involved in this sector of the tourist industry, which earned K130 000 for Zambia in 1968, one quarter in fees directly to government. These earnings are a tenth of those earned similarly in Kenya, where tourism is far older and more developed.

In the past Zambia's foreign tourists came mainly from South Africa and Rhodesia. Such visitors looked for economical rather than luxurious accommodation and facilities, many preferring to camp and 'rough it'. Since Rhodesia's Unilateral Declaration of Independence (November 1965), Zambia has lost almost all her annual visitors from the south and has become all the more anxious to attract European and American tourists. These are often older, wealthier and more demanding visitors; many will in future glimpse Zambia very briefly during inclusive air tours. This change of clientele particularly affects Livingstone, largely dependent on tourists, where the numbers of visitors slumped from 52 000 in 1962 to 12 000 in 1967.

The ZNTB faces considerable difficulties arising from this loss of visitors and from changes in the nature of services demanded of it. There is also a lack of private investment capital available for tourism (the state provides services through ZNTB only until viable private firms can do so). Above all, tourist accommodation and facilities are entirely inadequate: for example, there were only 138 beds with hotel facilities in the game parks in 1969. In these circumstances the total number of foreign visitors actually fell from 22 167 in 1964 to 5964 in 1968, while East African tourism was booming. Quality hotel accommodation has recently increased with the opening of two modern hotels at Lusaka and Livingstone, current expenditure is improving several smaller rural hotels and plans have been announced to build a chain of motels across the country. Nevertheless tourism in Zambia is under-developed. Its future growth may well depend as much on creating a new kind of African tourism by opening up remote but beautiful areas such as the Barotse Plain and the Bangweulu Swamps, with their rich bird and aquatic life, as on continuing to depend so heavily on recognized beauty spots and upon traditional game parks, where East Africa has a long lead.

N D McGLASHAN

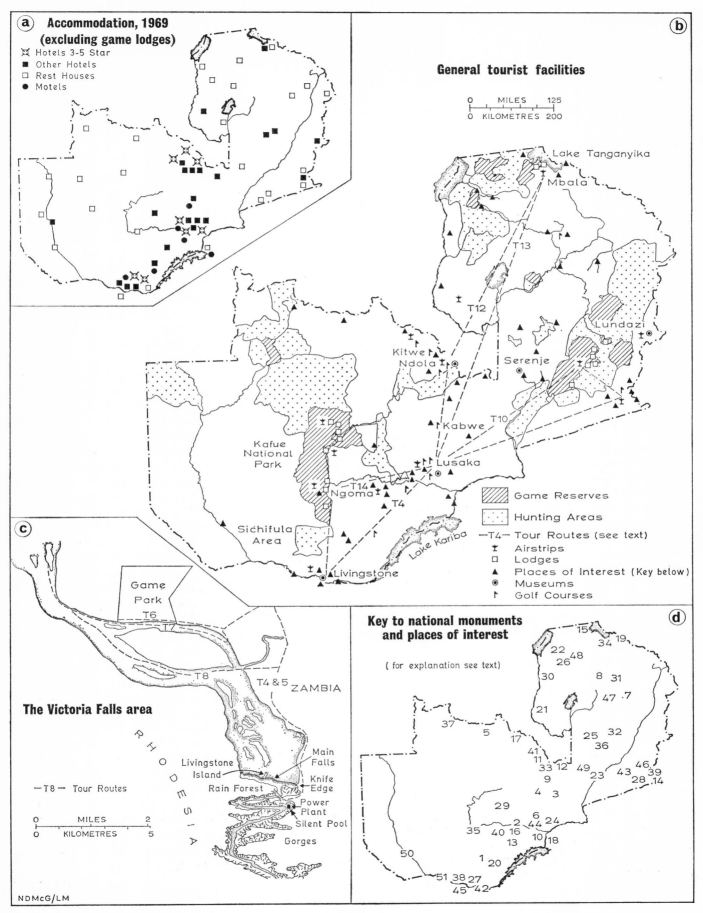

Accommodation, 1969
(excluding game lodges)

⋈ Hotels 3-5 Star
■ Other Hotels
□ Rest Houses
● Motels

b **General tourist facilities**

```
0        MILES      125
0   KILOMETRES   200
```

Lake Tanganyika
Mbala
T13
T12
Lundazi
Kitwe
Ndola
Serenje
Kabwe
T10
Lusaka
Kafue
National
Park
T14
Ngoma
T4
Sichifula
Area
Lake Kariba
Livingstone

▨ Game Reserves
⠂⠂ Hunting Areas
—T4— Tour Routes (see text)
⚲ Airstrips
□ Lodges
▲ Places of Interest (Key below)
◉ Museums
⌐ Golf Courses

c **The Victoria Falls area**

Game
Park
T6
T7
T8
T4 & 5 ZAMBIA

R H O D E S I A

Livingstone
Island
Main Falls
Knife Edge
Rain Forest
Power Plant
Silent Pool
Gorges

—T8— Tour Routes

```
0       MILES        2
0    KILOMETRES      5
```

d **Key to national monuments and places of interest**

(for explanation see text)

15
34 19
22 48
26
30   8   31
47 .7
21
37
5   17   25   32
41   36
11
33 12 49 23   43 46 39
9   28 14
4   3
29
2   6
35   44 24
40 16   10 18
13
50
1 20
51 38 27
45 42

NDMcG/LM

51 ROADS AND THE RAILWAY

Roads

The key to Zambia's road and rail network is the Great North Road, a truly significant factor in African history. Historically a general routeway rather than a road, this forms a link in a tenuous transportation chain stretching from Cairo up the Nile valley, across the desert to Kenya, via the East African lakes into Zambia and south to the Cape of Good Hope. This route was probably followed by Bushmen and Hottentots and by Arab slavers pushing into southern Africa, while Boers trekked northward along it into Tanganyika and Kenya. Staging posts for the inter-war pioneer air route across Africa lay partly along it—in Zambia at Mbala, Samfya and Livingstone. The abortive 'Cape to Cairo' railway would have followed much the same route.

The motor car turned the route into a road of sorts, its first motorist travelling from Dar es Salaam to Swakopmund between 1907 and 1909.

Recently the Great North Road became popularly known as the 'Hell Run' when, following sanctions against Rhodesia, Zambia sought new trade routes through northern countries. The main practical route was the Great North Road from Kapiri Mposhi to Dar es Salaam in Tanzania. This graded gravel road, with the Great East Road to Malawi, had to bear heavy loads of petroleum products, copper and general goods and became difficult in places during the rains. Today this stretch has been newly tarred and the road is now surfaced from the Rhodesian border at Chirundu to Tunduma on the Tanzanian border, as are its main branches to Livingstone and to the Copperbelt. Zambia–Tanzania Road Services operate a fleet of over 400 trucks carrying some 200,000 tons of goods annually over the road. The Great East Road is also almost fully tarred.

The roads tie Zambia together politically and economically. Except for those mentioned and those of the Copperbelt, nearly all are graded gravel or dirt, some of them due for improvement. Road construction in parts of western Zambia is made difficult by floodplain and dambo and by large rivers. In eastern Zambia the situation is also difficult, with the Bangweulu Swamps, the Luangwa and Luapula Rivers and great escarpments as barriers. Because of these barriers the main road network is broadly aligned to plateau and watershed country, leaving parts of Zambia inadequately served. Both dry and rainy seasons take their toll. During the rains stretches may become impassable and localities are occasionaly cut off. When dry, untarred roads become severely corrugated, while patches of sand can halt vehicles. In Western Province the deep Kalahari sand is notoriously difficult.

Road maintenance is restricted by shortage of skilled labour and by great distances between service facilities. Away from the line of rail, petrol stations may be a hundred miles apart and the few hotels and rest houses far more separated. In the west and north-west, traffic is still slowed by pontoons (as opposed to bridges) across many rivers.

Nevertheless great progress has recently been made in road improvement. In 1963 there were only 788 miles of paved roads, but by December 1969, 1880 miles (3025 km.), including all in relatively heavy use (fig. b), had been paved. Graded roads increased from 2702 miles in 1963 to 3991 miles (6421 km.) in 1968. Road developments feature largely in the First National Development Plan (p. 119 [b]).

The railway

Zambia's solitary railway line stems from Cecil Rhodes' ambition to build a Cape to Cairo railway and from her landlocked location. It was the principal instrument of European penetration and colonization.

In 1905 the line from Cape Town bridged the Zambezi River at Victoria Falls, the gateway to the future Republic. The Cape to Cairo dream had already faded and the immediate objective, much more modest, was to reach the new mine at Broken Hill (Kabwe). The Kafue River was crossed and the site of Lusaka reached in 1905, the line terminating temporarily at Kabwe in 1906. Meanwhile, a railway was completed from Beira to Salisbury which, renamed the Beira-Mashonaland Railway, joined the main line many years later at Bulawayo, making Beira a major port.

Development of copper mines in Katanga further stimulated railway construction. To serve this region a railway was begun from Lobito in Angola in 1905. It did not reach the Congo border at Luao until 1928. The southern railway had previously been extended northward from Kabwe to reach the Northern Rhodesia-Congo border in 1909. By 1910 it had reached Elizabethville (now Lubumbashi), capital of Katanga. The Congo line was extended to Tenke in 1918 and to Port Francqui in 1928: with the link-up with the Benguela Railway in 1931 the present network was essentially complete. It stretched across underdeveloped Africa from Cape Town to Lobito and to Port Francqui (a distance of 3400 miles (5471 km.). Four substantial ports had been connected to it; later a line from Rhodesia to to Lourenço Marques added that major port to the system.

The unified Rhodesia Railways had early been formed to link Northern and Southern Rhodesia, Mozambique and South Africa. Following Zambia's independence and Rhodesia's UDI (in 1965) this arrangement became politically inoperable and the Zambia Railways Act of 1967 established an independent national system. This began operations with 87 locomotives, 70 coaches and 1200 wagons and by 1969 had added 26 diesel locomotives and 1300 wagons. During the first year of independent operations (1967–68) some 2 000 000 tons of general goods, 1 300 000 tons of coal (principally from Wankie in Rhodesia) and 3 900 000 tons of minerals (mostly copper) were transported.

Southward traffic is gradually being shut down and the future lies largely with the projected Tanzania–Zambia (TanZam) railway from Dar es Salaam (figs. a, c). To be built with Chinese aid from 1970 to 1975, this will cross most difficult terrain. When completed the new line should end Zambia's dependence on rail outlets through Rhodesia, Angola and Mozambique, but its use will add considerably to shipment costs as long as the Suez Canal remains closed.

J W SNADEN

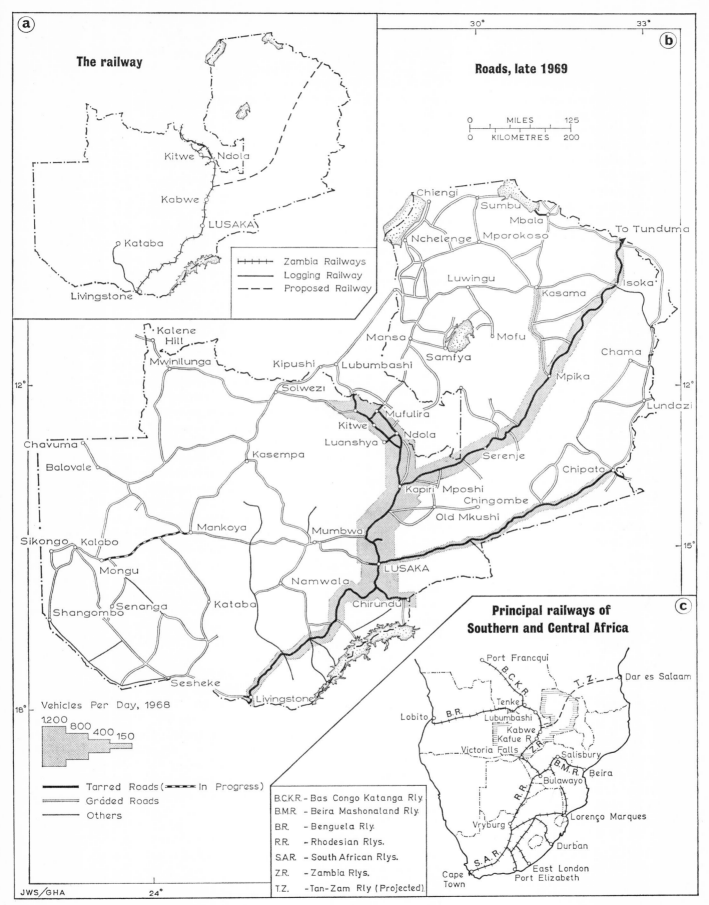

(a)

The railway

Kitwe Ndola
Kabwe
○ LUSAKA
○ Kataba
Livingstone

├┼┼┼┼┤ Zambia Railways
───── Logging Railway
─ ─ ─ Proposed Railway

(b)

30°   33°

Roads, late 1969

MILES
0   125
0   200
KILOMETRES

Chiengi   Sumbu
                          Mbala
Nchelenge   Mporokoso   To Tunduma
                                        Isoka
        Luwingu   Kasama
Mansa   Mofu
        Samfya   Chama
Kipushi Lubumbashi   Mpika
Solwezi   Lundazi
                    Mufulira
        Kitwe   Ndola
Chavuma   Luanshya   Serenje   Chipata
Balovale   Kasempa
                    Kapiri Mposhi
                          Chingombe
Sikongo Kalabo   Mankoya Mumbwa   Old Mkushi
    Mongu
Shangombo Senanga Kataba   LUSAKA
            Namwala   Chirundu

Kalene
Hill
Mwinilunga

12°   12°

15°   15°

18°

Sesheke
            Livingstone

Vehicles Per Day, 1968
1,200 800 400 150

──── Tarred Roads (─▪─▪─ In Progress)
▭▭▭▭ Graded Roads
──── Others

(c)

**Principal railways of
Southern and Central Africa**

Port Francqui
                    B.C.K.R.   T.Z.   Dar es Salaam
Lobito   B.R.   Tenke
            Lubumbashi
        Kabwe
        Kafue R.
Victoria Falls   Z.R.   Salisbury
                          B.M.R. Beira
                    Bulawayo
                R.R.
            Vryburg   Lorenço Marques
                          Durban
        S.A.R.
Cape   East London
Town   Port Elizabeth

B.C.K.R. – Bas Congo Katanga Rly.
B.M.R. – Beira Mashonaland Rly.
B.R. – Benguela Rly.
R.R. – Rhodesian Rlys.
S.A.R. – South African Rlys.
Z.R. – Zambia Rlys.
T.Z. – Tan-Zam Rly (Projected)

JWS/GHA   24°

III

52 AIR SERVICES

Zambia is a large, sparsely populated country with underdeveloped and, in places, difficult surface transportation routes largely restricted to plateau and water-shed terrain by large rivers, lakes, swamps and escarpments. It is landlocked in the vast southern African hinterland. Consequently air services, domestic and international, are vital to national development.

Domestic air services play an essential part in tying the country together politically and economically, contributing greatly to the maintenance of effective contact between politicians and civil servants in Lusaka and the provinces. Scheduled domestic air services are provided by the state airline, Zambia Airways, which began independent operations in September 1967 under a five-year management contract with Alitalia. Zambia Airways, Air Malawia and Air Rhodesia together comprised Central African Airways in Federal days, finally breaking up following Rhodesia's Unilateral Declaration of Independence (UDI) in 1965.

Two aircraft types flew the airline's domestic services in 1969. Livingstone, Lusaka and Ndola were linked by the *BAC 1-11* jet airliner, which also flew internationally to East Africa. Elsewhere the venerable Douglas *DC3* (*Dakota*) was used, being replaced by the *HS 748* in 1970 (not shown on the map). Preparatory to this change-over certain improvements were made at several provincial airfields, and others are planned. Only fully commercial airfields are mapped.

Fig. *b* shows that by far the busiest route links Lusaka with Ndola, regional airport for the Copperbelt, with eighteen flights a week by the larger aircraft (1969). Some of these, however, are also international flights to East Africa. The Lusaka-Livingstone route ranks second, emphasising line of rail dominance. Flights elsewhere are still very limited in frequency and available seats.

Air services are, however, growing vigorously throughout the country, as shown by the following passenger figures for outlying airfields:

Airfield	1963		1969	
	embarked	disembarked	embarked	disembarked
Mbala	958	956	1 171	1 305
Chipata	1837	1869	3 414	3 465
Mansa	687	638	1 910	1 632
Kasama	941	939	4 999	4 197
Mongu	1988	2254	5 565	5 331
	6411	6656	17 059	15 930

Along the main line of rail route comparable growth has occurred, except for Livingstone. Because the *BAC 1-11* flights continue to East Africa, however, the following figures embrace some international as well as domestic passenger traffic:

Airport	1963		1968	
	embarked	disembarked	embarked	disembarked
Lusaka	25 741	25 885	89 712	89 694
Ndola	37 615	36 081	69 870	66 087
Livingstone	14 608	14 464	11 354	12 442
	77 964	76 430	170 936	168 223

Lusaka overhauled Ndola after its large international airport opened in 1967. Livingstone's decline reflects its virtual closure as an international airport and a severe decline in tourism (p. 108).

Non-scheduled commercial and private flights are also increasing rapidly, including some Zambia Airways flights and those of charter firms, government, the mines and private owners:

Aircraft movements, all airfields	1964	1968
Commercial non-scheduled	4668	11 804
Private	4915	15 113

Domestic air freight is limited by the small load capacity of most aircraft used, largely reflecting the inadequacy of small outlying airfields, many only cleared grass strips. Speciality goods feature prominently in air freight, particularly medicines and foodstuffs into isolated areas. The Flying Doctor Service, based on Ndola, provides medical aid to remote localities (p. 100).

International air services have profoundly changed since independence. Previously, Zambia's main airports were essentially stops to and from Salisbury and Johannesburg. After UDI these services were eventually stopped completely by Zambia, since when Lusaka has become primarily a terminal airport. The Flight Information Centre at Salisbury, which previously served the entire Central African Federation, has also been replaced for Zambia by a new centre at Lusaka.

Zambia has two fully international airports in Lusaka and Ndola, the latter presently restricted pending runway repairs. Livingstone is no longer so classified, although used as a stopover between Gaberones and Lusaka. Small peripheral airfields, such as Chipata, do in fact handle flights to neighbouring countries. Lusaka airport is dominant, since all long-distance international flights originate or terminate there and it houses the principal servicing facilities in the country.

Nine international airlines operated in Zambia late in 1969 (see key, fig. *a*—Sabena's limited licence expired during 1969). Most international flights are to European termini, with African stop-overs, especially in East Africa. In addition to East African flights, Zambia Airways recently inaugurated a service to Europe, flying a *DC 8* in association with Alitalia, and a tourist service to Mauritius. Air services to Rhodesia, South Africa and Mozambique are now available only indirectly via Gaberones and Blantyre, connecting via Johannesburg to Australia, South America and New York. It now takes longer to fly to Salisbury than to motor there.

Sanctions against Rhodesia also curtailed cargo traffic between Rhodesia and Zambia. To replace this, Zambian Air Cargoes Ltd was created to operate a cargo run from Dar es Salaam, using *Hercules* freighters. General cargo and, for a time, petroleum products were flown in and copper bars exported before road improvements permitted phasing out this costly operation in March 1969.

J W SNADEN

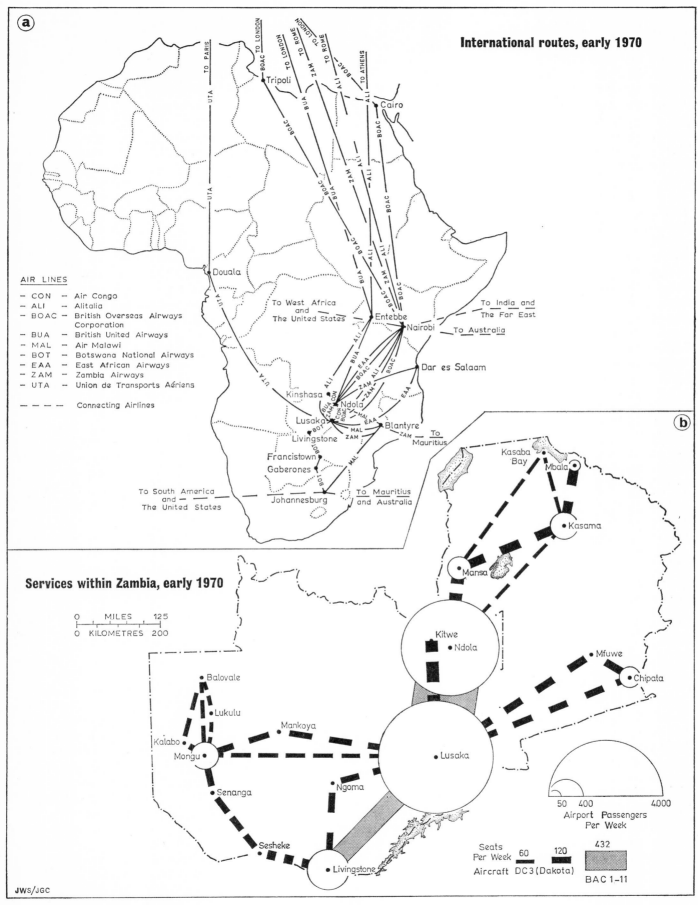

(a)

International routes, early 1970

AIR LINES

- CON — Air Congo
- ALI — Alitalia
- BOAC — British Overseas Airways Corporation
- BUA — British United Airways
- MAL — Air Malawi
- BOT — Botswana National Airways
- EAA — East African Airways
- ZAM — Zambia Airways
- UTA — Union de Transports Aériens

— — — — Connecting Airlines

TO PARIS
TO LONDON
TO LONDON
TO ROME
TO ROME
TO ATHENS

Tripoli
Cairo

Douala

To West Africa and The United States

To India and The Far East
To Australia

Entebbe
Nairobi

Dar es Salaam

Kinshasa
Ndola
Lusaka
Livingstone
Blantyre
To Mauritius

Francistown
Gaberones

To South America and The United States
Johannesburg
To Mauritius and Australia

(b)

Services within Zambia, early 1970

```
0    MILES    125
0  KILOMETRES  200
```

Kasaba Bay
Mbala
Kasama
Mansa

Kitwe
Ndola

Mfuwe
Chipata

Balovale
Lukulu
Mankoya
Kalabo
Mongu
Senanga
Ngoma
Lusaka

Sesheke
Livingstone

Airport Passengers Per Week
50 400 4,000

Seats Per Week 60 120 432
Aircraft DC 3 (Dakota) BAC 1–11

JWS/JGC

53 FOREIGN TRADE

Zambia's rapid economic growth since independence is reflected in her foreign trade statistics. From calendar year 1964 to the twelve months' period August 1968 to July 1969, total exports rose from K335·5 millions to K621·3 millions, or over 85 per cent by value. Imports increased similarly by over 90 per cent, from K156·4 millions to K301·2 millions (fig. *c*). Zambia's favourable export surplus thus increased from K179·1 millions to K320·1 millions over the same period. This is because Zambia is still a producer of primary products, with copper accounting for some 95 per cent of domestic exports by value (fig. *b*). Due mainly to continuing high prices, the total value of copper exported has risen greatly since independence to a peak of K586·4 millions in the period August 1968 to July 1969. This value represents 772 500 short tons, or 12·4 per cent of world production, placing Zambia third among producing countries.

Other exports are minor, totalling some 5 per cent by value. Chief among them, in descending order of value, are zinc and manganese ore, lead, cobalt, tobacco, maize (in some years) and hardwood timber: minerals thus dominate exports. The underdeveloped agricultural sector provides few exports.

Rhodesia's Unilateral Declaration of Independence (UDI) in 1965, however, her share has dwindled to a position where Zambia, in 1969, was virtually importing only hydro-electricity and coal. Since 1965 Zambia has progressively disengaged from traditional pre-independence trade links with southern Africa and developed new ties elsewhere in Africa and overseas. Thus imports from the United Kingdom, Europe, North America and Japan are increasing at the expense of the southern neighbours.

Total sales of copper (the only significant export commodity) to Zambia's eight largest customers in 1968 were (in short tons): United Kingdom 219 000; Japan 156 000; West Germany 92 000; Italy 71 000; France 61 000; Sweden 20 000; United States 10 000; Switzerland 10 000. Total world sales were 708 000 short tons.

Trade Routes

Limited trade figures differentiated by routes are contained in the *Annual Statement of External Trade, 1968* (Central Statistical Office, Lusaka), on which the following table is based: Imports overland from South Africa were temporarily in first place in this period following UDI, with those passing through Mozambique ports in second place. Imports through Lobito come third and those through Tanzanian ports fourth, while overland imports from (not through) Rhodesia fell drastically

ROUTE ANALYSIS	Imports				Exports			
	Value (K·000)		Gross weight (short tons)		Value (K·000)		Gross weight (short tons)	
Route and method of transport	1967	1968	1967	1968	1967	1968	1967	1968
BY SEA THROUGH								
Tanzanian ports	28 150	41 319	69 885	180 542	135 940	188 429	205 880	252 722
Mozambique ports	63 908	70 029	313 392	342 948	220 006	216 379	497 516	364 150
Lobito (Angola)	48 382	47 889	112 306	139 864	77 472	121 859	124 664	169 828
South African ports	8 120	10 234	10 904	10 902	6	94	23	194
Other ports	1 052	1 412	5 367	2 316				
BY ROAD OR RAIL FROM					By road or rail to			
Tanzania	9 120	6 404	237 185	208 329	26	9	142	47
Rhodesia	23 326	8 986	1 300 786	876 773	1 723	669	11 573	15 271
South Africa	69 876	80 721	402 989	464 066	23 684	8 504	77 588	50 711
Other countries	9 126	13 479	83 089	143 659	7 724	4 407	102 305	59 078
BY AIR	24 194	24 335	n.a.	n.a.	395	359	n.a.	n.a.
OTHER	21 096	20 376	79 769	63 335	40	35	4 626	412
TOTAL	306 350	325 185	2 615 672	2 432 734	467 016	540 744	1 024 317	912 413

Source: Annual Statement of External Trade, 1968 (Central Statistical Office, Lusaka).

Imports into Zambia embrace a variety of manufactured goods, over 75 per cent by value comprising machinery, transport equipment, other manufactured goods and mineral fuels. Others include foodstuffs, chemicals and miscellaneous goods.

Origins of imports: destinations of exports

Most imports come from the Sterling Area, followed by the EEC, EFTA and Dollar Areas (fig. *d*): but trade with Japan is important and that with East Africa growing rapidly. In 1968 the United Kingdom was the biggest sterling area trading partner, followed by South Africa and Rhodesia (fig. *a*). Since

in value. The importation by air reflects emergency measures pending improvements to the main roads to East Africa.

As regards exports (95 per cent copper by value), the traditional movement pattern through Beira and Lourenço Marques (Mozambique) can still be seen in the figures, but these ports are being overhauled by those of Tanzania. Lobito, in third place, had expanded her Zambian export traffic even more rapidly to 1968. The rapid decline of exports to South Africa is explained by the fall in copper exports from 30 000 to 6 000 short tons from 1966 to 1968, due to local replacement. Combined with temporary increases in imports from that country, this explains South Africa's highly favourable trade balance.

Fig. *a* shows Zambia's unfavourable trading balances with nearer partners, and favourable ones with European countries.

These figures are limited and already somewhat dated, but they indicate broad trends referred to above. During the nineteen-seventies the foreign trade pattern will continue to change. As young local industries expand there may be some decrease in manufacturerd imports. Similarly, agricultural developments may reduce food imports and Zambia may even export some agricultural commodities. The next decade may also see a final break in trade with South Africa and Rhodesia, particularly when the new railway to Dar es Salaam is completed around 1975, when Kariba North Bank, Kafue and the additional Victoria Falls hydro-electric power stations are functioning, and when the coal-washing process at Maamba brings Zambian coal into wider use. Trade with East Africa should continue to increase correspondingly, especially when Zambia joins the East African Common Market. Copper is likely to dominate Zambia's exports for some time : her foreign trade, and indeed her entire economy will depend heavily upon maintenance of foreign markets and prices for copper for years to come.

M M KAUNDA

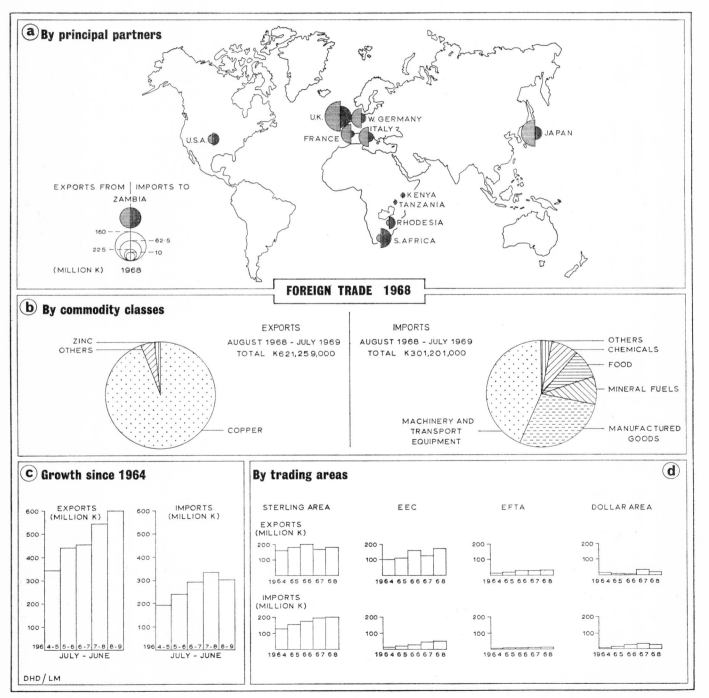

54 REGIONAL INEQUALITIES AND THE FIRST NATIONAL DEVELOPMENT PLAN, 1966-70 1

Two dominant geographical facts emerge from this study. Firstly, Zambia's location in south-central Africa critically influences its prospects for prosperity and stability: this is discussed in the opening chapter. Secondly, its internal development geography is dominated by a well-established regional inequality between the zone of the line of rail (including the Copperbelt) and outlying regions. Various indications of this inequality appear throughout the book, but here the point is specifically, although briefly, examined.

In the available space regional inequality can be indicated only by sampling. Six representative indicators have been selected for mapping (from many possibilities), partly using data from other maps in the book, partly additional data. Administrative provinces have been chosen as the areal units or 'regions', although they by no means form 'natural' planning units. However, because they alone provided a reasonable data base they were chosen for this purpose in the First National Development Plan (FNDP) and are, perforce, similarly used here. Only provinces provide a reasonable basis for comparison between different parts of Zambia for all the selected indicators. A measure of comparability is sought by plotting on a common basis of *per capita* effect, although unavoidably the actual units of measurement vary from literal per head to per 100 000. Standardized gradations of shading have been used to facilitate visual comparison, although they relate to different value ranges on different maps. The maps should, in short, be regarded as merely crude indications, yet sufficient to demonstrate certain obvious points concerning regional inequality.

Figs. *a* to *d* clearly demonstrate spatial imbalances and the dominance of the line of rail. Here is the classic pattern of Zambian regional inequality. The *urbanization* map merely re-states the 'Towns of Zambia' distribution (p. 81) in another form, but the proportions of provincial populations living in towns do demonstrate spatial variation in general availability of urban jobs, services and amenities and hint broadly at the distribution of such non-material factors as social and cultural outlooks. The *manufacturing* map is based on the only spatially differentiated data available in this sector since 1966. Calculated solely on numbers of establishments (which vary greatly in size and hence in job opportunities) it is crude, but unmistakably emphasizes the same pattern. Manufacturing industry (p. 95) is overwhelmingly located in the towns (although it created none of them) and significant towns are overwhelmingly located along the line of rail. Consequently, good job opportunities in the modernized sector of the economy are predominantly available in this favoured zone, a major cause of the crisis of expectations creating the present drift from outlying rural areas.

Bank services, derived from the map on p. 107, reflect present opportunities for developing a modern business outlook among the people, which chances were and are being eagerly seized. The map suggests localities where private funds are most readily available for banking and where private loans can most readily be sought for personal advancement into a commercialized society. Regional variations are less marked than in the preceding figures and the (still private) commercial banks are gradually spreading into rural centres. It is important to notice, however, the very thin spread of banks in all provinces, which does not justify drawing firm conclusions on distributional variations. *Personal levy payments* collected represent the best available indication of extent of paid employment by province (1967 figures were used because no payments were collected in 1968, while 1969 figures were not to hand at the time of writing). In 1967 all men earning more than K120 per annum (and women earning over K400) paid a personal levy on a sliding scale to a maximum of K5 per annum. The map averages total payments received on a *per capita* provincial basis and makqes no allowances for numerous smaller earnings from the sale of agricultural surpluses or intermittent labouring, or for certain other factors. However, it suffices to illustrate the brutal fact of line of rail dominance. (The 1969 levy, based on a new scale, rising to a maximum of K20 on an annual income of over K1000, may well modify this picture.)

The last two maps differ from the others in showing imbalances which are beginning to break down under redressive developmental pressures during the plan period. *Secondary school places* (see p. 105) are more evenly distributed. Similarly *hospital beds* show a better-balanced distribution. These two maps reflect some priority accorded to education and health in the FNDP and also comparative success in actually spending development funds, often a problem in developing countries. In short, the plan was already beginning to 'bite' in these sectors in 1968 and 1969. The (unusually) favourable position of Northwestern Province is interesting, but not readily explained.

These two maps lead naturally to consideration of the FNDP itself and to the figures on p. 119. The full implications of the FNDP—a vast document of 288 pages—cannot even begin to be considered in the space available, nor would this be wholly relevant in this basically descriptive study of existing resource distribution. Suffice to say that the plan aims at wholesale expansion of the national economy, is regarded as one of the most ambitious in independent Africa, and has, thanks to copper, been backed by capital resources that have permitted some success in implementation, despite difficulties. One major aim of the FNDP, and the only one considered here, is to redress the regional imbalances illustrated above. It has been shown that in some limited sectors the plan is, indeed, beginning to 'bite' in this respect. How far is this true across the entire national economy?

The point may be considered, although only sketchily, by studying fig. *a*, on p. 119. Here circle sizes are calculated proportionally to planned government capital expenditure per head by province during the plan period (1966–70), the national picture being shown in the key. It is necessary to emphasize all the limitations stated in the preceding sentence. *Planned*, not actual expenditure is shown. The latter has frequently fallen short of the former because of various difficulties and is not easy to quantify. However, planned expenditure indicates intent, which is being considered here. The map also shows only

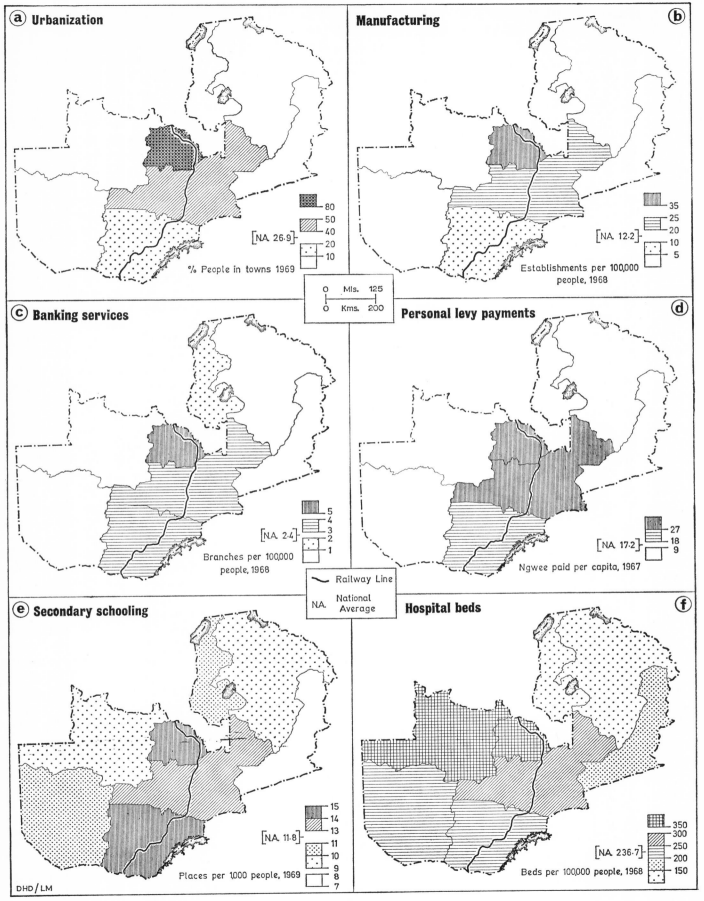

a **Urbanization**

80
50
40
20
10

[N.A. 26·9]

% People in towns 1969

b **Manufacturing**

35
25
20
10
5

[N.A. 12·2]

Establishments per 100,000
people, 1968

O — Mls. — 125
O — Kms. — 200

c **Banking services**

5
4
3
2
1

[N.A. 2·4]

Branches per 100,000
people, 1968

d **Personal levy payments**

27
18
9

[N.A. 17·2]

Ngwee paid per capita, 1967

Railway Line

N.A. — National Average

e **Secondary schooling**

15
14
13
11
10
9
8
7

[N.A. 11·8]

Places per 1,000 people, 1969

f **Hospital beds**

350
300
250
200
150

[N.A. 236·7]

Beds per 100,000 people, 1968

DHD/LM

planned *government* expenditure, although optimistically anticipated private investment is allowed for in designing expenditure in the plan. Unlike many developing states, however, Zambia has a plan depending comparatively little upon private investment or foreign loans. Thanks to copper, no less than 84·5 per cent of public sector expenditure (capital and recurrent) was estimated to be available from taxation. Finally, *capital* but **not recurrent expenditure is shown.**

The spatial pattern on the map is not immediately apparent, there being no clear-cut dominance of either line of rail or outlying regions. In fact this is the right conclusion to be drawn from the map. For the planned expenditure pattern (only the capital part being indicated) reflects a conflict between warm socio-political ideals concerning equal opportunity and well-being for all citizens within the context of the official philosophy of humanism and cold economic reality concerning relative investment advantages to be enjoyed along the line of rail. If socio-political criteria alone were applied the map would show most government expenditure in the outlying provinces, not only the more backward, but also the almost wholly deprived of *private* investment capital. This is not the pattern shown. Conversely, if purely economic criteria prevailed, expenditures would be predominantly concentrated along the line of rail, where a comparatively developed infrastructure, modest resources of skills and established domestic markets offer the best available investment returns. To essay a sweeping generalization, it is nobler for government to invest in the bush, but more **effective to do so along the line of rail. This dilemma has re-**sulted in a compromise decision to spend more on outlying pro-**vinces than may be wholly justifiable in terms of scarce resource** investment criteria, yet less than relative need demands. It should be re-emphasized that, apart from other limitations, the map possibly distorts the picture in two ways. Firstly, it does not show *private* capital investment; secondly, it does not show *actual* expenditure under the plan which, it has been pointed out, has tended to lag behind planned expenditure. Both concealed factors would tend to favour the line of rail, so that the *actual* development picture by late 1969 is probably more concentrated along the line of rail than the map suggests.

Circle segments are proportional to distribution of expenditure by sectors in each province. The pattern is quite self-evident. It may be noted, *inter alia*, that planned development in manufacturing industry is still directed to the line of rail, where transport and communications expenditure is also quite heavy, much of it on large-scale projects (e.g. Lusaka International Airport) reflecting the role of the line of rail as the national focus of transport and communications. It should be recorded that sub-division of the circles has entailed some simplification at the map scale adopted. Non-appearance of—for example—the health or agricultural sectors does not imply total lack of expenditure in these sectors in a given province, but only that

smaller sectors have been grouped together as 'other categories' for cartographic reasons.

Fig. *b* locates selected individual development projects under the plan. The selection is somewhat arbitrary, the main criteria being size and a quality of 'visibility'. This does not permit the map to be interpreted as a distribution map, for as such it misleads in unduly favouring the line of rail, where most larger and more spectacular projects are located. This conceals quite large expenditures divided among smaller projects in outlying areas, for example on grain mills in several provincial centres. The figure is thus merely a location map.

Space permits no description of individual projects, most of which are in any case mentioned elsewhere in the book. Here they are given symbols according to categories. Perhaps the most spectacular are the *hydro-electric* power projects (p. 98). The largest of these is the Kafue Dam (fig. *d*), whose regulating dam at Iteshi-Teshi will be built at a future stage after completion of Zambia's north bank power station at Kariba (not a Plan project). Another major project entails further harnessing of the Victoria Falls, while the Lushiwashi Dam will produce power for Eastern Province towns.

Transportation and communications projects are immensely important to landlocked and regionally underconnected Zambia. The most costly are upgrading of the Great North, Great East and the Lusaka-Mongu roads. Others include a new road from the Copperbelt to the new mine at Kalengwa and the already completed tarred road down the formidable Zambezi escarpment to the new Maamba coalfield, which will also be served by an overhead cableway to the railway. (Apart from surveying costs, the immense Zambia–Tanzania railway project does not fall under the FNDP, although mapped). Other large projects include the International Airport at Lusaka and the railway workshops at Kabwe.

Manufacturing developments are discussed on page 94. The most spectacular concentration will be at Kafue, where a new industrial town is emerging, planned to grow to 100 000 people by AD 2000 (fig. *c*). *Health* and *education* developments include hospital expansion at Ndola and Lusaka and the University of Zambia in the capital. A striking, large agricultural project is the Industrial Development Corporation/Tate and Lyle sugar estate at Nakamabala, near Mazabuka, in which government has only a minority holding. Another joint, primarily private enterprise project is the new copper industries' fabrication plant at Luanshya.

These are only some of the projects now transforming the face of Zambia. Progress to date has not been without setbacks. In particular Rhodesia's Unilateral Declaration of Independence forced diversion of spending into emergency measures such as short-run improvements to the Great North Road and transportation and petrol subsidies. In general, UDI greatly added to development costs in Zambia. Nevertheless, despite the obstacles much success has already been achieved. The second national development plan has been deferred for a time: it is likely to emphasize rural development even more than does the first. Hopefully it may place regional aspects of development planning on a sounder scientific basis than hitherto.

D HYWEL DAVIES

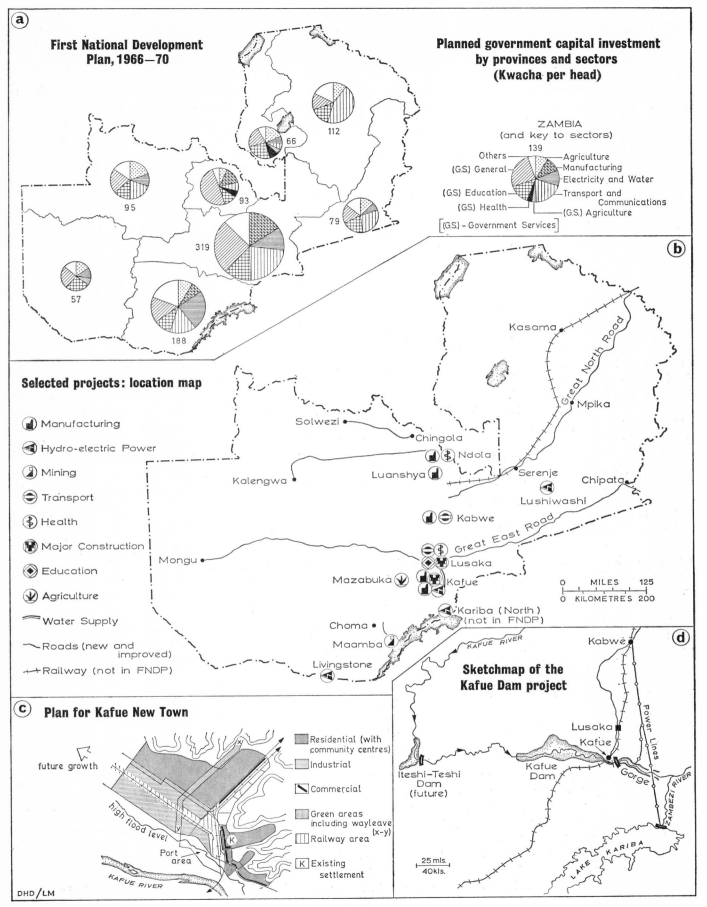

a

First National Development Plan, 1966—70

66

112

95

93

79

319

57

188

Planned government capital investment by provinces and sectors (Kwacha per head)

ZAMBIA
(and key to sectors)

139

Others

(G.S) General

(G.S) Education

(G.S) Health

Agriculture

Manufacturing

Electricity and Water

Transport and Communications

(G.S.) Agriculture

(G.S) - Government Services

b

Kasama

Mpika

Great North Road

Solwezi

Chingola

Ndola

Luanshya

Serenje

Chipata

Kalengwa

Lushiwashi

Kabwe

Great East Road

Lusaka

Mongu

Mazabuka

Kafue

Choma

Kariba (North)
(not in FNDP)

KAFUE RIVER

Maamba

Livingstone

```
0        MILES        125
0    KILOMETRES    200
```

Selected projects: location map

- Manufacturing
- Hydro-electric Power
- Mining
- Transport
- Health
- Major Construction
- Education
- Agriculture
- Water Supply
- Roads (new and improved)
- Railway (not in FNDP)

c

Plan for Kafue New Town

future growth

high flood level

Port area

K

KAFUE RIVER

- Residential (with community centres)
- Industrial
- Commercial
- Green areas including wayleave (x-y)
- Railway area
- K Existing settlement

DHD/LM

d

Sketchmap of the Kafue Dam project

Kabwe

Power Lines

Lusaka

Kafue

Iteshi-Teshi Dam (future)

Kafue Dam

Gorge

ZAMBEZI RIVER

LAKE KARIBA

```
25 mls.
40 kls.
```

RETROSPECT AND PROSPECT

In Zambia today practically everything seems to be changing quickly. Many changes stem from planned national development, in which the achievement since independence in 1964 has, despite severe difficulties, been impressive. Development has been financed mainly from the proceeds of the world's third largest copper industry, proceeds that mostly left the country under the colonial régime. The state, assuming increasing control of the means of production following the Mulungushi national policy declaration of 1968, is playing the major part in harnessing the considerable national wealth of natural resources —minerals, water and land—and in seeking new resources to exploit it. A small but growing manufacturing industry, together with agricultural commercialization and diversification programmes, aim for, but have yet to achieve, much more self-sufficiency. Rural evolution from a subsistence to a commercial economy, begun under colonial rule, is accelerating under the spur of heavy government investment and activity. However, with co-operatives, credit organizations and other rural sector developments in difficulties and with marketing facilities under-developed, the rather meagre results to date have not been commensurate with the effort expended.

Correspondingly far-reaching changes, largely unplanned, are taking place in society, and some give cause for concern. These include the breakdown of certain tribal customs and values (with their inherent stability), particularly in association with urban immigration. The drift to the towns has vastly increased since independence, and failure, to date, to accommodate unskilled and disorientated rural migrants in urban homes, in jobs and in society, is apparent in the mushrooming peri-urban shanty settlements, with their growing social problems. Here, above all, the crisis of expectations stemming from the euphoria of recently-won independence can threaten stability and internal security. Unemployment poses a serious and growing problem. In the critical agricultural sector paid employment has actually decreased in recent years, mainly because many large-scale expatriate commercial farmers have left the country. The construction industry, employing at its peak about a fifth of the working labour force, has been experiencing a recession. Because of high wages by African standards and in relation to productivity, low levels of education and technical skills, and a general absence of a well-developed artisan tradition, there is a tendency to substitute labour, despite high importation and maintenance costs for mechanical equipment of all kinds. A majority of today's primary school leavers thus face unemployment, particularly in the larger towns to which many will be drawn.

Nevertheless, there have been notable achievements in the social field, particularly in the intensifying attack on disease and, more recently, on malnutrition, with which it is closely bound up. Provision of mass educational opportunities has made comparable strides, at least in quantitative terms, while more relevant school curricula now being discussed should contribute to qualitative improvement. Everywhere, too, one sees an energetic, if under-co-ordinated search for knowledge on which to base further development. Along with the inevitable erosion of many aspects of traditional life by planned modern progress the desire for national identity has given rise to a hunt for an identifiable, indigenous Zambian culture among such threatened conditions.

Politically the government, active in international affairs, has gained wide recognition for the new state, its problems and its principles. The latter are now being codified into the evolving official credo of Zambian Humanism, to which all key government servants, at least, are required to subscribe. No longer in any sense a northern extension to white-ruled southern Africa, the state has quickly achieved a political identity that colonial Northern Rhodesia could never have matched. A policy of non-aligment, and opposition to racialist policies to the south, have led to the loosening of traditional ties with the United Kingdom and with white-ruled southern Africa and to greatly widened trading partnerships: Rhodesia's seizure of independence dramatized and hastened this process, but did not create it. Internally, the major political objective is national unity, the welding of a new nation from notably diverse tribal, linguistic and historical elements. The government sees the one-party state as an important means to this end and expresses confidence that this is attainable at the polls; the opposition thinks otherwise. However, the still novel concept of an over-riding Zambian nationalism remains fragile and vulnerable, for parochial loyalties run deep and are potentially destructive, so that controlling them is perhaps the most crucial internal problem. In this area of national development, where change is most urgently needed, there is as yet too little in evidence. Viewed in the perspective of her colonial history, Zambia's policy of non-racialism has been remarkably successful, although local tensions have surfaced occasionally, much exacerbated by the continuing impasse over Rhodesia. Zambia has responded to Rhodesia's declaration of independence with much diplomatic activity and by hastening her trade re-orientation from southern to northern routes, at heavy short-run costs; she could well close the southern border entirely in due course. Further than this, however, she is as yet unable to venture alone, while the activities of freedom fighters/terrorists (to use both terms) increasingly expose her to physical retaliation from Angola and Mozambique.

The future, then, has its uncertainties, being subject to the successful maintenance of national security in face of the threat of racial war in southern Africa, of internal stability in face of the reality of sectional interests, and of continuing satisfactory copper sales and prizes. Given these pre-conditions, however, it seems likely that the broad lines firmly laid down since independence for socio-economic development and political nation-building will continue to be followed for some time to come. For, unlike some other new African states, Zambia possesses many of the essential internal material resources for self-advancement. Above all, she needs time and peace—including industrial peace—to marshal and equip her limited manpower for this task.

During the coming decade, therefore, the landscape should reveal increasing evidence of national development. In major towns and cities, public buildings and office blocks—and, hopefully, many more low-cost houses—will continue to rise. Here opportunities and living standards should continue to improve for some, although unemployment will surely be the lot of many.

In rural areas the raw new buildings of clinics and schools will continue to spring up while, hopefully, vastly improved marketing and distributional facilities and organization, presently most deficient, will enable increasing quantities and varieties of food, consumer goods and services to appear in rural centres. More roads will be tarred or graded the better to link the line of rail, with its centres of government, industry and commerce, to outlying areas, while in north-eastern Zambia, completion of the Tanzania–Zambia Railway should stimulate general development within its zone of influence. The already familiar heraldic devices of numerous national and international agencies—the Zambian Food and Nutrition Commission, UNICEF, foreign volunteer organizations, imported consultants, and many others —will be borne ever deeper into the bush, their activities stimulating further development.

It is a tenet of national policy to bring the material benefits of development to the mass of the people, in particular to that large proportion of the population living in the hitherto deprived remoter rural areas. Strong and increasing planning emphasis is laid on rural development projects and government administration has been considerably decentralized in support of this policy. All this is admirable in itself and essential if rural living standards are to be raised. But it is difficult to accept that this can achieve the declared major aim of halting the present population drift to the line of rail and so alleviate growing pressures of unskilled labour in the larger urban centres. Strong rural development can surely at best only slow down this process, and may whet the appetites of rural folk for more sophisticated amenities and imagined opportunities available only in true towns. Indeed, there are sound, if currently unfashionable, economic arguments in favour of concentrating relatively more (not less) investment along the line of rail, for within that zone the concentration of much of the limited available private capital, of semi-skilled labour, of internal markets and comparatively developed infrastructure ensure the best returns. It has been pointed out that the most important fact of Zambia's internal geography today is the marked contrast between the zone of the line of rail and the remainder of the country. While the gap in living standards between urban African and urban expatriate is narrowing, the rural/urban gap continues to widen. This fundamental regional contrast is, unfortunately, likely to sharpen rather than blur in the foreseeable future.

Security and stability apart, Zambia's main concern must be the development and wise use of her human resources, so neglected before independence. The government is acutely aware that in addition to the provision of general education (including basic literacy training) and vocational training on a massive scale, a sense of self-reliance has to be instilled into a people caught up in rapid social change and hitherto conditioned by government promises and handouts to think that Lusaka will provide, come what may. Furthermore, the aims of a notably progressive government will in future have to be attained by more efficient tactical means: there must be less waste of resources and better returns in expenditures of money, skill and effort. Moreover, functional efficiency should not be sacrificial so much to the political imperative of 'Zambianization' (localization): while this policy is wholly understandable and strongly justifiable, bearing in mind the serious shortage of trained manpower at independence, it in effect decrees that many Zambians *must* run before they can walk. However, all in all, a remarkable amount of good has been achieved in six short, crowded and exciting years of independence: Zambia needs, first and foremost, to continue advancing along her chosen and logical path.

D HYWEL DAVIES

SELECTED REFERENCES

A considerable literature, particularly rich on society, is available on Zambia, but to date no large-scale, multi-disciplinary bibliography appears to have been published. The works listed below are limited to major references used by the present authors. Because of the breadth of the present study, however, these provide fairly representative introductory source material on the country, although in general authors have drawn heavily on personal investigations and on scattered original sources (in particular official documents) that are not generally available and which it has not been thought useful to cite here. Many of the references contain their own bibliographies. For further information on Zambian source material the reader is recommended to contact the following:

The Government Printer, Box 136, Lusaka (government printed documents)

Map Sales, Survey Department, Box RW 397, Lusaka (most official maps)

Library of the University of Zambia (designated the national reference collection), Box 2379, Lusaka

Zambian National Archives, Box RW 10, Lusaka (historical material)

Publications Officer, University of Zambia, Box 900, Lusaka (university research publications, particularly those of the Institute for Social Research—formerly Rhodes-Livingstone Institute)

Documentation and Information Retrieval Centre, National Council for Scientific Research, Box RW 166, Lusaka (pure and applied science)

A. General

CENTRAL STATISTICAL OFFICE, LUSAKA *Statistical Yearbook*, Lusaka, 1967, 1968, 1969
CENTRAL STATISTICAL OFFICE, LUSAKA *Monthly Digests of Statistics*
DAVIES, D HYWEL 'Zambia', in *Developing Countries of the World* (ed. Chatterjee, S P). Special Publication of the 21st International Geographical Congress, India, 1968
GRIFFITH, I L 'Strategy for Zambia', *Geographical Magazine*, vol. 42, 1969, p 3
HALL, R *Zambia*, London, 1965
KAUNDA, K D *Zambia's Guidelines for the Next Decade*, Lusaka (Government Printer) 1969. (Address to the United National Independence Party's National Council, Mulungushi, November, 1968
KAY, G *A Social Geography of Zambia*, London, 1967

B. Physical Environment and Natural Resources

BALLANTYNE, A O (ed.) *Soils of Zambia*, Mount Makulu, Zambia, 1968
BOND, G 'Pleicestocene environments in Southern Africa, in *African Ecology and Human Evolution*, London, 1964
DEPARTMENT OF AGRICULTURE, LUSAKA *Soils Map of the Republic of Zambia*, Lusaka, 1967
DEPARTMENT OF GAME AND FISHERIES, LUSAKA *Annual Reports*, Lusaka (Government Printer), 1959–
DEPARTMENT OF METEOROLOGY, LUSAKA 'The Climate of Zambia; A general survey', *Climate Data Publication*, No. 6, Lusaka, 1969
DIXEY, F 'The geomorphology of Northern Rhodesia', *Transactions Geological Society of South Africa*, vol. 48, 1944, p. 9
—— 'The geology of the upper Zambezi Valley', in *The Stone Age Cultures of Northern Rhodesia* (ed. Clark, J D), Claremont, Cape, 1950
—— 'Some aspects of the geomorphology of central and southern Africa', annexure to *Transactions Geological Society of South Africa*, vol. 58, 1955
FANSHAWE, D B 'Evergreen forest relics in Northern Rhodesia', *Kirkia*, 1, Salisbury, 1960, p. 20
FORESTRY DEPARTMENT, LUSAKA *Annual Report*, 1967, Lusaka, 1968
HATTLE, J B 'Meteorology of the Africa region', *Meteorological Officers' Forecast Course Supplementary Paper*, No. 4, Salisbury, 1950. Rhodesian Meteorological Department
KING, L 'On the origin of African land surfaces', *Quarterly Journal Geological Society, London*, vol. 104, 1949, p. 439
—— *The Morphology of the Earth*, Edinburgh, 1962.
LAMBERT H H J *The Groundwater Resources of Zambia*, Lusaka (Department of Water Affairs), 1965
LINEHAM, S 'Variability of rainfall', *Meteorological Notes*, Series A, No. 7, Salisbury, 1955
—— 'Date of onset and end of the rains in Zambia', *Meteorological Notes*, Series B, No. 21, Salisbury, 1955
—— 'Expected dates of planting rains in northern Rhodesia and northern Mashonaland', *Notes on Agricultural Meteorology*, No 3, Salisbury, 1960
MENDELSOHN, E (ed.) *The Geology of the Northern Rhodesian Copperbelt*, London, 1961
MORTIMER, M A E (ed.) 'The Fish and Fisheries of Zambia', Lusaka (Department of Game and Fisheries, Ministry of Lands and Natural Resources) 1965
RATTRAY, J. M and WILD, H 'Vegetation Map of the Federation of Rhodesia and Nyasaland', *Kirkia*, 2, Salisbury, p. 94, 1961
REEVE, W H 'The geology and mineral resources of Northern Rhodesia', *Bulletin Geological Survey*, Lusaka, 1963
SIMPSON, J G, DRYSDALL, A R and LAMBERT, H R J *The Geology and Groundwater Resources of the Lusaka Area*, Lusaka (Government Printer), 1963
de SWARDT, A M J and DRYSDALL, A R (with a section by GARRARD, P) 'Pre-Cambrian geology and structure in central Northern Rhodesia', *Memoirs Geological Survey Northern Rhodesia*, Lusaka, 1964
TAGUE, M *The Groundwater Reserves of the City of Lusaka*, Lusaka (Ministry of Lands and Natural Resources), 1965
TORRANCE, J D 'A review of cyclones passing over or near to the South of Nyasaland', Meteorological Notes, Series A, No. 3, Salisbury, 1955
TORRANCE, J D and LINEHAN, S *Report on the Meteorology of the Kafue Basin*, Salisbury (undated)
TRAPNELL, C G, MARTIN, J D and ALLEN, W *Vegetation–Soil Map of Northern Rhodesia*, Lusaka, 1947 (2 sheets, 1 : 1 000 000, 1952 ed., with text)
TRAPNELL, C G *The Soils, Vegetation and Agriculture of North-eastern Rhodesia*, Lusaka, 1953
TRAPNELL, C G and CLOTHIER, J N *The Soils, Vegetation and Agriculture of North-western Rhodesia*, Lusaka, 1957
TRAPNELL, C G 'Ecological results of woodland burning experiments in Northern Rhodesia', *Journal Ecology*, vol. 47, Oxford, 1959, p. 129
WEBSTER, R 'Soil Genesis and classification in central Africa', *Soils and Fertilisers*, vol. 23, 1960, p. 77
WHITE, F *Forest Flora of Northern Rhodesia*, London, 1962 'Conservation of vegetation in Africa south of the Sahara', *Acta Phytographica Suedica*, vol. 54, Uppsala, 1968

C. Pre-history and History

ARNAT, F S *Garenganze, or Seven Years' Pioneer Mission Work in Central Africa*, London, 1889
BURTON, R F *The Lands of Cazembe*, London, 1873
CAPELLO, H and IVENS, R *De Angola a Contra-Costa*, Lisbon, 1886
CLARK, J D *Stone Age Cultures of Northern Rhodesia*, Cape Town, 1950
—— *Prehistory of Southern Africa*, Harmondsworth, 1959
—— *Kalambo Falls Prehistoric Site*, Cambridge, 1969 (3 vols)

COILLARD, F *On the threshold of Central Africa*, London, 1897
DEPELCHIN, A and CROONENBERGHS, C *Trois Ans dans l'Afrique Australe*, Brussels, 1883
FAGAN, B M *Southern Africa in the Iron Age*, London, 1966
FAGAN, B M (ed.) *A short history of Zambia*, Nairobi, 1966
GAMITTO, A C P *King Kazembe*, Lisbon, 1960
GANN, L H *The Birth of a Plural Society*, Manchester University Press, 1958
—— *A History of Northern Rhodesia*, London, 1964
GELFAND, N *Northern Rhodesia in the days of the Charter*, London 1961
GIRAUD, V *Les Lacs de l'Afrique Equatoriale*, Paris, 1890
GLAVE, E J Articles in *Century Magazine*, New York, 1896–7
HOLUB, E *Von der Kaapstadt ins Land der Maschukulumbwe*, Vienna, 1890
JOHNSTON, J *Reality Versus Romance in South Central Africa*, London, 1893
LANGWORTHY, H W *Zambia in the Pre-Colonial Era*, London (forthcoming)
LIVINGSTONE, D *Missionary Travels and Researches in South Africa*, London, 1857
LIVINGSTONE, D and C *Narrative of an Expedition to the Zambesi*, London, 1865
MOIR, J W *Mambera's to the Besenga Country*, July 1879, Edinburgh, 1880
NORTHERN RHODESIAN GOVERNMENT *Ordinances and Orders in Council*, Lusaka
PHILLIPSON, D W 'The early Iron Age in Zambia', *Journal African History*, vol. 9, 1968, p. 191
RANGER, T O (ed.) *Aspects of Central African History*, London, 1969
ROTBERG, R J *Christian Missionaries and the Creation of Northern Rhodesia, 1880–1924*, Princeton University Press, 1965
SELOUS, F C *Travel and Adventure in South East Africa*, London, 1893
—— 'Twenty years in Zambesia', Geographical Journal, London, 1893
de SERPA PINTO, A *How I crossed Africa*, London, 1881
SHARPE, A Articles in *Proceedings of the Royal Geographical Society* and *Geographical Journal*, London, 1890, 1892, 1893
SHAW, J R 'The Baldwin diary', *Northern Rhodesia Journal*, Lusaka, 1962–63
Silva Porto e a Travessia do Continente Africano, Lisbon, 1938
SUMMERS, R (ed.) *Prehistoric Rock Art of the Federation of Rhodesia and Nyasaland*, London, 1959
TABLER, E C (ed.) *Trade and Travel in Early Barotseland*, London, 1963
—— *Richard Thornton's Zambesi Papers, 1858–63*, London, 1963
THOMSON, J *To the Central African Lakes and back*, London, 1881
—— 'To Lake Bangweolo and the unexplored regions of British Central Africa', *Geographical Journal*, 1893
VARIAN, H *Some African Milestones*, Oxford (Ronald), 1953
WALLER, H (ed.) *Last Journals of David Livingstone*, London, 1874
WIESE, K 'Expediçao Portugueza a M'Pesene, 1889', *Boletim da Sociedade de Geographica de Lisboa*, 1891–2
ZAMBIAN NATIONAL ARCHIVES, LUSAKA Various district notebooks, tour reports and correspondence on native affairs

D. Society and Settlements

ADSHEAD, S D *Report on the selection of a site and the preparation of a plan for the new Capital City and Government Centre in Northern Rhodesia*, Salisbury (National Archives), 1931
ANGI, C and COOMBE, T 'The primary school leaver crisis and youth programmes in Zambia, Lusaka, University of Zambia School of Education, *Youth Training and Employment Project, Discussion Paper No. 3*, December 1969
ANON *Report on a Survey of Christian Medical Work in Zambia, September 11th–October 17th, 1968*, Lusaka, 1969
BOLINK, P *Towards Church Union in Zambia*, Wener Franeker, 1967
BRELSFORD, W V *The Tribes of Zambia*, Lusaka (Government Printer), 1965
—— *Catholic Directory of Southern Africa*, 1968
CENTRAL STATISTICAL OFFICE, LUSAKA *Final Report of*

the May/June 1963 Census of Africans, Lusaka, 1968
—— Preliminary Returns of the *1969 Zambian National Census*
—— Census of Population and Housing (1969): First Report, August 1970
CENTRAL STATISTICAL OFFICE, SALISBURY *Preliminary Results of the Federal Censuses of Population and Employees*, Salisbury, 1961 (3 parts)
CHRISTIAN COUNCIL OF ZAMBIA *Report of the Twelfth Meeting*, Lusaka, 1967
COLLINS, J 'Lusaka, the myth of the garden city'. *Zambian Urban Studies*, No. 2, Lusaka (Institute for Social Research), 1969
COLSON, E and GLUCKMAN, M (eds) *Seven Tribes of British Central Africa*, Manchester (for Rhodes Livingstone Institute), 1951
CUNNISON, I *The Luapula Peoples of Northern Rhodesia*, Manchester, 1959
DAVIES, D HYWEL 'Lusaka, Zambia: Some town planning problems in an African capital city at independence', *Zambian Urban Studies*, No. 1, Lusaka (Institute for Social Research), 1969
DEPARTMENT OF HEALTH, LUSAKA *Annual Report* for 1968, Lusaka
FORTUNE, G *A Preliminary Survey of the Bantu Languages of the Federation*, Lusaka (Rhodes Livingstone Institute), 1959
KAY, G 'The Towns of Zambia', in *Liverpool Essays in Geography*,
—— 'Maps of the distribution and density of the African population in Zambia'. *Institute for Social Research Communication* No. 2, Lusaka, 1967
MINISTRY OF EDUCATION, LUSAKA *Annual Reports*, 1964–7, Lusaka (Government Printer)
—— *Report on Educational Developments in 1966–7* (presented to the 30th Session of the International Conference on Public Education, Geneva, July 1967—cyclostyled)
MINISTRY OF FINANCE, LUSAKA *Preliminary Report of the May/June 1963 Census of Africans in Northern Rhodesia* Lusaka, (Ministry of Finance) 1964
—— *Second Report of the May/June 1963 Census of Africans in Zambia*, Lusaka (Ministry of Finance) 1965
MINISTRY OF HEALTH, LUSAKA *Annual Reports* for 1964, 1965–6, and 1967, Lusaka
MULFORD, D C *Zambia: The Politics of Independence, 195 –64*, London, 1967
OHADIKE, P O 'Some demographic measurements for Africans in Zambia: an appraisal of the 1963 census administration and results', *Institute for Social Research Communication No. 5*, Lusaka, 1969
RASMUSSEN, T 'Political competition and one-party dominance in Zambia', *Journal of Modern African Studies*, vol. 7, 1969, p. 407
ROTBERG, R J *The Rise of Nationalism in Central Africa, the making of Malawi and Zambia, 1873–1964*, Cambridge (Mass.) 1966
SCOTT, J and MOLTENO, R 'The Zambian General Elections', *Africa Report*, vol. 14, 1969, p. 42
SHEANE, H and GOULDSBURY, C *The Great Plateau of Northern Rhodesia*, London, 1911
TURNER, V W *Schism and continuity in an African Society*, Manchester, 1957
WERNER, A *The natives of British Central Africa*, London, 1906
WILLIAMS, S 'The distribution of the African Population of Northern Rhodesia', *Rhodes–Livingstone Institute Communication No. 24, Lusaka*, 1962
ZAMBIA GEOGRAPHICAL ASSOCIATION Report on Second Annual Conference, Ndola, in *ZGA Newsletter*, Lusaka, 1969

E. Economy

ALLEN, W *The African Husbandman*, London, 1965
BOSSE, T *Notes on the National Beef Scheme*, Lusaka (Department of Agriculture)
CABINET OFFICE, LUSAKA. *Manpower Report: A Report and statistical handbook on manpower, education, training and Zambianization, 1965–6*, Lusaka (Government Printer), 1966
CENTRAL STATISTICAL OFFICE, LUSAKA. *Census of Industrial Production*, 1965 and 1966

—— *Report on Passenger Road Transport in Zambia*, Lusaka, 1968

CHARLTON, L 'Great North Road', *Horizon*, vol. 8, 1966, p. 20

COPPER INDUSTRY SERVICE BUREAU LTD *Copperbelt of Zambia Mining Industry Yearbook, 1968*, Kitwe 1968

DEPARTMENT OF AGRICULTURE, LUSAKA *Agricultural and Pastoral Production, 1966, and 1967*, Lusaka, 1968

—— *Tobacco Section Annual Report, 1st October 1966–30th September 1967*, Lusaka, 1968

DUFF, C E (ed.) *First Report on a Regional Survey of the Copperbelt 1959*, Lusaka (Government Printer), 1960

INDUSTRIAL DEVELOPMENT CORPORATION OF ZAMBIA (INDECO) *Annual Report 1968–9*, Lusaka, 1969

LITTLE, A D LTD *Zambia's Tourism—The Way Ahead*. Lusaka (Report to the Zambian National Tourist Bureau), 1968

MINISTRY OF LANDS AND NATURAL RESOURCES: COPPERBELT PLANNING AUTHORITY *Copperbelt Development Plan*, Lusaka, 1965

OFFICE OF NATIONAL DEVELOPMENT AND PLANNING, LUSAKA *First National Development Plan, 1966–70*, Lusaka, 1966

—— *Zambia's Plan at Work, 1966–70*, Lusaka, 1967

OFFICE OF THE VICE-PRESIDENT, DEVELOPMENT DIVISION *Zambian Manpower, 1969*, Lusaka (Government Printer) 1969

An Outline of the Transitional Development Plan, Lusaka (Government Printer) 1965

MINISTRY OF FINANCE, Lusaka *Economic Reports, 1965–* , Lusaka (Government Printer)

TRACEY, L T *An Approach to Farming in Southern Rhodesia*, London,

UNO/ECA/FAO Report on an Economic Survey Mission to Zambia, Ndola, 1964

WILSON, A T, BALLANTYNE, A O, BROCKINGTON, N D and REES, A M *Report of a Soil and Land Use Survey of the Copperbelt*, Lusaka (Government Printer), 1956

YOUNG, A 'Patterns of development in Zambian manufacturing industry since independence', *East African Economic Review*, Nairobi, vol. 1, 1969

Zambian Industrial Directory, 1969, Lusaka, 1969

APPENDICES

1: TABLE: PARLIAMENTARY CONSTITUENCIES
(1968) (*Chapter 22*)

Balovale East 68
Balovale West 69
Bangweulu North 49
Chadiza 32
Chama 35
Chikankata 83
Chililabombwe 88
Chingola East 90
Chingola West 89
Chinsali North 52
Chinsali South 53
Chipata East 30
Chipata North 31
Chipata West 29
Chitambo 26
Choma 74
Gwembe North 78
Gwembe South 77
Isoka East 54
Isoka West 55
Kabompo 70
Kabwe 12
Kabwe South 13
Kabwe West 15

Kalabo 2
Kalomo 79
Kalulushi 91
Kantanshi 99
Kasama North 56
Kasama South 57
Kasama West 58
Kasempa 71
Katete North 34
Katete South 33
Kawambwa 43
Kawambwa East 44
Kitwe East 95
Kitwe North 94
Kitwe West 93
Libonda 3
Livingstone 81
Luampa 11
Luanshya 96
Luapula 48
Lukanga 14
Lukona 1
Lukulu 6
Lundazi Central 36

Lundazi East 37
Lundazi South 38
Lusaka City Central 20
Lusaka City East 19
Lusaka City West 21
Lusaka Rural East 16
Lusaka Rural North 17
Lusaka Rural West 18
Luwingu East 60
Luwingu West 59
Malambo 28
Mankoya 4
Mansa 47
Mazabuka 82
Mbabala 75
Mbala North 61
Mbala South 63
Mkushi North 22
Mkushi South 23
Mongu 5
Monze Central 85
Monze East 84
Monze West 86
Mpika East 65
Mpika West 64
Mporokoso North 66
Mporokoso South 67
Mpulungu 62
Mufulira East 100

Mufulira West 98
Mumbwa East 25
Mumbwa West 24
Mununshi 45
Mwense 46
Mweru 42
Mwinilunga 72
Nalikwanda 7
Namwala 87
Ndola Central 105
Ndola North 103
Ndola Rural East 102
Ndola Rural West 101
Ndola South 104
Pemba 76
Petauke Central 39
Petauke South 40
Petauke West 41
Roan 97
Samfya 50
Samfya East 51
Senanga East 9
Senanga West 8
Serenje 27
Sesheke 10
Solwezi 73
Wusikili/Chamboli 92
Zimba 80

2: TABLE: SIZE, ADMINISTRATIVE STATUS AND MAJOR FUNCTIONS OF ZAMBIAN URBAN CENTRES WITH A POPULATION OVER 4000 (*Chapter 36*)

Size and administrative status rankings	Urban centre	Population in Thousands 1969	1963	Principal functions
Over 200 000 (City)	Lusaka	238·1	121·1	National capital, manufacturing, commerce and services, transportation, education
150 000–200 000 (City)	Kitwe	179·3	117·3	Manufacturing, mining, commerce and services, education
	Ndola	150·8	86·1	Manufacturing, commerce and services, administration, transportation, education
40 000–150 000 (Municipality)	Mufulira	101·2	76·1	Mining, commerce and services
	Chingola	92·8	56·3	Mining, commerce and services
	Luanshya	90·4	71·4	Mining, commerce and services
	Kabwe	67·2	45·7	Mining, commerce and services, transportation
	Livingstone	43·0	32·7	Tourism, administration, commerce and services
4000–40 000 (township)	Chililabombwe	39·9	30·1	Mining
	Kalulushi	24·3	13·2	Mining
	Chipata	13·3	8·0	Outlying administrative and /or rural service centres (except Chambishi = mining)
	Choma	11·3	6·8	
	Mongu	10·7	5·0	
	Mazabuka	9·4	5·1	
	Kasama	8·9	6·7	
	Mansa	5·7	5·4	
	Mbala	5·2	3·7	
	Chambishi	5·0	0·0	
	Monze	4·3	3·1	

1. 1963 figures compiled from 1963 Census of Africans and 1961 Census of Non-Africans and African Employees. 1969 figures from 1969 Census (some figures provisional).

2. Administrative townships below 4000 population are not shown.

3. Since the 1969 census the populations of some centres have been increased by expanding municipal boundaries.

hood infections have continued for some years, both at health centres and by local health authorities; fig. *d* shows the magnitude of this work.

Pulmonary tuberculosis has remained fairly stationary in recent years, causing nearly 5000 admissions and over 400 hospital deaths annually; about 3000 new cases are notified each year. Mass BCG vaccination (about 1 500 000 children were vaccinated from mid-1966 to late 1969), improved case-finding and early treatment will take several years to show significant results. Non-pulmonary tuberculosis, however, has declined markedly; in 1969 under 600 new cases were notified, compared with over 1300 in 1965.

The major threat to Zambia's health is undoubtedly malnutrition—particularly kwashiorkor (protein malnutrition), avitaminosis, marasmus (calorie malnutrition) and iron-deficiency anaemia. Nutritional deficiencies, alone or associated with other diseases, cause much suffering, disability and death among babies and young children. In women they cause ill-health and births of unhealthy babies and, in association with frequent pregnancies, contribute to early death. Kwashiorkor and iron-deficiency are widely prevalent, especially where fish and meat are not locally available; in addition, marasmus is common where cassava is the staple diet. The problem is social and educational as well as medical—for example, taboos on women eating eggs still persist in places. Even among comparatively well-paid mineworkers' families in the Copperbelt, malnutrition is prevalent. Malnutrition and anaemia cause 9000 admissions and nearly 900 hospital deaths (mostly children) and overload health centres and clinics. Government is tackling this serious problem from several angles. A major campaign by the Department of Health, the National Food and Nutrition Commission and the Ministry of Rural Development aims to introduce improved food-growing to peasant farmers, bring nutrition demonstrators to rural areas, and teach mothers about protein diets, food preparation and hygiene. Health and nutrition education is also given to schoolchildren. Maternal and child health care is organized in 'under-five' clinics, which over half of all health centres and hospitals already operate. However, the mothers' participation rate is still low—only about 9 per cent of the under-five population is brought to clinics—and re-attendance averages only 3·4 visits per child. Low participation is due partly to custom and tradition (which attributes a child's sickness to a parental moral lapse and therefore not medically treatable), and partly to far distances to clinics. The Department of Health and UNICEF are initiating a five-year expansion programme of maternal and child health promotion.

Despite the diseases described above, the general health of Zambia's adult and school population compares well with other African countries. The crude mortality rate (estimated from census and other sources) is around 22 per 1000 total population, and, despite high infant and child mortality, the estimated average expectation of life at birth is nearly 45 years. Preventive measures introduced since independence have greatly changed Zambia's disease pattern; but malnutrition, in association with measles, malaria, gastro-intestinal and other infections, is undoubtedly responsible for great loss of life at ages under five and for lowered function subsequently. Health improvement and disease eradication will depend more on universal health education and full participation of the rural population than on medical services alone.

LILLI STEIN

Key to National Monuments (fig. *d*, p. 109)

1 Administrator's House, Kalomo
2 Ayrshire Farm
3 Bell Point
4 Big Tree, Kabwe
5 Chifubwa Stream
6 Chilenje House 394
7 Chipoma Falls
8 Chishimba Falls
9 Chirenga Lake
10 Chirundu Fossil Forest
11 Collier Monument, Luanshya
12 Fort Elwes
13 Fort Monze
14 Fort Young
15 Good News Monument
16 Gwisho Springs
17 Hippo Pool
18 Ingombe Ilede
19 Kalambo Falls
20 Kalundu Mound
21 Kasamba Stream
22 Kundabwika Falls
23 Kundalila Falls
24 Leopards Hill Cave
25 Livingstone Memorial
26 Lumangwe Falls
27 Maramba Quarry
28 Mkoma Rockshelter
29 Mumbwa Cave
30 Munwa Stream
31 Mwelu Rocks

32 Nachikufu Cave
33 Nachitalo Hill
34 Niamkolo Church
35 Nkala Camp
36 Nsalu Cave
37 Nyambwezu Falls
38 Old Government House, Livingstone
39 Rooklands Farm
40 Sebanzi Sebanzi Hill
41 Slave Tree, Ndola
42 Sutherlands Farm Site, Livingstone
43 Thandwe Rockshelter
44 Twin Rivers, Kobje
45 Victoria Falls Gravels
46 Zawi Hill

Key to Places of Interest (fig. *d*, p. 109)

47 Safwa Rapids
48 Yangumwila Falls
49 Chipota Falls
50 Sioma Falls
51 Mambova Rapids

Key to Tour Routes (figs. *b* and *c*, p. 109)

T.4 Day trip to Victoria Falls and Livingstone
T.5 The Eastern Cataract, Knife Edge, Palm Grove and Victoria Falls Bridge
T.6 Livingstone Museum and Game Park
T.7 Cruise on Zambezi River to Palm Island
T.8 'Sundowner' cruise
T.10 Four, five or eight day stay in the Luangwa Valley National Park
T.12 Four, five or eight days at Kasaba Bay
T.13 An overnight excursion to Mpulungu, Mbala and the Kalambo Falls
T.14 A three, four, five or seven day stay in the Kafue National Park